Mexican Solidarity

Jacqueline Butcher
Editor

Mexican Solidarity

Citizen Participation and Volunteering

 Springer

Cemefi
CENTRO MEXICANO
PARA LA FILANTROPÍA
20 AÑOS

Editor
Jacqueline Butcher
Centro Mexicano para la Filantropía (Cemefi)
México D.F.
México
rivasjb@prodigy.net.mx

ISBN 978-1-4419-1077-6   e-ISBN 978-1-4419-1078-3
DOI 10.1007/978-1-4419-1078-3
Springer New York Dordrecht Heidelberg London

Library of Congress Control Number: 2009932415

Printed on acid-free paper

Springer is part of Springer Science+Business Media (www.springer.com)

Foreword

During the nearly 20 years of its existence, the *Centro Mexicano para la Filantropía, A.C.* (Cemefi, acronym in Spanish for the Mexican Center for Philanthropy) has promoted a varied agenda of research about civil society in Mexico.

Cemefi has produced and published information on the characteristics of the social organizations that make up the Mexican nonprofit sector, as well as information about the type of legal, fiscal, and economic factors that promote or hinder organized citizen participation based on the principles of solidarity, social responsibility, and philanthropy.

Once again, with the aim of bringing together information regarding the importance of practices of solidarity in the country, Cemefi has decided to contribute to understanding, making known, and ultimately promoting volunteer action and acts of solidarity undertaken by citizens in this country.

The end result of this effort is portrayed in this book, *Mexican Solidarity: Citizen Participation and Volunteerism*, edited and coordinated by Doctor Jacqueline Butcher. It is the product of a joint effort on the part of different people and institutions with a common goal: finding out about the characteristics of volunteerism and, in general, citizen participation in acts of solidarity in Mexico.

We are convinced that the distribution of this first work will encourage other research that will be able to deepen and complement what is presented here from a variety of perspectives and methodologies. Social development and democracy are aspirations that are built every day within the scope of public life, understanding this to include not only the governmental apparatus and forms of citizen participation, but also all actions on the part of men and women who voluntarily seek everyone's well-being. These aspirations may become realities to the degree to which each Mexican assumes our responsibility as citizens: to obey the law, vote in the elections, pay the taxes we owe, and voluntarily participate in actions for the public good.

Mexican Solidarity is a first approach and diagnosis of the situation with regard to volunteerism and civic participation expressed in acts of solidarity in our country. The results it offers will make it possible to evaluate the scope and potential of a wide range of acts of solidarity that contribute to the social cohesion of our society on a daily basis. Likewise, we hope that this study motivates later research work from other perspectives and also promotes reflection about the best ways of consolidating and increasing the social capital we have.

This work will make it possible for public and private actors to identify the challenges and possibilities we face as a country in regard to the promotion of volunteer activities.

The Centro Mexicano para la Filantropía considers that the first step toward promoting expressions of generosity, social solidarity, and citizenship is to find out about the composition of this social universe, which is often underestimated. For this reason, it has promoted this research. As Cemefi approaches the second decade of its existence, all of its members reiterate their commitment to continue promoting the development and communication of information about the nonprofit sector and civil society, with the aim of strengthening organized participation by society in the solution of common problems.

Our thanks and congratulations to Doctor Jacqueline Butcher for her great enthusiasm promoting this research, for bringing together a team of first-rate researchers, and for her participation and coordination of the work. Our recognition goes out to Doctor Guadalupe Serna from the *Instituto Mora* (Mora Institute), to Doctor Gustavo Verduzco from *El Colegio de México* (College of Mexico), and to Engineer Ernesto Benavides from the *Tecnológico de Monterrey* (Monterrey Institute of Technology), for all the hours of work and reflection dedicated to this effort. And, of course, our great thanks to those who made it possible: Clemencia Muñoz from the W.K. Kellogg Foundation, Jorge Hierro from Banamex, Samuel Kalisch and Pablo Cuarón from the *Fundación del Empresariado Chihuahuense* (Chihuahua Business Foundation), Pilar Servitje, and several private donors, for having believed in this project. Our deepest thanks to all of them.

Executive President   Jorge V. Villalobos Grzybowicz
Cemefi

Preface: Reflections Based on Practice

More than 30 years of participation as a volunteer and advisor to volunteer organizations and social help groups in Mexico motivated me to pose different questions about this work. This activity has allowed me to observe visible effects in the attitudes of those who are devoted to a cause and are able to dedicate part of their lives to serving others. I consider myself to be a witness to the advances, not only on the part of the people doing volunteer work, but also on the part of the groups and individuals who receive the fruits from that work. As the product of an effort that involves sharing resources and experience, these transformations have many times been mutual, which shows that changes are possible and that it is probable that there is a relation between the way they are initiated and their results. It also seems to suggest that it is relevant to understand the way that volunteers work both inside and outside of the organizational structures of social help groups.

At the same time, among solidarity and voluntary activities, I have observed many impositions affecting the rights and lives of others, with the excuse of helping and of satisfying unfelt needs. I have seen resources of time and energy wasted, where egoism and the desire to be the center of attention are so great that they obscure any attempt to serve. In the name of "development" and "progress", many times what is achieved is simply to disorient the people assisted and leave them in a precarious state when the "project" undertaken disappears. This is why it is essential to learn how to do this work in a professional and respectful way, with greater awareness of the responsibility it implies.

My personal experience in the field of voluntary action has had an important impact on my perceptions concerning attitudes of solidarity and my own actions in this regard. Once, in a Mexico City neighborhood marked by the lack of resources, we decided, together with a group of young people, to work jointly to build a house for an elderly man in that community. Every Saturday morning, our group came to work on that project. A woman from the neighborhood helped us, bringing rice water and hibiscus flower drinks for the young people and working together with us, laying brick. One day, sweating under the sun, the woman and I stopped to think: there were big social differences between the two of us, but in human terms we were the same, just people.

We shared concerns about what our children were doing, about the city's pollution, the future, and death. We saw ourselves as two human beings doing something for someone else, working together, shoulder to shoulder, simply because we chose to do so. That day we decided that each one of us – within our own worlds and with the resources available – would continue doing "something" for others, because it was a good way to live, because we agreed it was worth the time and life invested in it, and also because we felt useful and satisfied.

We agreed that the path of service and solidarity may be the path of accompanying and facilitating processes, of being a witness and companion – offering what one is, and at times, what one has – of being available to..., open to..., present...; what it finally shows us is that you cannot live for another, grow or suffer for another, but it is possible to be with and be there for another person.

In practice, it is possible to dispose of common resources by means of encounters and relationships. Solidarity and voluntary activity open the door to infinite possibilities for sharing and growing, not only as individuals, but as a society.

The experience of voluntary action led me to embark on a long road that made me to pose questions, now no longer from *praxis*, but rather from within the university. I had to go back to the classroom and obtain the academic degrees necessary to back up my writing and inquiries. The sparse information available about voluntary practices in Mexico was the motivation for beginning a process that would provide an account of these activities. I recognized that the good intentions that we assume to be implicit in participation in acts of solidarity were not enough; it was necessary to dig away at what this activity represents specifically for present-day Mexican society. It was evident that in order to approach and deal with these kinds of actions, a profound review and a theoretical basis were necessary that only the objective point of view of academic research is able to offer. In order to look for support for a nation-wide project covering this subject, it was essential to convince researchers in different fields of its importance, so that they might contribute their experience and knowledge to achieving this objective.

The study presented here represents this journey. We think that it is time to reflect on and pay attention to this relational and associative phenomenon that – it seems – may change, in some way, the way in which we participate with one another to build that which we call citizenship and democracy. Those are big words. Our contribution does not attempt to be so ambitious, but we do not consider it to be any less important because of that. In our research, the interactions that occur in acts of solidarity and volunteer work in Mexico are the motive; understanding what happens in and through them is the challenge.

General Organization of the Text

As editor, I have organized this text keeping in mind the complexity involved in articulating it for a broad public consisting of those who study this sector, as well as those interested in it due to their practice. As I mentioned earlier, the research that gave rise to this text was an effort that combined my experience and knowledge of the sector as a practitioner and researcher involved with it, together with that of specialists from many different social science disciplines, in which we have collaborated in order to structure a far-reaching research project. The process of doing the research was carried out by parts, in which the members of the team that was organized worked and took responsibility for their particular parts. The result is that this text includes chapters prepared by each one of the members of the team. It should be noted that the opinions expressed in this book are the responsibility of each one of the authors.

In my role as the general coordinator for the project, I devoted myself to the task of establishing overall guidelines and concerns for the project, as well as the theoretical concerns underlying it, while at the same time I was responsible for drawing up the survey and conducting two of the case studies.

While compiling the text, I considered it to be appropriate to organize it based on the National Survey on Solidarity and Volunteer Action (ENSAV, Spanish acronym), and then to consider the members participating in groups of volunteers, and conclude with an attempt to characterize the organizations wherein these members participate. Finally, by this means, I seek to provide the reader with an overall picture of the volunteer actions and acts of solidarity that are carried out by different groups in Mexican society.

In Chap. 1, I present the background of this research effort and establish the theoretical basis, the assumptions, hypotheses, definitions, and general concepts that guide and underlie the study. An international and regional panorama of these activities is also provided, and a focus is provided – by means of some historical background on the third sector in Mexico – on the state of knowledge concerning volunteer actions and acts of solidarity in Mexico.

In Chap. 2, the National Survey on Solidarity and Volunteer Action (ENSAV) is analyzed. This survey was conducted among the over 18-year-old population and is the first attempt to determine the characteristics of this sector in the case of Mexico. At the beginning of the chapter, both the historical and cultural reasons for some generalized precepts about solidarity and voluntary activities by Mexicans are presented. Then the methodological procedure used for preparing this survey is explained. Following this, a detailed analysis is presented that covers each one of the substantive questions in the survey, aimed at responding to some of the main concerns related to the extent of volunteer actions and acts of solidarity in the country, their main activities, their geographical distribution, and the time that Mexicans invest in them.

Chapters 3–5 analyze the results of 15 case studies that include a total of 66 in-depth interviews with people who participate in nonprofit organizations, as well as with one person performing acts of solidarity as an individual. Chapter 3 explains the methodology employed for carrying out the qualitative part of the project. The characteristics of the case studies among nonprofit organizations are discussed, and the information derived from 66 in-depth interviews with people who are members of these organizations in which groups of volunteers hold different positions is then analyzed.

The socio-demographic characteristics of those interviewed are also analyzed, the individual trajectories and life experiences of those who participate in volunteer groups are discussed, the importance and significance that the subjects attribute to their activities is delved into, as well as the process by which these individuals give new meaning to these activities in their daily lives. There is also an analysis of the conceptual map presented in the chapter, where some specific hypotheses arise from the relations among the codes noted which allows a better understanding of volunteer attitudes based on what each of them has expressed.

Chapter 4 returns to the 66 interviews included in 15 case studies of nonprofit organizations, and one point in particular is analyzed: the act of giving. The majority (98.48%) of those interviewed – whether volunteers or not – who participate in the organizations studied expressed that this kind of action was the most meaningful one for them. A conceptual map of volunteer actions is included in the chapter, and the act of giving is analyzed based on the expressions of those interviewed from the standpoint of different theoretical perspectives.

Chapter 5 discusses the characteristics of the organizations that provided the subject matter for 14 case studies carried out in different regions of the country and oriented toward different spheres of action. The data is organized in terms of four main themes: how the organizations began and the kind of objectives expressed when they started out; the goals proposed and accomplished during their efforts; the characteristics of the structure with which they have operated, and their decision-making process, as well as their mode of financing.

Finally, in Chap.6, the fundamental discoveries of this research are brought together. The main ideas of the study are posed and the data and contributions of both the survey and the case studies are presented, as well as verification of the hypotheses of the research. Based on the results obtained, challenges and recommendations are proposed in relation to the government and the market in order to promote volunteer actions and acts of solidarity. Future actions corresponding to both organized civil society and those who express their solidarity and participate in these activities in an informal way are also proposed.

Jacqueline Butcher

Acknowledgements

This book is the result of a show of confidence on the part of many people who supported the research from the beginning and encouraged this process up until the end. We acknowledge their encouragement for providing precise information that increases the store of data about the third sector in Mexico.

My special thanks go to the institution that endorsed and published this research, the Centro Mexicano para la Filantropía (Cemefi), and also, to the 2002–2005 Board of Directors, headed up by María Luisa Barrera de Serna, who considered it to be a priority to add this research project to the organization's strategic planning process, giving the Research Committee their approval to begin.

It is imperative to thank the people and the representatives of sponsoring institutions that provided the resources necessary for the complex and multifaceted project that is presented here. I would like to express my appreciation to all of them for their contributions and for their great interest in this study.

This project would not have been possible without the support of both individuals and institutions. Thanks to Hilda Catalina Cruz and Pilar Servitje de Mariscal, as well as to Samuel Kalisch and Jorge Hierro, who planted the first seed. My thanks also go out to Manuel Arango, Maite Orbe de Gárate, Pín Toutolli, Clemencia Muñoz Tamayo, Pablo Cuarón, and Dr. Rafael Rangel Sostmann for their support.

Acknowledgment also goes to the sponsoring institutions for their contributions: Banamex, the W.K. Kellogg Foundation, the Fundación del Empresariado Chihuahuense, FECHAC, A.C., and the Tecnológico de Monterrey; my thanks to them, their support was essential.

The anonymous mentors, assistant researchers, readers, evaluators, and institutions that worked hand in hand in developing this study merit gratitude and congratulations. Thanks to Ernesto Benavides from the Tecnológico de Monterrey for his voluntary support and spirit of cooperation. I also want to thank Gustavo Verduzco, from El Colegio de México, for his careful analysis and his vision, María Guadalupe Serna, from the Dr. José María Luis Mora Research Institute, for her professional ability, her unconditional dedication and her careful observations, and Miguel Basáñez, for his experience and professionalism.

Our recognition also goes out to the Cemefi Research Committee, witness to the multiple reports on the progress of the work, as well as to Virginia Hodgkinson, a world pioneer in studies on acts of solidarity and voluntary action, and to Cuauhtémoc

Valdés, for his accurate and sensible comments and suggestions. We thank the Cemefi operational personnel, who were always present and ready to help, read, express an opinion, and support the project at all times. I express additional gratitude to Marian Olvera, Consuelo Castro, Sergio García, Carlos Cordourier, and Jorge Villalobos their Executive President, for their patience and words of encouragement. Many thanks to the editors, proofreaders, and in particular, to Carlos Noriega for his contribution to the sector, for his recommendations and friendship. I owe my friends and family a special mention: Eduardo, Ernesto, Ana Paula, Ramón, Magdalena, Pedro, and especially Ernest Butcher. To all, many thanks for many hours of listening, accurate feedback, and respect for my work, as well as their tolerance for the time dedicated to this research.

Finally, I offer my warmest gratitude to the Mexican people who have provided, through their responses and their dedication to serving others, a panoramic and convincing vision of volunteer activities and acts of solidarity.

Editor   Jacqueline Butcher

Contents

Contributors

Miguel Basáñez
Global Quality Research Corporation, Princeton, NJ, USA

Ernesto Benavides
Tecnológico de Monterrey, Monterrey, México

Jacqueline Butcher
Centro Mexicano para la Filantropía (Cemefi), México D.F., México

María Guadalupe Serna
Instituto de Investigaciones Dr. José María Luis Mora, México D.F., México

Gustavo Verduzco
El Colegio de México, México D.F., México

Chapter 1
Conceptual Framework for Volunteer Action and Acts of Solidarity

Jacqueline Butcher

Introduction

This book is the result of research carried out with the hope of taking the first steps toward discovering and opening society's eyes to the universe of both formal and informal practices of solidarity in Mexico and the characteristics that define them. This work is the product of a study that the *Centro Mexicano para la Filantropía, A.C.,* (*Cemefi*, Mexican Center for Philanthropy) decided to encourage in order to understand, explain, make known, and eventually promote the actions undertaken by the citizens of this country in solidarity with others and as volunteers.

In the course of these pages it will be possible to outline some of the main volunteer activity and acts of solidarity practiced by Mexicans. Basic coordinates will be traced to contribute to elucidating where and how they are distributed in the country. Also, the value of the time this voluntary work represents will be covered. It will also be possible to observe the map of regional differences and become acquainted with a diagnosis of different ways in which people collaborate, both horizontally and vertically, in social organizations. The dynamics of voluntary actions of solidarity inside organizations – the privileged place of analysis in order to locate the volunteer – and outside of them will also be examined. It is important to point out that, as we shall see later, there are subjects who practice solidarity with others outside formal spheres and the organizations of civil society, and this activity is also important to recognize and validate within the scope of social investigation. This book is a joint effort, as well as an interdisciplinary effort, in connection with a shared concern: getting to know the many-sided and, until now, little explored trend of volunteers and voluntary actions of solidarity in Mexico. Hence, the purpose of this research is to analyze these activities. Both the subject of study and the unit of analysis of these actions are in and of themselves.

J. Butcher(✉)
Centro Mexicano para la Filantropía (Cemefi), México D.F., México
e-mail: rivasjb@prodigy.net.mx

J. Butcher (ed.), *Mexican Solidarity: Citizen Participation and Volunteering,*
DOI 10.1007/978-1-4419-1078-3_1, © Springer Science+Business Media, LLC 2010

The lack of information in the country about the role of these activities translates into insufficient awareness, resulting not only in an underestimation of volunteer practices and volunteerism in society, as well as the participants that give them meaning, but also in a lack of recognition of the potential – and the contributions – that this set of activities can have in consolidating an evolved civil society.

This is why it was decided to study this participatory trend in the Mexican context by means of a nation-wide investigation that would be able to comprehend the present participation of Mexicans who, by their own choice, without expecting any economic remuneration, and on the basis of the attitudes of solidarity, work for the good of society. As a result, what is shown here are the findings regarding solidarity and voluntary activities as one more form – among others – of citizen participation in Mexico, a product of individual and group efforts in selfless actions for the solution of community problems of all kinds.

The original research project regarding volunteer actions and acts of solidarity in Mexico entitled *Citizen Participation in Solidarity and Volunteer Service in Mexico* arose from the editor's concern to improve the understanding regarding these kinds of activities which – apparently – occur on a daily basis in our country. From within this very activity, observations emerged that led to questions and concerns such as: Who are the citizens who become interested in participating in their communities, and why? Who are the people who commit their time to volunteer actions and acts of solidarity for the benefit of the community without receiving any remuneration? What are these practices of solidarity like in Mexico and how can they be described? Do they correspond to volunteer practices and practices of solidarity in other parts of the world? What is volunteer work? How many volunteers are there in the country and how are they distributed? How much time do they devote to volunteer activities? What are these people like, what is their profile? Do they work in groups or alone? How do they organize themselves to form informal groups and non-profit institutions? What are their roles within the organizations to which they belong? In order to respond to these questions, it was necessary to analyze and formulate these and other concerns, translate them into research questions and propose an academic study covering this kind of participation in the Mexican context.

Exercises that arise from practice and then acquire the form of academic enquiry are not very common; it is much more common to find experts and scholars who observe and explain different social phenomena in an objective manner and from a theoretical standpoint. In this case, the journey from practice to academia, although long, was systematic. First it was necessary to search out and study the existing literature in Mexico regarding these kinds of activities in the country, and also to simultaneously take a global perspective of the same phenomenon so as to understand similar experiences in other parts of the world. Then the information had to be brought together that would allow us to develop a deep understanding of expressions of solidarity by the Mexican people, which are considered to be voluntary actions, and to consider what is understood to be social volunteerism. This is the reason why it was also important to establish definitions that were useful for demarcating the universe of study. Finally, it was essential to structure a flow for the research that would provide an appropriate and adequate methodology for each component of the project.

What began as an individual endeavor became an institutional one when Cemefi adopted the project and approved it as part of its 2002–2007 Strategic Plan. The next step consisted of inviting a team of experts and academics capable of utilizing their abilities and knowledge to analyze the information produced. This is how the final format of an exploratory and descriptive study of volunteer actions and attitudes of solidarity among Mexicans was developed, which is what is presented below.

Background

Contemporary societies are more and more characterized by the existence of associative phenomena in which social organizations play a determinant role, distinguished by their intermediate position between the government and the market. When explaining the evolution of the concept of civil society, Bobbio (1988, 1575) observes that "civil society is the sphere of relations among individuals, groups, and organizations that develop outside the power relations that characterize governmental organizations."

This set of relations in civil society and of actions by individuals, institutions, and organizations that are not within governmental structures constitutes a third nonprofit sector that corresponds to a formal reality that is neither under government nor is it commercial (Weisbrod 1974). This sector moves along the vectors of assistance and social and political promotion and development. In some countries it has also been called the volunteer sector or the solidarity sector, owing to the principles governing it and to the individuals participating within its structures.[1]

So-called volunteer actions and acts of solidarity are distinguished from other activities by their particular characteristics of providing both the drive and initiative without receiving remuneration, as well as having an impact on the well being of society and contributing to what has been called the common good. The volunteers reflect different forms of participation by individuals who use their rights of expression – in some cases, in association with others – in order to exercise their ability as common citizens to participate in public life with regard to matters affecting their communities. Thus, the third sector appears as a collection of private agents who

---

[1]See the book: *Más allá del individualismo: el tercer sector en Perú* (Portocarrero et al. 2002, 20–76), which explains the main economic theories about the sector, such as: (1) those referring to the existence of the sector (the theory of public goods, Hansmann's confidence hypothesis, theories of public choice, theories of industrial organization, the theory of consumer control, business and social offer theories), and (2) those that analyze how the state and the market operate in relation to social organizations (altruistic behavior, the function of ideology, stakeholders). It also presents social theories that have to do with the sector we are concerned with: (1) proposals that attempt to explain, from an overall perspective, how historical and social coordinates influence the nature and dynamics of the sector (the theory of social origins, the third sector of developing countries), and (2) the other theoretical approximations that concentrate on the specific role of some social actors, such as the church and the state (the theory of the welfare state, the theory of interdependence, religion, and the third sector).

are indispensable for the management of collective goods, i.e., who have public ends (Serna and Monsiváis 2006, 26–32).

Therefore, when speaking of organized and private volunteer activities with social and non-profit aims, the third sector is being referred to as a category distinct from the commercial sector (the market) and the public sector (the state), which poses as its main object the search for social wellbeing by dealing with identified human needs and promoting society's participation (Butcher 2003, 111–125). Based on its self-organizing function, and also fulfilling the task of sustaining public communication and debate (Young 2000, 164–180), relational elements are promoted in this sector that strengthen collective wellbeing, on the basis of social norms such as solidarity, confidence, and reciprocity.

Solidarity activity to the benefit of third parties exists in Mexico, but not all the activity involved can necessarily be considered to be of an altruistic nature. There are organizations in the third sector that promote different forms of participation and association, such as: universities, labor unions, minorities, professional associations, and political clientele. The majority are organizations having social and developmental ends, as they are based on providing services to vulnerable populations. Other groups have been formed around resources that exist for the sector. It is possible that some people who start these organizations to provide services to social organizations see it as a future source of employment. There are groups that start off as volunteer organizations and over time look for professionals to help with the organization's cause; others are nonprofit groups of professionals who get organized to support or provide different services to the sector.[2]

Although the importance of the presence and *praxis* of volunteer activity as a fundamental part of some organizations and structures making up the third sector in our country may have been recognized, the construction of formal conceptual elements was needed, supported by the findings of social science research, to determine the role fulfilled by solidarity and voluntary activities in the Mexican reality. Other formats are also used for naming the range of groups and institutions in this sector with group and associative participation, such as: civil society organizations (CSO), nonprofit organizations (NPO),[3] social assistance institutions, philanthropic organizations, nonprofit institutions (NPI), civil organizations (CO), and nongovernmental organizations (NGO), among others.

The appearance of social organizations on the national scene provided space for the proliferation of solidarity and voluntary activities on the part of individuals,

---

[2]The main objective of this investigation is to study volunteer actions and acts of solidarity by Mexicans. Formal and informal organizational structures serve as a framework for performing the different roles that individuals play within them. Civil organizations in Mexico have been well studied and are not the subject of this investigation. However, Chapter 5 of this work presents an analysis of the non-profit organizations (NPO) involved in this study in terms of their aims, internal structure, operational mechanisms, funding mechanisms, and the decision-making process on the part of their members.

[3]NPO, nonprofit organization. This term will be used from now on as a group reference for this investigation.

especially in the beginning. Although there are an endless number of studies about social movements and the formation of civil organizations, there is no register of studies about activities of this nature conducted outside the organizational sphere. Starting with the colonial period, social forms in Mexico were imported from Europe, such as the brotherhoods that functioned as lay organizations supporting ecclesiastical work, although they were always monitored by the Catholic Church. Since the creation of the Jesus Hospital, founded by Hernán Cortés in 1524, the Church took the reins of social assistance in hospices and orphanages, as well as providing multiple services in terms of education, catechesis, and, on occasion, even government. This is the institution that in some way came to shape life and the social fabric during the colonial period, without supporting the creation of autonomous secular organizations.

After the colonial period, during the period of independence, volunteer organizations and activities were very limited because of disputes with the new Mexican state. Later, with the advent of the liberal government and the disentitlement or forced sale of the property of the clergy, the state acquired – at the same time – the responsibility of administering the programs to meet the social needs of the population and the activities related to development. Different authors have recounted the history of the social movements and the formation of civil organizations in the course of the history of Mexico. In *Abriendo veredas, iniciativas públicas y sociales de las redes de organizaciones civiles* [Opening paths: Public and social initiatives of networks of civil organizations] (1998), Rafael Reygadas provides an extensive history of charity in Mexico, and hence of the creation of all kinds of civil organizations, as well as the participation of these groups in promoting the development of the country.[4] In the historical account provided by the author, expressions of solidarity and volunteer efforts come to confirm later organizational structures. In the process of institutionalization in the nineteenth century, the Public Charity Administration was created in 1861 under the Ministry of the Interior, with the intention on the part of the liberals of transforming what had been up until that time church assistance into public assistance. In this regard, Reygadas notes that:

> [T]he liberal state could not fill the vacuum left by the clergy, since it simply did not have the material structure or the experience necessary to fully attend to matters of public assistance. This is why Porfirio Díaz finally left it to the church to continue with part of the important work that it had been doing for three centuries (Reygadas 1998, 19).

From this historical perspective, it may be observed how a significant component of current volunteer activity comes from structures that were not so much civil as ecclesiastical. This religious influence, we note, continues up until the present day. The influence of these institutions on Mexican solidarity activities is explained in depth later in the following chapter. Many of the first volunteer activities had a

---

[4]The first two chapters of this book explain the social and theoretical genesis of social assistance in Mexico, as also the evolution of the ideas of promotion and development, as understood and interpreted from a Latin American, especially, Mexican perspective.

religious hue, for example, in 1868, the Ladies' Charity Association had 12 thousand active and honorary volunteers (Marina 2002). However, after the Revolution (1911–1921), with the formalization of social rights in the Constitution of 1917, the government took an active part in the promotion and creation of institutions and programs in favor of the poor and vulnerable, under the auspices of the Institutional Revolutionary Party (PRI, Spanish acronym), which constituted a corporative political system, creating a culture of paternalism and social assistance that discouraged the formation of autonomous volunteer organizations in the country. Health, education, housing, and rural development policies were promoted and "volunteer" groups were created that were useful and loyal to the party.

The *Casa del Estudiante* [Student House] was founded in the decade of the 1930s, an institution which encouraged social work by students. In this way, the Association of Infant Hospital Volunteers and the National Association of Volunteer Social Service were founded in 1943.The social service requirement in higher education institutions was introduced in 1945 under the auspices of Doctor Gustavo Baz, which was supposedly "voluntary", although in reality it was designed as a way for students to repay society for the higher education they received almost for free. Even today, social service is a requirement in order to receive a bachelor's degree from both public and private institutions in Mexico.

The government has played a role in "officially" promoting volunteer actions (Becerra and Berlanga 2003, 13–42). The organizations formed by Emilio Portes Gil in 1929 are an example of this kind of support: the National Infant Protection Association and the private charity organization, *Gota de Leche* [Drop of Milk], manned by volunteers and established to attend to nutritional problems in children. However, it is during the government of Lázaro Cárdenas that the concept of social assistance as a right had an effective impact:

> His main concern consisted of guaranteeing the social rights of the population and assistance for the destitute classes as one of the responsibilities of the government, orienting his governmental policy toward attacking the causes of poverty and not only attenuating its effects... As a result, in 1937, in the exposition of motives that gave rise to the Act creating the Ministry of Public Assistance, it is recognized that the concept of charity should be changed to that of public assistance (*Ibid*, p. 30).

The institutions promoted by the government continued to change. In 1961, the National Infancy Protection Institute (INPI, Spanish acronym) was created and, in 1968, the Mexican Child Assistance Institute (IMAN, Spanish acronym). Similarly, in 1977 the National System for the Integral Development of the Family (DIF, Spanish acronym) was founded, and that same year the National Council of Volunteer Promoters was created in 31 states, with 121 volunteer units established with the collaboration of the federal government, the private sector, and the nonprofit sector. The Council established significant work in the training of volunteers and was the first organization of its type to come up within the public sector. It was headed up by the wife of the president in office with the purpose of "promoting and orienting, on a national level, the voluntary participation of people committed to greater collective wellbeing" (*Ibid*, p. 37). At the end of 1993, this entity involved the participation of 180,000 people and supported 17,104 communities in the country. This organization disappeared in 1995 owing to a decree by President Ernesto Zedillo, and the actions of its "volunteers" ceased to be supported with public funds.[5]

It is essential to mention the government social programs that on occasion included citizen participation and free labor on the part of many individuals. This was the case with the *Solidaridad* [Solidarity] program promoted during the administration of President Carlos Salinas de Gortari, which brought communities – especially the most isolated ones – new forms of cooperation and mutual aid. Based on this relation with governmental entities, the improvements in the populations have been effective and many times more expeditious. This type of program has been slowly transformed, changing name and orientation. *Pronasol* became *Progresa* and finally the current *Oportunidades* [Opportunities] program, which is administered by the Ministry of Social Development in collaboration with other government entities like the Ministry of Public Education and the Ministry of Health. Similarly, national health programs have evolved in terms of their approach and scope.

In the case of the DIF, its base includes a certain number of communities helped by Community Development Centers and in which elements of citizen participation and volunteer training were included as part of the 2000–2006 National Development Plan (PND, Spanish acronym). In the new 2007–2012 PND, opportunities for citizen participation in the political, cultural, economic, and social life of their communities are included in the seventh objective. In the ninth objective, the importance of consolidating the democratic regime through agreement and dialogue among the different branches and levels of government, the political parties, and the citizens is indicated (PND 2007–2012, 25–26). Although it is true that opportunities have existed for volunteer participation in governmental entities, it is also true that this participation has not been entirely autonomous.

In this fashion, it is considered that a large part of volunteer participation in Mexico, unlike in other countries, has occurred under the protection of governmental entities and not in the form of voluntary individual association, in addition to constituting a more "corporative participation combined with acceptance of authoritarian forms" (Verduzco 2003). This is owing to the characteristics that developed in the colonial past already mentioned, with the strong presence of the Catholic Church and its intolerant attitudes, the factor of subordination that continued during the era of independence, and, after the Revolution, the corporation of social organizations around a single party which remained in power until very recently.

Beginning in the second half of the twentieth century, diverse social organizations were formed that had an influence on the struggle for democracy. In this sense, new

---

[5]This document does not analyze these activities. In this sense, it may be considered that the action arising in this framework was not entirely voluntary, but rather constituted a sort of "pseudo-volunteer work", because a certain degree of compulsion existed. The wives of public officials preside over these activities in many states through governmental entities or federal institutions. Nevertheless, this category is included in the classification of volunteer activity in Mexico, because, even though this first premise is true, it is also the case that this has been a way that many subjects linked to the government bureaucracy who began within this framework have been introduced to and have continued with these kinds of activities.

rules were established for the state–society relationship in the Mexican scene initiating with the student movement of 1968. That period served as a detonator for other social sectors that had been left behind, such as women, labor union members, and factory workers – to mention a few – to create their own civil organizations, which stimulated the creation of new social organizations throughout the nation.

The earthquake of 1985 is considered by many authors who have studied the subject to be a watershed in terms of volunteer participation by Mexicans (Alonso 1996; Méndez 1998; Reygadas 1998; San Juan Victoria 1999; Olvera 1999; Verduzco 2003). The spontaneous volunteer and solidarity action among people who were not necessarily part of some civil organization was very evident and visible in the face of this natural disaster. From that time on, other citizen movements arose to change the political and social scenario of the country. Groups and organizations interested in promoting social change also arose. According to a study made by Cemefi, as many NPO's were created between 1984 and 1994 as in the previous one hundred years. Monitoring of elections began in 1991 on the part of organizations like Citizen Power and the Convergence of Civil Organizations for Democracy, along with key milestones like the emergence of the *Zapatismo* social movement. At the same time, many new citizen networks were formed to help people living on the streets or whose human rights had been violated. In this way, the first social organizations law to emerge from civil society itself arose, which came to be known, thirteen years later, as *the Federal Act for the Promotion of Activities Undertaken by Civil Society Organizations*, published in the *Official Daily of the Federation* on February 9, 2004.[6]

New relations between organized civil society and the government began to develop starting in the year 2000, where it is possible to observe that some of the processes of social change occur by means of citizen groups interested in the field of multiple social action and other fields (Butcher 2002).[7] However, all Mexican social groups and NPO's are not necessarily made up exclusively of volunteers, although, often, these are the people who take the initiative or have the concern to create them and find ways to help and serve others in an organized way. It is essential to remember that forms of pressure and protest are also manifest through civil associations because, in the end, they are the legal mechanisms that the citizens have at hand in order to participate in public affairs.

The historical background shows that the characteristics of political, social, and economic change in Mexico today, established a timely context for carefully

---

[6]This law was promoted by several Civil Society Organizations: the Fundación Miguel Alemán (Miguel Alemán Foundation), Convergencia de Organismos Civiles por la Democracia (Convergence of Civil Organizations for Democracy), Foro de Apoyo Mutuo (Mutual Support Forum) and Cemefi, among others.

[7](2002) V Encounter of the International Society for Third Sector Research (ISTR) in Cape Town, South Africa. There was an attempt to present a brief analysis on the state–civil society relationship in Mexico from the democratic transition until the change of government in the year 2000 in the panel: *Civil Society, Citizen Participation and the Dawn of a New Era: the Third Sector in Mexico in Light of a New Political Regime.*

studying the participatory activities of the Mexican people in the continual construction of civil society. There is a need to know how and how often citizen participation actions considered to represent solidarity and volunteer work, occur because the aim is to understand how they influence the search for present-day solutions to the country's social and community problems.

In Mexico, the first steps taken in the field of philanthropy and organized civil society research have been mainly oriented toward defining the size and the specific activities that characterize the third sector, most of them focused on the NPO's. With regard to the international work reviewed, the most relevant is the John Hopkins University Comparative Nonprofit Sector Project. According to that research, Mexico is the country with the least number of "formal" volunteers and the smallest nonprofit sector in a comparative study of 22 countries.[8] The same study presents the following in its results for Latin America:

> "Duality" is the main characteristic in Latin America. There are two independent nonprofit sectors in this region: one of them is made up of more traditional charity organizations and other entities linked to the social and economic elite, and the other is related to a type of organization of recent creation called "non-governmental organizations" (ONG's) (Salamon and Anheier 1999, 19.)

Some Mexican studies that have taken up the subject of volunteer action and served as predecessors of the present study are: the metropolitan survey carried out by the Mexican Association of Volunteers, A.C. (AMEVAC, Spanish acronym), (Alduncin et al. 2003), the National Philanthropy Survey (ENAFI 2005) carried out by the Metropolitan Autonomous Technological Institute (ITAM, Spanish acronym) and the Banamex Bi-national Survey (Moreno 2005).[9] Other surveys that have also contributed to finding out more about associative and citizen participation practices include those of the Ministry of the Interior, the so-called ENCUP (the Spanish acronym for the National Survey on Political Culture and Citizen Practices) for the years 2001, 2003, and 2005.[10] Other sources used as reference points for designing this investigation and survey are mentioned later on in detail in this same section.

Up until now, little precise information has been available about the number of nonprofit organizations in Mexico (Verduzco 2003). Depending on the criteria applied for counting them, calculations indicate the presence of about 20 to 35

---

[8] See Verduzco, List, and Salamon (2001), *Perfil del sector no lucrativo en México*, for the main findings of the comparative study on the scope, structure, financing, and role of the non-profit sector in Mexico. In the comparative study by John Hopkins University, five parameters were considered to select the organizations that would be used for measuring the sector. These are: private (institutionally separated from the state); organizations (possessing an institutional structure and presence); that do not distribute benefits; are autonomous (essentially controlling their own activities); and have volunteer participation (membership is not legally imposed and they attract a certain level of voluntary contributions of time and money).

[9] See Moreno (2005), *Nuestros valores. Los mexicanos en México y en Estados Unidos al inicio del siglo XXI*. Banamex. Chapter seven contains the author's conclusions about confidence, social capital, and solidarity, as well as volunteer activity and altruism among Mexicans.

[10] http://www.gobernacion.gob.mx/encup.

thousand NPO's in the country. More than 10,000 institutions are now registered in the Cemefi's Directory of Philanthropic Institutions. According to Layton (2006, 170), if the ENAFI data for 2005 is compared to Chilean data, where there are 50 organizations for every 10,000 inhabitants, in Mexico there is only one organization for the same number of inhabitants.

This background, also, contributed to forming the guiding hypothesis for this investigation, insofar as it indicated that participation in solidarity exists among the people, although this does not always occur through formal groupings. We consider that the sum of the actions both inside and outside NPO structures in terms of hours of volunteer work as well as the donations resulting from this work represent the total solidarity effort on the part of the population.

Research Proposal

The main hypothesis for this study was formulated on the basis of reflections arising from an exhaustive review of the literature related to these activities and it was considered that by virtue of the small number of civil society organizations and their low level of institutionalization, Mexican social solidarity expressed through volunteer actions and acts of solidarity would tend to present itself in an informal context. As will be seen later on, this hypothesis is corroborated by analyzing the data of the survey done, which indicates that 66% of the people surveyed have participated in these kinds of activities. Of this, 44% do so through an organization, 24% in an informal way with friends and/or neighbors, and 32% as individuals . Adding the last two figures together tells us that 56% of the total engages in solidarity activities in an informal way.

On the basis of this idea, a set of research questions and the main aims of the study were developed, as well as the general objective of this study, which is: *To undertake an exploratory study in order to analyze the characteristics of the paths followed by citizens who carry out solidarity-type activities, as well as to identify the reasons and motives of the volunteers for participating in non-profit organizations.*

The aims established reflect the original questions for investigation and include: (a) analyzing and evaluating both the social and economic contributions of citizen participation acts of solidarity and voluntary service in Mexico; (b) establishing the number of "man hours" that are donated through volunteer work and calculating the economic contribution of Mexican volunteerism; (c) bringing together qualitative and quantitative information on the national level that will be useful for future research on acts of solidarity, citizen participation, volunteer service, and the third sector in Mexico; (d) deepening knowledge about citizen participation in acts of solidarity and volunteer service in both formal and informal spheres as regards motivation, participation, levels of association, and spheres of action; and also, (e) generating greater understanding about socio-cultural processes that influence the kinds of volunteer and solidarity-type actions found in Mexico, by means of analysis of different contexts of volunteer action and its operative structures.

The situation in regard to volunteer, solidarity, philanthropic, and service-to-third-party activities in Mexico is very complex. It was not sufficient to determine the profile and number of volunteers participating in the NPO's, their geographic distribution, the heterogeneity and frequency of their activities; it was also necessary to deepen understanding about informal acts of solidarity in order to find out about their particular characteristics and motivation. The size of the study required the formation of a research team including experts from different fields and the search, within academia, for appropriate methodologies for the task.

The team was composed of Jacqueline Butcher, from the Centro Mexicano para la Filantropía (Cemefi), as director and general coordinator of the project; Gustavo Verduzco, from El Colegio de México; and María Guadalupe Serna, from the Dr. José María Luis Mora Research Institute. The support group consisted of Ernesto Benavides, director of Social Formation of the Tecnológico de Monterrey and Miguel Basáñez, President of Global Quality Research of Princeton, N.J. The research assistant was María Abeyami Ortega.

For the field-work phase, which included participatory observation and information gathering from in-depth interviews, we had the participation of professionals from the Social Formation area of the Tecnológico de Monterrey, who were located at different campuses, and whose active participation and knowledge about the organizations facilitated gathering qualitative information. Sandra Díaz, Luis Manuel López, Norma Buen, Violeta Sandoval, Vivian Rentería, Rosario Wendoline Guerrero, Adria Placencia, Alicia Pérez, María Concepción Castillo, Consuelo Luna, Gabriela Martínez, and Alejandra Delgado participated in this team. José Sánchez, from the Social Science Research Center of the University of Guanajuato and Soledad León, from the University of Guanajuato, carried out the data run to search for the enunciation context using the NVivo program.

Concepts and Definitions for the Study

Volunteer Actions and Acts of Solidarity

There are any number of manifestations of solidarity toward others among Mexicans, in addition to a tradition of volunteer practices. However, the conceptual vision of volunteerism utilized for this study was derived from practice itself. A biased conception that misrepresents the multiplicity and richness of how they are manifest is often detected as a product of the limited knowledge in Mexico concerning volunteer actions and acts of solidarity. It is not uncommon to find that, when one thinks about this subject, the first images evoked may frequently be ones of religious groups or of women from the more well-to-do classes. These are indeed volunteers. But other diverse social actors are also volunteers, who are rarely linked to these kinds of actions in the traditional cultural imagination.

Volunteer actions are so varied and heterogeneous that they cover an extremely broad spectrum of actions: from civic and religious education, through interest in and defense of human rights, to the solution of specific health and education problems in unprotected populations. Attitudes and actions in favor of others take on many expressions, from the formation of associations dedicated to solving evident and obstinate problems like cancer, blindness, mistreatment, or orphans, to isolated and simple actions of an individual character like teaching someone how to read, displaying a work of art, helping to build a school, or attending someone who is dying.

Today, two fundamental types have been identified for these activities: the first consists of those undertaken through citizen organizations and groupings around the globe that participate in all spheres of social activity, from culture and sports to the most basic social assistance. The second, the dominant form in most cultures, are spontaneous or informal expressions of solidarity.[11]

In many countries, especially developing ones, such as in the case of South Africa,[12] it has been demonstrated that the number of volunteers of the latter type surpasses that of those who work in formal, registered structures. A recent African study including four countries – Zimbabwe, South Africa, Namibia, and Mozambique – (Wilkinson-Maposa et al. 2006) has attempted to classify the different forms of philanthropy, help, and donations to individuals in precarious economic circumstances, taking into consideration the different forms of expression of mutual aid, solidarity, and reciprocity among individuals, including actions considered to be volunteer actions.

Authors who have studied this phenomenon, such as Hodgkinson, Salamon, Reed, Butcher, Dekker, and Halman, among others, have tackled the need to understand this action:

> People are guided not only by their passions and self-benefit, but also by their values, standards, and belief systems... altruism may be one of those values, but solidarity, reciprocity, charity, injustice, equality, and inequality, are too, and finally, religious values may also be mentioned in connection with volunteer work (Dekker and Halman 2003, 6).

The importance of the value and cultural dimensions are recognized, as elements to be taken into account for analysis: "[A]s is ever more evident and clear, culture matters..., and because values are an important attribute of culture, it seems reasonable to assume that collective values are also important for volunteer service actions" (*Ibid*, 7).

Recently, social researchers have begun to classify volunteers according to their interests or their motivations (Handy 1988; Van Daal 1990; Meijs 1997). These authors agree that it is possible to distinguish three kinds of volunteerism: reciprocal help, with the motivation being solidarity through common interest;

---

[11] *Medición del servicio voluntario: una guía práctica. Independent Sector* y Voluntarios de las Naciones Unidas (2001). This guide classifies them as managed or unmanaged.

[12] For more information on this case, see the study: *The Size and Scope of the Non-Profit Sector in South Africa,* developed by Swilling and Russell (2002). "Informal" groups mainly made up of volunteers represent 53% of the non-profit sector in that country.

providing services, motivated by the urge to donate time and talent to others; and, finally, social commitment, motivated by the idea of an active citizenry which participates.

The main point of reference for the effort to understand the set of volunteer actions and volunteerism on a global level in many different spheres and geographical regions is the year 2001, which the United Nations declared to be the International Year of Volunteers. This was a way of seeking to promote research about these activities and of achieving greater publicity regarding their social impact, as well as encouraging volunteer contributions around the world. In the case of Mexico, we can ask ourselves: Why promote these activities and not others? Are they a positive influence on Mexican society because of the fact that they are volunteer activities or acts of solidarity? How do they contribute to the development of the country and the promotion of citizenship? In answering these questions, the UN recognized the role of volunteer activity in social development when it declared that:

> [V]olunteerism represents an enormous reserve of abilities, energy, and local wisdom that can help governments to carry out more focused, efficient, participative, and transparent public programs and policies. However, it is not very common for volunteerism to be recognized as a strategic resource that can positively influence public policy, and even less common for it to be taken into account in international development strategies... [T]he International Year of Volunteers (2001) offers a unique opportunity, on the one hand, to confirm an ancestral tradition with recognition of its potential and, on the other hand, as a major asset in the promotion of social development (UN Social Development Commission, 2000).[13]

Similarly, world knowledge of volunteer activities and their value are considered in surveys like the European Values Survey (EVS) and the World Values Survey (WVS). For its part, the Report on *Follow-up to Implementation of the International Year of Volunteers* (2005) from the General Assembly of the United Nations, reports that:

> There are, however, wide variations in trends among countries and regions and this unevenness needs to be addressed if volunteerism is to realize its full potential for contributing to many of today's global challenges. Volunteerism, when properly channeled, is a powerful force for the achievement of the Millennium Development Goals.

There are sufficient reasons then to justify the need to investigate these kinds of actions in a specific and ordered way, since, as is established by the book *Medición del servicio voluntario: una guía práctica* [Volunteer Service Measurement: A Practical Guide], prepared by experts of the Independent Sector and Volunteers of the United Nations (2001), a study of this nature demonstrates to both government and society the contributions of volunteer actions and expressions of solidarity to society in all aspects: social, political, and economic. The guide mentioned indicates that volunteer service is important because it "helps to create a stable and cohesive

---

[13] Report of the Comisión de Desarrollo Social. December, 2000. *El papel del Voluntariado en la promoción del desarrollo social* in : http://www.iyv.org/iyv_span/policy/unitednations/csd_document/csddocument_htm/csd_document_span.htm

society" and "add value to the services offered by the government". According to this guide, there are three criteria that cover practically all forms of volunteer activity, which in turn describe the universe of activities in the Mexican context:

1. *It is not carried out mainly for monetary gain.* This means that if the monetary reimbursement that people receive for the work they do is equal to or greater than the "market value" of the work, it cannot be considered to be volunteer activity. However, volunteers may receive payment to cover their basic expenses; this avoids a situation in which people with few financial resources cannot offer themselves as volunteers.

2. *It is carried out based on individual decision.* Free will is a basic principle of volunteer action. However, it may be said that there are pressures to undertake this kind of activity, such as social pressures or the person's own feelings of moral obligation. This criterion helps to distinguish actual voluntary service from that where there is external coercion and one is obligated to participate. This is the case with "voluntary" social service to receive an academic degree or community service that replaces military service.

3. *It provides benefits for third parties and also for the people who provide the volunteer service.* This criterion makes it possible to distinguish volunteer activity from purely recreational activities like soccer. The criterion covers a broad range that includes everything from individual beneficiaries, such as friends and neighbors, to the society that is benefited by these activities. Providing services for one's family is excluded here, since this activity is considered to be part of the normal responsibilities of an individual.

The most recent classification by the United National proposes four categories of volunteer activity: (1) mutual aid or self-help; (2) philanthropy and service to others; (3) citizen participation; and (4) advocacy or campaigning (Independent Sector and United Nations Volunteers 2001). These terms were explained in a meeting on volunteer action and development called by the United Nations in 1999 (United Nations Volunteers, 1999, 3–5.)

Mutual aid or self-help. In many parts of the developing world mutual aid or self-help constitutes the main system of social and economic support. From small informal kinship and clan groupings to more formal rotating credit associations and welfare groups, volunteering as an expression of self-help or mutual aid plays a primary role in the welfare of communities. Self-help also plays an important role in countries of the industrialized North, particularly in the health and social welfare field, where numerous organizations have been established to provide support and assistance to those in need, often organized around a particular disease or illness not covered by government health services.

Philanthropy or service to others. Philanthropy or service to others is distinguished from self-help in that the primary recipient of the volunteering is not himself/herself a member of the group, but an external third party, although most people would acknowledge that philanthropy includes an element of self-interest. This type of volunteering takes place typically within voluntary or community organizations, although in certain countries there is a strong tradition of volunteering within the public sector and a growing interest in volunteering in the corporate sector. There is also a long-standing tradition of volunteers being sent from one country to another to offer developmental and humanitarian assistance.

Participation. Participation refers to the role played by individuals in the governance process, from representation on government consultation bodies to user-involvement in local development projects. As a form of volunteering it is found in all countries, although it is most developed in countries with a strong tradition of civic engagement. Participation was recognized as an essential component of good governance at the Copenhagen Summit and has become the watchword of development in recent years, although there is a forceful critique which argues that much of what has passed for participation has been little more than token involvement and a means of legitimizing outsiders' decisions.

Advocacy or Campaigning. Advocacy or campaigning may be instigated and maintained by volunteers, sometimes described as activists, for example, lobbying government for a change in legislation affecting the rights of disabled people or pushing for a worldwide ban on landmines, or for the introduction of anti-racism measures. Volunteers have paved the way for the introduction of new welfare services in the field of HIV and AIDS, have raised public consciousness about abuses of human rights and environmental destruction, and have been active in the women's movement and in democracy campaigns in many parts of the world.

Volunteer actions and acts of solidarity cover an enormous range of different service and community help activities, and are not the exclusive component of formal civil society groups. Individuals also practice them in an informal way, in many cases without belonging to any organization whatsoever. When a group of volunteers in Mexico wishes to become associated and constitute themselves as a formal non-profit organization, they may adopt a number of different kinds of legal status, such as civil associations (*asociación civil*, A.C.), institutions or associations for private assistance or charity (*institución de asistencia privada*, I.A.P., *Institución de beneficencia privada*, I.B.P., or *asociación de beneficiencia privada*, A.B.P.), and civil societies (*sociedad civil*, S.C.). The one that is most predominant among all of these is the A.C., and the least utilized is the A.B.P. (Castro 2005 and Tapia and Robles 2006).

Volunteer action and acts of solidarity are phenomena that possess universal characteristics and particular features at the same time – it represents action inserted into the social settings of concrete cultures to which the subjects belong, adapting themselves to the contextual shadings in a complex way at the local, national, regional, and global levels. This underlines the importance and pertinence of producing information to analyze particular realities of solidarity and voluntary activity in specific contexts and locations on their own terms, to understand the many different ways in which volunteer action and expressions of solidarity may be built among the population.

International studies on the third sector[14] have demonstrated that the more the number of nonprofit organizations, the more the economic and human resources invested, and therefore, the more volunteering there is, implying that more professionals will be trained in this field. Proportionally, there is more non-profit activity and a greater number of volunteers in more developed societies, even though the fields of activity include the categories of culture and sports and the society participates in these to manifest its customs and cultural expressions.

Definition of Volunteer

In our country, little is said about the individuals who make up the NPO's, those who initiate them, and those who sustain them. There are even fewer commentaries about the motives behind these social initiatives, which in some countries constitute an activity that complements governmental activities, sometimes contributing to covering the needs of the citizenry. Insufficient attention is also paid to the people who contribute their efforts and enthusiasm in an isolated way to resolving problems in their communities.

With regard to this point, it is important to conceptualize volunteer praxis as the phenomenon of actions and activities in which individuals do not receive payment for their work and freely choose to give their resources of time, talent, and money for the well-being of others who are outside the circle of their family relations. Who are these people and what distinguishes their activities from others?[15] The first concept established is that of the *volunteer* – who is the subject who undertakes the action? "A volunteer is a social actor who provides unremunerated services. They donate their time and knowledge and dedicate themselves to a work of solidarity, whether in response to the needs of their fellow man or due to their personal motivations, which may be emotional, religious, political, or cultural."[16] The authors of

---

[14] Salamon *et al.* (1999). *Nuevo estudio del sector emergente: resumen.* This comparative study of 22 countries, including Mexico, presents some facets of voluntary individual participation. These authors argue that the size of the non-profit sector is a good indicator of the number of formal volunteers in existence. In another related article, *Volunteering in Cross-National Perspective: Evidence from Twenty-four Countries* (2003), by Salamon and Sokolowski, the findings reveal that in countries where the government spends more on social services for its citizens, there are also a greater number of volunteers. The authors explain that volunteer actions are concentrated in two areas of activity: the area of service to others –which is the Mexican case – and the expressive area – which includes cultural, recreational, and lobbying activities. This international study indicated that volunteer actions and acts of solidarity like those included in this investigation need to be studied deeply to better understand the non-profit sector.

[15] See Butcher (1999). "La solidaridad organizada: el voluntariado social como agente de cambio social en México", in *Sociedad Civil*, for an analysis of this definition and for a description of volunteer action in Mexico both inside and outside formal organizational structures.

[16] www.risolidaria.org.ar. Fascículo del Tercer Sector 04. "Todo lo que usted necesita saber sobre Voluntariado", *Tercer Sector* (2004).

this informative booklet suggest that these acts of solidarity many times serve to consolidate the exercise of public rights and awaken civic awareness about different social problems.

> The following is a description of the volunteers who donate their time in an organized way for society:
> Citizens who, once having fulfilled the duties of their situation (studies, family, profession) and their civil duties (administrative, political, or trade-union life), unselfishly place themselves at the service of the community, promoting solidarity. In this, they offer their energies, capabilities, time, and, at times, the means available to them, as a creative response to emerging needs of the territory and, as a priority, to needs of marginalized people. All of this, preferably, through the action of a group that provides permanent training and continuity of service in collaboration with public institutions and social forces (*Manual de Formación de Voluntarios* 2002, 11).

The definition of volunteer proposed by the United States Red Cross (Smith 1989), has been particularly useful for our investigation, because it refers specifically to individual activity:

> Volunteers are individuals who go beyond the confines of their remunerated employment and their normal responsibilities to contribute with time and service to a non-profit cause in the belief that their activity is beneficial for others, as well as satisfying to themselves (Smith 1989).

However, developing a broad and functional definition of volunteer action for the Mexican context was a fundamental point of departure for this investigation. Aspects related to volunteer actions and acts of solidarity were studied in both the formal and informal spheres. In this way, a definition of volunteer was established for this study that was inclusive of the different modalities of voluntary participation and solidarity in Mexico, activities that arise from the free will of individuals with diverse motives:

> Volunteer: A person who, by his/her own choice and without receiving any remuneration, contributes time to an activity that goes beyond the family sphere to provide service to others for the benefit of others and of the society as a whole.

With this definition, it is possible to include both volunteers inside the organizational structures of the third sector and those persons who undertake voluntary activities by way of solidarity outside the formal non-profit organizations in Mexico.

Volunteers are the protagonists of volunteer action and acts of solidarity. These are actions that individuals choose to undertake in their daily lives. It is not suggested that these people represent an ideal of citizen activity; they are rather considered as a set of individuals who undertake these activities as a form of citizen expression and social participation. We are aware that this description covers a very broad range of possible activities and includes Mexicans who, by this definition, contribute time, talent, and different resources for the common good.

Participation in Solidarity

The conceptual challenge for this study was to develop definitions that include volunteer and solidarity-type social participation activities in accordance with the socio-cultural specificities of the country, and the title of the investigation arose from this concern. For this first foray into participative solidarity phenomena in Mexico, the risk of adapting the traditional proposal for the concept of volunteer from the Anglo-Saxon perspective was accepted to arrive at an idea thereof that would contemplate the great richness and heterogeneity of volunteer activities exercised with an attitude of solidarity at the national level. It is considered that the definition of volunteer proposed for this study fulfills this objective.

It is important to be aware that problems and limitations may be found in any attempt to comprehend, explain, and quantify phenomena and the value of such activity. This work may be considered to be a pioneer study of an exploratory character; for descriptive purposes in this investigation, participation in solidarity shall be understood to be represented by the universe of both individual and group actions that occur outside formal NPO groups as one way in which common citizens freely express, without remuneration, voluntary attitudes of solidarity toward others. Expressing solidarity toward other citizens does not guarantee that the action, in addition to expressing solidarity, is ethical or specifically leads to a particular social good. However, solidarity represents – for our context – a way of acting for the benefit of others or of doing something for someone else. Although there are different uses of this term (Bayertz 1999), it is possible to indicate that, conceptually, solidarity presupposes the existence of a community to which one has specific duties.[17] In spite of a confused history owing to the lack of conceptual vigor in the use of the term, the notion of solidarity, as developed in the beginning of the first half of the nineteenth century, fundamentally lays claim to the idea that individuals have specific obligations in their community, obligations that are known in ethics as *positive* obligations (i.e., obligations that imply action). What began in the Aristotelian *polis*, where "*the interest of all is the same*", has evolved over time up until the term known today was coined.

The notion of solidarity has taken on even greater relevance today. As Valenzuela points out (2003, 504),[18] "it has become so important that it has become a generic

---

[17] In fact, the term "solidarity" has it origin in Roman law, where it was used to describe a type of legal situation in which individual subjects bound themselves as if they were a single subject, and therefore this type of obligation was called *obligatio in solidum*.

[18] See Valenzuela's text (2003), *La noción de solidaridad*, which undertakes a broad exploration of ideas and of the term "solidarity". In this theoretical-conceptual essay, the main theoreticians of the subject of solidarity are mentioned: Aristotle, Smith, Locke, Hume, Kant, Durkheim, de Tocqueville, Scheler, Rorty, Habermas, and Luhman, as well as mentioning the connotation it has in the current psycho-social trends of Eisenberg and Bandura, and the basis of Freud's psychoanalysis, also going into Kohlberg's y Piaget's moral training of individuals. It also includes an extensive bibliographical review of the use of the concept of solidarity over time, identifying the meanings and shades of meaning with which it has been used and presenting, by way of empirical evidence, some practical acceptations of the notion of solidarity expressed more or less explicitly in the Solidarity movement and other contemporary scientific theories.

term employed to refer to so-called "third-generation human rights". The idea of "participation in solidarity" in this study indicates, in addition to an attitude of solidarity, taking action as a consequence of this solidarity outside the family circle, without receiving remuneration. Such acts of solidarity suppose:

> ...an act of will,... an effort to transcend one's own limits, to transcend one's own individuality..., this effort also presupposes increased consciousness of the importance of solidarity, which is only really possible when anchored in feelings of empathy and compassion (Manual de Formación de Voluntarios 2001, 505.)

The citizenry expresses its solidarity with others in different ways. The *Volunteer Service Measurement: A Practical Guide* prepared by the United Nations – a key reference material for this investigation – used the notion of service considering it to be an essential and important component for describing volunteer action. In other words, voluntary service assumes a step beyond mere help. It implies both an open attitude and disposition toward the others and an orientation toward serving others instead of a utilitarian orientation. In this sense, Bolos (1997, 15–19) maintains that this kind of service ideally establishes and promotes the formation of horizontal relations and relationships among equals, which is an essential condition for the exercise of democracy. Horizontal or "service" interactions that occur during the experience of solidarity are not the exclusive province of groups of volunteers; they frequently occur in the case of any person with the willingness to give with the spirit of serving others.

Solidarity and voluntary activities do not guarantee, although they do evoke the ethical importance of, acting and achieving a common good for the society in which they are carried out. Our position is based, in principle, on the consideration that these actions are positive for society, within the variety of activities of organizations of a philanthropic nature, and those of social organizations that interact with one another in the third sector. However, we are also aware that there is a diversity of nonprofit dynamics, activities, and forms of participation, and association that attend to different interests, such as educational, political, and professional interests, among others.

Volunteer Work

According to what Morán (1997) points out, "work" is understood to be the expenditure of human energy oriented toward satisfying personal and social needs; therefore, not all work is found in the market. This author indicates that socially useful activities carried out outside commercial relations – such as domestic work or any work motivated by family ties, solidarity, or love – should be taken into consideration when conceptualizing the division of labor time.

There are several categories of unpaid work, and it is important to clarify that volunteer work does not represent the sum of these kinds of non-remunerated activities. Volunteer work, in addition to being free, is focused – at least in terms of its intention – on producing a social good, a good for everyone. The intention does not guarantee the results; however, it separates these activities from others that do not have the aim of achieving remuneration for the individuals who carry them out.

To consider work as only a human activity that is carried out in exchange for income is to assume a negation or ignorance of different kinds of labor done by thousands of people without receiving any remuneration whatsoever. In this investigation, volunteer work is defined as: *that which is not done according to the logic of obtaining economic benefit, i.e., without seeking material gain, in which time and energy are committed to the benefit of others, without expecting any remuneration in cash or in kind.*

From another perspective, it can also be said that the objective of volunteer work is not to maximize economic benefits for individuals but rather to generate certain services for the community or the public at large (Jerez 1997, 32). With regard to this last point, it is necessary to indicate that expressions of solidarity may involve volunteer work or donations or economic contributions. So the definition of volunteer work in this study does not include donations in cash or in kind – even though they may be voluntary – because this concept refers instead to effort and time dedicated to activities that do not result in any material gain whatsoever for the subjects carrying them out.

According to the definition of Portocarrero and Millán (2002, 2004), volunteer work is organized, unpaid work that is done for the benefit of others or the benefit of society as a whole, through some social organization. It should be questioned whether the existence of a social organization is always necessary in order to perform volunteer work, especially when it is known – as in the Mexican case – that many times actions of collaboration or support are performed outside these structures.

Volunteer work may have a role to play in promoting employment, by adding and developing abilities in those who do not have them. These actions also become ways of approaching the labor market, by creating new services that often become remunerated activities. When seeking to quantify the benefits of volunteer action, several restrictions have to be considered; in the first place, it should be noted that, from an economic viewpoint, volunteer work produces value – although it may be a nonmonetary value – for at least two groups; the volunteers and those receiving this service or the results of this work. In the second place, the limitations of using market costs to evaluate the supply of goods and services to those receiving them, when they do not pay the complete price, should be faced. If all kinds of volunteer work focused on the client are considered, there are forms of volunteer actions, such as political lobbying and actions oriented toward protecting the environment, for example, in which it is more difficult to identify the receiver of the service. In the third place, it is necessary to take into consideration the range of motivations that inspire people to be volunteers and give freely of their time, and some estimate of the value per hour of their actions, in line with their motives (Brown 1999, 5).

It is important to point out that official data, collected by all governments in a permanent way, is not available on volunteer work, as it is in the case of remunerated work. However, even though calculating it is complicated, it is not impossible. To achieve this, concepts must be defined and we must know what volunteer work is and what is not, in addition to establishing a more appropriate methodology for its study in Mexico.

The value and benefits of volunteer labor slowly began to be recognized, as volunteers' also contribute to the formation of social networks, promoting shared norms, and creating networks of mutual confidence. The individuals' attitudes of solidarity and the volunteers' actions represent some of the multiple activities that exist in present-day societies contributing to the development of more social capital (Putnam 2000, 21), which is an important indicator of the levels of participation and democracy in a country. Understanding, from the point of view of this author, social capital as the social networks that individuals build and the reciprocity norms associated with them, it follows that this may be both "a private good and a public good" (*Ibid*, 20).[19]

For this investigation, given the close conceptual relationship between these ideas and the lack of a theoretical consensus among the different authors who deal with this phenomenon, throughout the text volunteer action or acts of solidarity shall be used without distinction, referring to actors expressing solidarity and volunteer actors, whether they are engaged in formal or informal activities of this kind. In this study, what has been quantified, by means of a national survey, can all be considered to be volunteer work by the Mexican people. In the chapter about analyzing the interviews, the time people work inside and outside social organizations is specified.

Volunteerism

Our definition of "volunteers" complements the traditional group concept of volunteering or "volunteerism". Volunteerism systematizes volunteer action and links it to some type of organization or group. This assumes the idea of a collective that conceives of an organization of work called volunteerism or social volunteerism, as a set of volunteer actions and acts of solidarity carried out in an organized way in groups. It is considered to be a "movement of people who undertake actions for the common good without expecting remuneration, whether in the sphere of civil

---

[19]To delve more deeply into the concept of social capital, see Robert Putnam (2000), *Bowling Alone: The Collapse and Revival of American Community*, which emphasizes networks of reciprocity based on confidence and mutual aid, and explains that there are two kinds of linkages in the formation of these networks. The first occurs among individuals who are similar, with mutual and common interests, which is called *bonding social capital*, and refers to a close bond between equals. The second is called *bridging social capital,* and involves a bridge or connection between different and distinct people that goes beyond an intimate relation between peers. Putnam and Fieldstein's work (2003), *Better Together: Restoring the American Community*, should also be consulted, which establishes that the expression of bridging social capital is indispensable for the development of tolerance and openness in the construction of democratic societies. Both forms of relationship are considered by these authors as key to achieving active and inclusive participation in a democracy.

society organizations or in governmental and business entities."[20] The book *Voluntariados en Chile: lo plural y lo diverso* [Volunteerism in Chile: Plurality and Diversity], locates these actions "within a framework of a project belonging to a specific group" (Secretaría de Gobierno de Chile 2002, 39) and defines "volunteerism" as follows:

> ...the set of practices by means of which citizens make voluntary contributions or donations of work with the aim of satisfying essential unsatisfied human needs in concrete individuals, people, or groups, which action is carried out in the framework of special or discernible systematic processes of social intervention, linked to groups and organizations of civil society (*Ibid*).

In the international sphere, volunteerism is being more and more recognized as a fundamental social force. Countries like Canada, the United Kingdom, Holland, or the United States promote and support studies that deal with the phenomenon of the revitalization of civil society. These studies are also focused on the characteristics of an organized civil society that occupies participatory spaces which, in general, are not covered or attended to by other sectors of society. However, the views held on the third sector and the research undertaken – including studies on volunteer actions and acts of solidarity – represent, up until now, notions that have been built, for the most part, based on the mentality of the North (Fowler 1998.)

With regard to research on volunteerism in Latin American countries, a few relevant works may be cited. The Chilean government sponsored a study with a focus of a conceptual nature that deals with the subject of volunteerism; the study makes an analysis that considers the situation in that country and compares it with that of other nations, among them Brazil and the United States. In Peru, Portocarrero et al. (2004) conducted a survey in ten Peruvian cities to find out about the number of volunteers and the amount collected in donations of money and in kind. The authors recognize the difficulties due to the conceptual ambiguities about volunteerism and volunteer work, and comment that:

> In any case, it has been thanks to this broadness and indeterminacy, in which varied and ambiguous, old and modern social phenomena are brought together, that is probably its main attraction and, at the same time, its most evident weakness. In fact, the tendency to generalize the positive aspects and virtues of volunteer work has led to a situation in which perhaps too many expectations may have been placed on its ability to achieve social change, the strengthening of civil society, and economic development (Portocarrero et al. 2004, 9.)

In general, it could be said about this region that, together with the traditional volunteer benevolence and charity groups coming from religious-type groups – which were founded during the Spanish colonization – there has also been a system of "informal volunteerism", so that "when talking about volunteerism in Latin America and the Caribbean, it is necessary to recognize this permanent and silent form of donating personal time to the service of the common good" (Thompson and

---

[20]www.risolidaria.org.ar. Fascículos del Tercer Sector 04. "Todo lo que usted necesita saber sobre Voluntariado", *Tercer Sector* (2004).

Toro 1999, 31). Actions in the political field and those having religious motivation are today the most important incentives for the development of social volunteerism in Latin America, as distinct from other regions, according to these authors.

Also, beginning with the social movements in the decades of the 1960s and 1970s, a series of new actors arose seeking change of a political nature, who revolutionized the ways of perceiving participation. During the 1980's decade, both the emergence of "new social movements" and the NGO's associated with them may be mentioned, where volunteers got organized and acted, some in individual ways and others as groups, not only to fight against poverty and inequality but also to lobby for women's rights, environmental protection, and the promotion of citizen participation. Then this participation became a distinct kind of volunteerism, because in some of these activities, especially those with a political hue, the traditional concept of "charity" was transformed into the concept of "solidarity".[21] In more recent investigations in Latin America, we can see how ideas and concepts about solidarity are modified and transformed toward more modern forms of participation in solidarity based on the citizenry.

Components of the Study

This investigation includes two main components The first covers individual solidarity activities by the citizens themselves by means of a national survey. The questions were asked of people who, in an individual way on their own initiative and without being part of a specific group, undertake activities for others outside the sphere of the family. Chap. 2 presents an exhaustive analysis of the relevant questions in the survey.

On this basis, some of the questions developed as part of the general aim of the investigation are considered. However, it was necessary to develop a second component to express the reasons and motivations of people who work in social organizations and groups with a common aim, placing special emphasis on those considered to be volunteers. The methodology adopted in the case studies was chosen to broaden a qualitative perspective of the activities of these subjects. Case studies are relevant to this work, because it is possible, through them, to corroborate much of the quantitative data with qualitative data, increasing the reliability and

---

[21]As expressed in an article in the Argentinean newspaper *La Nación*, of April 21, 2000: "What elements does man have, at this point of transition from one millennium to another, to confront these evils, to contribute to the path toward a less unjust and more balanced society? He has, of course, his conscience and the values that illuminate it. Among these values, one of the most important is solidarity, understood as a generous force that moves human beings to do their utmost, unselfishly, to help their fellow man. Only to the degree to which people with more resources get organized to provide help and solidarity to the most unprotected sectors of the population will it be possible to advance toward a civilization less chastened by inequities and injustices."

validity of the investigation. For the Mexican case, case studies help to answer another series of questions that explain these motivations; they make it possible to find out the contexts of these individuals, at the same time as they deepen understanding of the profile of those people considered to be volunteers. The two components of this study complement one another, because they share a common subject of study – volunteer action. In this way, the investigation makes it possible to observe, analyze, and obtain information to understand the same actions from two distinct vantage points – in individual terms and in group terms.

I

To quantify this type of activity, a conceptual structure was developed by way of definitions to cover – as much as possible – all Mexicans performing these labors. Then, a national survey was developed including all solidarity and volunteer participation alternatives. The first component consists of the application and analysis of a national household survey. We sought to make this survey statistically representative to be able to establish parameters comparable to international studies, and also to be able to find a more reliable number, kind, location, and promoters of the main volunteer activities in Mexico.

The work of preparing the survey was the responsibility of the project director. One of the fundamental points when developing the battery of questions was not to use direct translations; experience indicated that people did not understand a substantial number of the questions. When some of them were employed, adaptations were made that made sense in the Mexican context.[22] In this, the *United Nations Guide* mentioned earlier was fundamental, because it had a clear warning on this problem. Alternative ways of asking the questions were also developed, and these referred more to people's activities than to their membership in organizations, which is the traditional way of asking about volunteerism.

In Mexico, the questions of the National Time Use Survey (*Encuesta Nacional del Uso del Tiempo*, ENUT 2002) were conducive to getting an idea of how people use their free time and their time at home. This survey was not designed for volunteers, but rather to differentiate work by men and women in the home, and it is useful insofar as it is possible to see how they use their free time. Among the

---

[22] For the ENSAV, 2005, the following documents, among others, were used for reference: *La medición del servicio voluntario: una guía práctica* (*Independent Sector y Voluntarios de las Naciones Unidas*, 2001), *Encuesta Nacional de Donaciones y Trabajo Voluntario 2002* (Portocarrero *et al.*), *Estudio sobre Trabajo Voluntario* (Gallup 2000, Argentina), the survey *Giving and Volunteering in the United States*, (*Independent Sector*, 1996) and the survey *Giving and Volunteering USA* (*Independent Sector,* 2001), the book *The Size and Scope of the Non-profit Sector in South Africa* (Swilling and Russell, 2002), *Encuesta Nacional sobre el Uso del Tiempo* (2002, México), and *Encuesta de Acciones Voluntarias del Manual de Cuentas Nacionales de Instituciones sin Fines de Lucro* (Universidad de John Hopkins, February, 2005, USA).

surveys done in Latin America, two stood out because of their contribution in terms of questions posed from the standpoint of a non-Anglo-Saxon mentality – The National Survey of Donations and Volunteer Work (*Encuesta National de Donaciones y Trabajo Voluntario*, Perú) and the Gallup survey done in Argentina in 2000. However, neither of them provided enough questions to cover the broad range of solidarity and voluntary activities; rather, they focused on membership in different social organizations. To delve into activities outside the formal sphere, recourse was had to a South African survey (Swilling and Russel 2002), because, although what the study measures is the third sector and not volunteer action in particular, it used a methodology in which the basis for the sample was not the existing NPO's, as the lists at that time were obsolete. It employed a representative sample of South African communities under the assumption that there was a direct correlation between the type of organization and the type of community. It took into account many aspects of informal groups like cooperatives, burial societies, religious organizations, and political parties.

The broad experience comprehended by the majority of Anglo-Saxon surveys could not be ignored, as they are the countries with the greatest number of studies of volunteer action. Although many were reviewed and are mentioned in the bibliography of this volume, the survey of the *Independent Sector*, 1996, from the U.S. was particularly useful because of its questions about confidence and its greater sample of populations not previously covered, such as higher-income individuals, Hispanics, and Blacks.

Finally, it was indispensable to maintain future international comparability among surveys, and for that reason an effort was made to include the basic questions proposed in the February, 2005, *Manual de Cuentas Nacionales de Instituciones sin Fines de Lucro* [Handbook on Nonprofit Institutions in the System of National Accounts] (John Hopkins University, 2003) from the Center for Civil Society Studies. The questions in this survey are basic for collecting information about volunteer action in the context where people know what volunteerism means; many of these questions were included in our national survey. In the final phase of preparing the survey, both specialists in the preparation of surveys and academics studying the sector were invited to be part of the team, and they gave it its present form. This survey was named the National Survey on Solidarity and Volunteer Action (*Encuesta Nacional de Solidaridad y Acción Voluntaria* or ENSAV), which will be used throughout this text.

The sample was developed from the conceptual framework and the definition of "volunteer" already described. A precodified questionnaire was tested on nine occasions until subtle aspects of the subject were captured, with 26 substantive batteries, 13 attitudinal ones, and 16 socio-demographic ones, taking advantage of the experiences and reactions tested by the most substantial national and international studies. The sampling framework was self-weighted. The size of the sample was 1,497 interviews with people over the age of 18, with a margin of error of ±2.5% and a level of confidence of 95%. The framework for the sample was probabilistic, on the basis of the electoral districts of the Federal Electoral Institute, updated to the elections of 2003. This kind of framework is recommended by experts from the United Nations.

The sample is considered to be statistically valid for establishing national and international comparisons and the results were organized in accordance thereof. The ENSAV was applied over one week, from September 19 to 25, 2005.

With regard to the accuracy of the concepts for applying the ENSAV, special emphasis was placed on the person being interviewed understanding that the questions were oriented toward a description of his/her activities. Therefore, after a series of deliberations and discussions among members of the research group and the group responsible for applying the survey, it was decided to present an introduction to the poll to ensure that the person interviewed would understand the intention of the questions posed. Hence, when beginning the questionnaire session with the survey, the following was indicated:

> I'm going to ask you about help in terms of time or services that you give or have given to other people who aren't part of your family, without receiving payment for that activity and which you have done in a voluntary way. It can be help of any kind: teaching how to read; organizing a neighborhood meeting; a school or church party; a sports team; a collection for the Red Cross or a clinic; helping a sick person who is not your relative; lending a neighbor a hand; helping with a pilgrimage or a political group; a project for the community. Anything that is to benefit others, without payment for you and done in a voluntary way.

The introduction to the survey cited above expresses a broad meaning of volunteer action and acts of solidarity and also contains three elements that are considered to be necessary to comprehend current participation by Mexicans who, of their own volition, without expecting economic remuneration, and with an attitude of solidarity, work for the common good. Thus volunteer actions developed in formal organizations are only a point of departure. This is why it was necessary to broaden the definition of "volunteer" beyond the formal sphere, with the aim of identifying how to incorporate volunteer actions by individuals who do not "officially" belong to a third sector organization.

Questions were asked in the ENSAV relating to the amount of contributions by Mexicans, especially in terms of time, but also in terms of economic resources and contributions in kind. Questions were included to get information on all forms of donations and contributions made by Mexicans in favor of others, an important point to meet the expectations of the study with regard to the number of hours contributed on a voluntary basis so as to be able to account for them in accordance with their market value. The analysis of the survey is presented in Chap. 2 of this book.

II

The second component of the investigation consists of 15 case studies carried out in different regions of the country so as to delve in a qualitative way into the reasons and motivations volunteers in Mexico have for undertaking this kind of work and offering their services to others. Fourteen of these case studies were done in relation to organizations with volunteers, and one case study was done on an individual basis. A specialist in case studies was invited to participate, given that this methodology was the appropriate one for this part of the investigation. A total of

66 interviews were done with different actors who participate in organizations that include volunteers. In the study, it was also possible to analyze the participative and associative dynamics of different social actors who participate in these organizations, whether or not they were volunteers.

This part of the investigation is not statistically representative. However, the number of interviews and cases considered is sufficient to show some significant tendencies and trends in terms of these kinds of activities in Mexico. The organizations were selected on the basis of a territorial distribution that included different parts of the country, to note and compare regional participative tendencies for these kinds of activities.

In the selection of organizations, 12 of the NPO's where case studies were done are or have been linked to the social service program of the Tecnológico de Monterrey at some of their 33 locations. The specialist in the area of Social Formation of that institute actively participated in executing and following up on this. For follow-up, feedback, and concentration of this group of interviews, the Blackboard platform was used, monitored by the Tecnológico de Monterrey and coordinated with the investigator responsible. The other three case studies were done in the traditional way.

Although it is true that typologies and classifications for social organizations exist at a world level, for the Mexican case in the investigation that concerns us, practice tells us that we will find a larger population of volunteers in health organizations than in business associations and professional associations. Even though all the organizations used for our investigation are nonprofit institutions, this classification does not indicate if there are volunteers active in them or not, so for our selection criterion, spheres of action were chosen that the team of investigators considered represented the broadest array of volunteer action and solidarity activities in Mexico and we developed our own classification taking into account the priority of finding greater volunteer activity in the organization.[23]

Both our own and foreign classifications exist for volunteer activities and civil organizations. We found a typology of nonprofit organizations based on the United Nations' International Standard Industrial Classification (ISIC) called the International Classification of Non-Profit Organizations (ICNPO), prepared for Phase II of the John Hopkins University Comparative Nonprofit Sector Project,[24] which consists of: (1) culture, (2) education and research, (3) health, (4) social services,

---

[23]Arredondo (1997) in "Naturaleza, desarrollo y tipología de la sociedad civil organizada" in *Sociedad Civil*, no. 1, vol. II, pp 164–184, offers a classification of civil organizations. A typology of civil associations by Alberto Olvera appears in: "Representaciones e ideologías de los organismos civiles en México: crítica de la selectividad y rescate del sentido de la idea de sociedad civil", pp 31–37, in Cadena Roa, J. (2004) (Coordinador) *Las organizaciones civiles mexicanas hoy*, which presents different forms of civil association in Mexico; the same author comments on the difficulties of covering the entire gamut of possible combinations of citizen associative activities. The typology in our study covers 12 spheres of action which were selected because of being considered as having the greatest volunteer work content.

[24]Salamon and Anheier (1999), *Nuevo estudio del sector emergente; Resumen*, p. 3, Baltimore: Universidad de John Hopkins, Instituto de Estudios Políticos, Centro de Estudios sobre Sociedad Civil.

(5) environment, (6) development, (7) civil rights and legal advice, (8) philanthropic activities, (9) international aid, (10) religious denominations, (11) business, professional, and trade union associations, (12) other.[25]

The categories considered for classifying the spheres of volunteer work in non-profit organizations in Mexico used in the qualitative section of the study are indicated in Table 1.1.

To analyze the qualitative information, four different roles were defined for those interviewed in the organizations, so as to understand the dynamics of their structure and get to know the processes of participation and interaction that occur inside these organizations. In this way, it was possible to observe the relation between those who participate in an organization of this type and some external factors such as the circumstances and life stages of these actors, their management of their available time, the opportunities for participation manifest in each case, as well as an analysis of the reasons and motivations of the subjects interviewed for getting involved in these activities.

The interviews were done between December, 2005 and April, 2006, and included direct and constant feedback from the investigator responsible for this phase to the interviewers. The interviewers were also trained during the months of September and October, 2005. At the beginning of the phase of interviews, there was a period of participatory observation. The information from the interviews was correlated with the *NVivo* program and a data run was performed in search of the enunciation context to obtain relevant information about the aspects directly mentioned by those interviewed when referring to volunteer actions. Chaps. 3–5 of this book cover the results of these interviews.

The appendices are an important part of the information produced by this project, and work by specialists in each case has been included so that it may be used as a reference point for future projects. In addition to analysis of the survey and of volunteer action, these appendices include the methodology applied, the survey graphics, and the questionnaire used, as well as the themes around which the in-depth interviews were structured. Also included, is the statistical data from the national survey which is available on the Cemefi web page.[26]

We then include the sections analyzing the information from the two components of this study. We believe that the point to emphasize is the richness of the material accessible to the reader. We hope that this pioneering effort will place the data arising from this investigation on the table of conceptual and analytical discussion concerning the third sector and citizen participation. We trust that this book will benefit, not only those studying the sector, but, also all those interested in exploring the activities and experiences of its protagonists.

---

[25]The ISIC and, hence, the ICNPO, classify organizations according to their main economic activity, i.e., the one that consumes the largest part of their operational expenses. So if an organization carries out activities in more than one area, it will be classified based on the area with the greatest operational expenditures. This is particularly important in the case of Mexico, since there are many organizations that work simultaneously in several areas or in areas of activity that are not easily identifiable.

[26]www.cemefi.org

Table 1.1 Spheres of action of non-profit organizations in Mexico

Business	Organizations engendered by business associations with quite varied purposes that get their operational funds from the private sector, even while maintaining their non-profit character.
Religious	Organizations engendered by religious institutions, whose objectives may include the strengthening of values and beliefs or assistance to unprotected groups.
Sports/recreation	Organizations that have the objective of promoting sports culture, especially among children.
Youth	Organizations formed to serve a diverse and complex sector like that of youth; they are particularly focused on serving their needs.
Rural/community	Organizations formed with the purpose of helping to develop projects for groups of peasants.
Vulnerable groups	Organizations created to serve children, women, seniors, and indigenous peoples in highly vulnerable conditions.
Urban	These are organizations that have been created to attend to specific demands of groups and/or populations in marginalized conditions that may have either a temporary or permanent character.
Health	Organizations formed with the specific objective of openly promoting the health of the population in precarious conditions that does not have the possibility of using public or private health services.
Educational	Organizations whose purpose is to strengthen education in all its forms and offer this kind of service to a broader sector of the population.
Cultural	Organizations whose objective is to contribute to knowledge, appreciation, and diffusion of different cultural expressions.
Causes	Organizations that have been engendered to fulfill specific objectives according to the requirements of groups of citizens interested in supporting others in different ways.
Environmental	Organizations that have been developed around concerns related to caring for and preserving the diversity of natural resources.

Source. Developed by the authors for this study.

References

Alduncin y Asociados. 2003. "El voluntariado en el Valle de México". In: Este país, 47–53

Alonso J (1996) La sociedad civil en óptica gramsciana. In: Sociedad Civil, no. 1, vol 1. pp 11–29

Arredondo V (1997) Naturaleza, desarrollo y tipología de la sociedad civil organizada. In: Sociedad Civil, no. 1, vol II. pp 165–185

Bayertz K (1999) Four Uses of 'Solidarity'. In: Bayertz K (ed) Solidarity. Kluwer Academic Publisers, London, pp 3–28

Becerra T, Berlanga R (2003) Voluntariado en México: una nueva visión. Noriega Editores, México

Bobbio N et al (1988) Diccionario de Política, vol II. Siglo XXI Editores, México

Bolos S (1997) ¿Actores sociales o actores políticos? El dilema de la democratización. In: Prometeo, Revista mexicana de psicología humanista y desarrollo humano, verano, pp 15–23

Brown E (1999) Assessing the value of volunteer activity. In: Nonprofit and voluntary sector quarterly, no. 1, vol 28, March, pp 5–17

Butcher J (1999) La solidaridad organizada: el voluntariado social como agente de cambio social en México. In: Sociedad Civil, no. 9, vol. III, pp 51–80

Butcher J (2002). A New Perspective in Voluntarism and Citizen Participation in Mexico: Recreating Civil Society/Government Relationships. Panel: Civil Society, Citizen Participation and the Dawn of a New Era: the Third Sector in Mexico in Light of a New Political Regime, V ISTR Conference, Cape Town, South Africa. (http://www.istr.org/conferences/capetown/volume/index.html)

Butcher J (2003) A humanistic perspective on the volunteer-recipient relationship. In: Dekker P, Halman L (eds) The values of volunteering: cross-cultural perspectives. Kluwer Academic/Plenum Publishers, New York, pp 111–125

Butcher J (2004) Building Citizenship and Voluntary Participation in Mexico: Social and Economic Implications from a National Study, VI ISTR Conference, Toronto, Canada. (http://www.istr.org/conferences/toronto/workingpapers/index.html)

Butcher J, Serna MG (coord.) (2006) El Tercer Sector en México: perspectivas de investigación. Cemefi-Instituto de Investigaciones Dr. José María Luis Mora, México

Castro C (2005) Manual de disposiciones legales y fiscales de las organizaciones de la sociedad civil en México. Cemefi, México

Cemefi (1994) La fundaciones norteamericanas y las instituciones no lucrativas en México. Cemefi, México

Dekker P, Halman L (eds) (2003) The values of volunteering: cross-cultural perspectives. Kluwer Academic. Plenum Publishers, New York

Fowler A (1998) Whither the third sector? A response to Stelle James. Voluntas 9(3):201–209

Gallup (2000) Estudio sobre trabajo voluntario en Argentina. Informe, noviembre

Govaart MM et al (ed) (2001). Volunteering worldwide. Institute of Care and Welfare, Holland, Netherlands

Handbook on Non-Profit Institutions in the System of National Accounts (2003). Appendix As(iii). United Nations

Handy C (1988) Understanding Voluntary Organizations. Penguin, London

Independent Sector y Voluntarios de las Naciones Unidas (2001) La medición del servicio voluntario: una guía práctica. Independent sector, Washington, DC. (http://www.independentsector.org/programs/research/toolkit/IYVspanish.pdf)

Independent Sector y Voluntarios de las Naciones Unidas (1996, 2001) Giving and volunteering in the United States

Inglehart R et al (2004) Human beliefs and values: 2000 world values survey. Siglo XXI Editores, Mexico

Instituto Nacional de Estadística, Geografía e Informática (2002) Encuesta Nacional sobre el Uso del Tiempo. INEGI, México

Instituto Tecnológico Autónomo de México (2005) Encuesta Nacional de Filantropía. ITAM, Mexico. (http://www.filantropia.itam.mx)

Investigator (2005) Placing a value on volunteer time. In: RKG Center for philanthropy and community service, no. 1, vol. 2, U.T. Austin, Fall, Texas. (http://www.rkgcenter.org/investigator/), (http://www.serviceleader.org/investigator/)

Jerez A (coord.) (1997). ¿Trabajo voluntario o participación? Elementos para una sociología del Tercer sector. Tecnos, Madrid

Layton M (2006) ¿Cómo se paga el capital social? In: Foreign Affairs en Español, no. 2, vol. 6, pp 163–172

Manual de Formación de Voluntarios (2002) Cultura de la solidaridad y voluntariado. (http://www.crefes.net/formacion/mdidacticos/descargas/asb/manual_voluntarios.pdf)

Marina S (2002) Las sociedades de San Vicente de Paul. In: Re-vista, giving and volunteering in the Americas, Spring, Harvard Review of Latin America

Meijs LCPM (1997) Management van vrijwilligersorganizaties. NOV-publicaties, Utrecht

Méndez J (1997). El Tercer sector y las organizaciones civiles en México: evolución reciente y perspectivas. In: Sociedad Civil, no. 1, vol. II, pp 103–124

Méndez J (coord.) (1998) Organizaciones civiles y políticas públicas en México y Centroamérica. Miguel Ángel Porrúa, México

Morán A (1997) El Futuro del trabajo, el empleo y el sector voluntario. In: Jerez A (coord.) ¿Trabajo voluntario o participación? Elementos para una sociología del Tercer sector. Tecnos, Madrid, pp 78–108

Moreno A (2005) Nuestros valores: los mexicanos en México y en Estados Unidos al inicio del siglo XXI. Banamex, México

Olvera A (1999) Los modos de la recuperación contemporánea de la idea de sociedad civil. In: Olvera A (coord.) La sociedad civil de la teoría a la realidad. El Colegio de México, México, pp 27–53

Olvera A (2004) Representaciones e ideologías de los organismos civiles en México: crítica de la selectividad y rescate del sentido de la idea de sociedad civil. In: Cadena Roa J (coord.) Las organizaciones civiles mexicanas hoy. UNAM, CIIICH, México, pp 23–47

Organización de las Naciones Unidas (2000) El papel del voluntariado en la promoción del desarrollo social. Reporte de la Comisión de Desarrollo Social. http://www.iyv.org/iyv_span/policy/unitednations/csd_document/csddocument_htm/csd_document_span.htm

Organización de las Naciones Unidas (2000) El papel del voluntariado en la promoción del desarrollo social. Consejo Económico y Social. (http://daccessdds.un.org/doc/UNDOC/GEN/N00/797/10/PDF/N0079710.pdf?OpenElement)

Organización de las Naciones Unidas (2005) Seguimiento de la observancia del Año Internacional del Voluntario. Sexagésimo periodo de sesiones, tema 64 del programa provisional, julio 18. Version in Spanish

Patronato Nacional de Promotores Voluntarios (1974) La acción voluntaria en el contexto histórico de la asistencia social. Gustavo Casasola, México

Portocarrero, F. et al (2002) Más allá del individualismo: el tercer sector en Perú Universidad del Pacífico, Perú

Plan Nacional de Desarrollo (2007–2012) Poder Ejecutivo Federal, Gobierno de los Estados Unidos Mexicanos, Presidencia de la República, México

Plan Nacional de Desarrollo (2000-2006) Poder Ejecutivo Federal, Gobierno de los Estados Unidos Mexicanos, Presidencia de la República, México

Portocarrero F et al (2004) Voluntarios, donantes y ciudadanos en el Perú: reflexiones a partir de una encuesta. Universidad de Pacífico, Perú

Putnam R (2000) Bowling alone: the collapse and revival of American community. Simon and Schuster, New York, NY

Putnam R, Feldstein L (2003) Better together: restoring the American community. Simon and Shuster, New York, NY

Reygadas R (1998) Abriendo veredas, iniciativas públicas y sociales de las redes de organizaciones civiles. Convergencia de Organismos Civiles por la Democracia, México

Salamon L, Anheier H (1996) The emerging sector. The John Hopkins University, Institute for Policy Studies, Civil Society Center of Studies, Baltimore

Salamon L, Anheier H (1999) Nuevo estudio del sector emergente: resumen. In: Proyecto de estudio comparativo del sector no lucrativo (Fase II). The Johns Hopkins University, Institute for Policy Studies, Civil Society Center of Studies, Baltimore

Salamon L, Sokolowski W (2003) Institutional roots of volunteering. In: Dekker P, Halman L (eds) The values of volunteering: cross-cultural perspectives. Kluwer Academic, Plenum Publishers, New York, NY, pp 71–90

San Juan Victoria C (1999) Tendencias de la sociedad civil en México: la puja del poder y la sociedad a fin de siglo. In: Olvera A (coord.) La sociedad civil: de la teoría a la realidad. El Colegio de México, México, pp 157–216

Secretaría de Gobernación (2001, 2003, 2005) Encuesta Nacional sobre Cultura Política y Prácticas Ciudadanas. Segob, Mexico. (http://www.segob.gob.mx)

Secretaría de Gobierno de Chile (2002) Voluntariados en Chile: lo plural y lo diverso. Sistematización de antecedentes generales en Chile y el exterior. Chile, Lom Ediciones

Serna MG, Monsiváis A (2006) Investigar el Tercer Sector. In: Butcher J, Serna MG (coord.) El Tercer Sector en México: perspectivas de investigación. Cemefi – Instituto de Investigaciones Dr. José María Luis Mora, México, pp 26–32

Smith M (1989) Taking volunteerism into the 21st century: some conclusions of the American red cross volunteer study 2000. J Volunt Adm III(1):3–10

Swilling M, Russell B (2002) The size and scope of the non-profit sector in South Africa. P&DM, University of the Witwatersrand, CCS, University of Natal, South Africa

Tapia M, Robles G (2006) Retos institucionales del marco legal y financiamiento a las organizaciones de la sociedad civil. Alternativas y Capacidades, México

Thompson A, Toro O (1999) El voluntariado social en América Latina: tendencias, influencias, espacios y lecciones aprendidas. In: Sociedad Civil, no. 9, vol. III. pp 27–49

Tocqueville A (1989) La democracia en América. Alianza, Madrid

Valenzuela R (2003) La noción de solidaridad. In: Portocarrero F, Sanborn C (eds) De la caridad a la solidaridad: filantropía y voluntariado en el Perú. Universidad del Pacífico, Centro de Investigación, Perú, pp 503–534

Van Daal HJ (1990) Vrijwilligerswerk. In: Informe le hule in Nederlands. NIMAWO, Den Haag

Verduzco G, List R, Salamon L (2001) Perfil del sector no lucrativo en México. Cemefi – The John Hopkins University. Institute for Policy Studies. Civil Society Center of Studies, México

Verduzco G (2003) Organizaciones no lucrativas: visión de su trayectoria en México. El Colegio de México-Cemefi, México

Weisbrod B (1974) Towards a theory of the non-profit sector in a three sector economy. In: Phelps ES (ed) Altruism, morality and economic theory. Russel Sage, New York, NY

Wilkison-Maposa et al (2006) The poor philanthropist. The International Business School in Africa, Africa. (http://www.gsb.uct.ac.za/gsbwebb/userfiles/Poor_philanthropist_screen.pdf)

Young I (2000) Inclusion and democracy. Oxford University Press, Oxford

Web Sites

Año Internacional del Voluntariado. Chile: http://www.chilevoluntario.cl.

Association for Research on Nonprofit Organizations and Voluntary Action (ARNOVA): http://arnova.org.

Association for Volunteer Administration (AVA). http://www.ava.org.

Canadian Centre for Philanthropy: http://www.nonprofitscan.ca

Fascículo del Tercer Sector 04. "Todo lo que usted necesita saber sobre Voluntariado": http://www.risolidaria.org.ar

Federación Catalana de Voluntariado Social (FCVS): http://www.fcvs.es.org

Foro virtual de ONG de acción social y el voluntariado: http://www.voluntariado.net.

Haces falta. Mexico: http://www.hacesfalta.org.mx.

Handbook on Non Profit Institutions in the System of National Accounts: http://www.jhu.edu/ccss/handbook

International Association for Volunteer Effort (IAVE): http://www.iave.org.

International Society for Third Sector Research (ISTR): http://www.istr.org.

Net Aid. http://www.netaid.org.

Participación ciudadana: http://www.participacionciudadana.cl

Red virtual de voluntarios reales: http://www.evoluntarios.net

The International Year of Volunteer: http://www.iyv2001.org

United Nations Information Technology Service: http://www.unites.org

Voluntariado: http://www.voluntariado.net

Voluntary Sector Initiative: http://www.vsi-isbc.ca

Chapter 2
Graphic "Acts of Solidarity in Mexico" (Analysis of the National Survey on Solidarity and Volunteer Action)

Gustavo Verduzco

Introduction

We usually think that most of our actions are governed by interests that bring us some kind of material benefit or by desires and intentions that are not economic but that are, however, selfish, where the final benefit is bestowed upon oneself or loved ones. It is true to a large degree that many human actions take place in this way. However, we rarely stop to think about the numerous actions we perform without any direct economic aim or without any self interest. These actions are carried out at times in different ways in diverse societies in accordance with the socioeconomic and cultural peculiarities of each place. In the western world, these kinds of activities commonly occur through nonprofit organizations, many of them religious, although the secularization of life has also allowed room for nonreligious organizations with humanitarian purposes. However, aside from what occurs based on secular organizations or within the institutional framework of churches, individual actions also take place that are not regulated by an organization or institution but rather are implemented by each individual to the benefit of others, in accordance with the volition of each person. These types of activities were known in earlier times as "charity", performed to alleviate some problem or other need of another person. Today, the secular world calls them "actions of solidarity" performed for the benefit of others. These activities are carried out either individually or in relation to various institutions. They are spontaneous expressions of support that occur either sporadically or regularly, but that occur with greater intensity when some event of catastrophic proportions takes place, such as a natural disaster.

Throughout the history of Mexico, we have seen different types of arrangements that have something to do, in some measure, with these kinds of expressions of solidarity. I will first mention several types so as to emphasize those that, although they have overtones of solidarity, more properly belong to a form of social organization

G. Verduzco (✉)
El Colegio de México, México D.F., México
e-mail: gverduz@colmex.mx

J. Butcher (ed.), *Mexican Solidarity: Citizen Participation and Volunteering*, DOI 10.1007/978-1-4419-1078-3_2, © Springer Science+Business Media, LLC 2010

that has generally persisted until our time with a certain sense of moral obligation arising from the socio-cultural framework to which some communities belong.

During the colonial era, the Crown imposed a type of social organization on the indigenous peoples that implied collective collaboration of the members of each village for common goals. This is why a system of posts and responsibilities generally referred to as the "stewardship system" (*sistema de cargos*) arose with the purpose of organizing different tasks that community members had to perform. This system was and continues to be a form of organization for dealing with common needs. The *tequio* (free community labor) and the *mano vuelta* (cooperative interchange of labor among community members) have been other forms of solidarity and collective organization among Mesoamerican indigenous peoples. These collective forms were a practical strategy for working together that made it possible to deal in a better way with conditions of a scarcity of goods in a world governed by colonial domination. For this reason, we should note that, in the strict sense of the term, these kinds of actions differ from others mentioned at the beginning insofar as these indigenous forms of organization, although expressing solidarity, had the aim of safeguarding their own conditions of social and economic reproduction as groups weakened by the actions of the colonial power imposed upon them. Some of these organizational forms have persisted up until the present, not only in indigenous communities, but also in *mestizo* (mixed race) communities in different regions of the country. Although these kinds of communal actions are still quite prevalent in the country, I want to make clear that they have not been the subject of our investigation, since they involve situations in which the actions occur under the pressure of a moral obligation arising from community life.

On the other hand, during the colonial era, there were also the so-called brotherhoods which, although wrapped in legal structures nominally corresponding to the Catholic Church, were organizations of laypeople, *criollos* (descendants of Spaniards), *mestizos*, and indigenous peoples with diverse religious, economic, and social background. Many of them were support institutions for the operation of schools, hospitals, and orphanages (Bechtloff 1996). They came to be what are now the foundations that also support these kinds of services. In the past as in the present, these kinds of organizations exist, because there are people who donate their time and money to these causes without any kind of personal profit or benefit involved. The support achieved through some brotherhoods for educational development and health care in the past had, in relative terms, greater importance than today, because modern public health and education institutions did not exist. This circumstance made the excellence of these support and solidarity institutions stand out even more.

In what is presented here, we will focus only on those actions that are carried out with certain regularity in favor of third parties without any payment whatsoever, both those in which an institution or group is involved and those carried out individually. We have not taken into consideration sporadic actions that are not done with certain regularity. It is important to note that, in the research on the subject, researchers often center solely on actions that people carry out for others within some institutional framework, leaving aside another set of actions that are carried out by informal groups or individuals. This has been the case with studies like the one by Portocarrero for Peru (2004) and Layton for Mexico (2006).

Before beginning this investigation, we had the hypothesis, based on field work experiences, that we Mexicans undertake intense solidarity activity, which for the most part occurs through informal groups or in a totally individual manner, in addition to other activities carried out through more formal institutions. Similarly, we had the impression that acts of solidarity performed individually or through informal groups with little structure were much more common and frequent than those taking place through more formal, institutional groups.

For example, one frequently hears of a neighbor who visits and helps some sick or disabled neighbor, with certain regularity with the aim of helping them in regard to some of their limitations. This is an individual type of act of solidarity. On the other hand, in rural communities and especially in poor urban neighborhoods, voluntary labor is commonly organized among the pauperized inhabitants in order to facilitate introduction of basic urban services such as drinking water or drainage. It is true that in these cases, there is a personal or family benefit from the free labor, but this does not mean that there is not also a broader public benefit served by this free personal collaboration. On the other hand, and in a different context, we often observe people in churches (more women than men) who voluntarily do different tasks, from catechesis work to multiple activities such as organizing processions, drawings and raffles, varied courses, help for the sick, and many other things. Similarly, in another sphere, one frequently hears of women workers who regularly leave some of their children with a neighbor while they are at work. These practices are, without doubt, exercises of solidarity In another sphere, there are, of course, actions that volunteers carry out through private assistance institutions (*instituciones de asistencia privada, I.A.P.*) such as orphanages, rehabilitation centers, or other kinds of organizations, either as simple collaborators or as part of administrative boards that help to organize activities and fundraising for the institutions. In this regard, a later chapter will deal more broadly with the trajectories of people who voluntarily contribute their time and efforts to these kinds of organizations, as well as the motivations that lead them to carry out this work.

Civil society organizations (CSO) also include the actions of many people acting as volunteers who carry out different unpaid tasks for the benefit of third parties in fields such as human rights, social development, and diverse citizen demands.

Daily life offers us multiple examples that go unnoticed most of the time. This is why the researcher faces a problem of mistaken conceptualization, because it is common for a good part of the activities we carry out voluntarily in favor of others to not be considered to be unpaid volunteer work (or work in solidarity[1]). But, rather we think of them simply as examples of "normal cooperation", without giving them any other content. It is even frequently the case that when someone is explicitly asked whether they do volunteer work, they respond negatively, even though that same person might respond positively when asked about some (volunteer or free)

---

[1]"Volunteer" and "solidarity" work are used as synonyms throughout the text.

"cooperation" they have performed. The words "to be a volunteer" or "do volunteer work" carry very concrete connotations that often induce people to think that they surely have not done this. However, it is clear that, because of the social importance of these actions, it was important to get to know the main characteristics of this kind of behavior. It was necessary to back up our perceptions with clear and extensive information about different ways in which Mexican people carry out acts of solidarity. It was also important to find out about the environments or situations in which they mainly occur, the time dedicated to them, their regularity, if they are carried out individually or in some kind of group, and other aspects. The first chapter pointed out the aspects of the social and economic importance of these kinds of actions, and the need to measure their scope in some way. In this sense, we emphasize the social value of these actions, since in most cases they probably involve collaboration and support of a horizontal type between equals or peers that normally occurs without coercion. For this same reason, these actions reinforce the social cohesion of the different groups of people who make up the society where each cultural environment has its own way of inventing, in social terms, the forms that develop in its midst. In some countries, of which the United States is a typical example, volunteer actions tend to occur mainly through formally constituted organizations (Corporation for National and Community Service, 2007). Historically, these have been a place for promoting horizontal social relations among similar actors that has not only allowed for broader democratic practices, but also brings together support for a common good with certain independence from governmental action. This allows for the possibility of developing relatively autonomous public projects, something that in the case of Mexico has not been able to develop because of the historically developed social and cultural environment in this country, as explained in the book by this writer: *Organizaciones no lucrativas. Visión de su trayectoria en México* [NonProfit Organizations: A View of their Development in Mexico] (Verduzco, 2003).

In New Spain, the presence of the Crown and of the Church, both strongly authoritarian institutions, emanating from a framework of colonial domination, imposed an equally authoritarian stamp on the population and the institutions that soon followed that suppressed any initiative that went beyond the bounds of vertical decision-making. Partly due to this, the social peace imposed by Porfirio Díaz after many years of conflict could only occur based on an authoritarian practice intensely centered on his person, and years later, also after a long period of conflict, this could only be replaced by another authoritarian practice based on a single party with unique characteristics that remained in power during almost the entire twentieth century: much longer than any other authoritarian regime in the world in that same period. This situation, which continued to encourage authoritarian forms, has denied us a freer and more spontaneous development of our own solidarity resources, including not only acts of solidarity in the strict sense studied herein, but also the spheres of social and political participation.

This is why, as will be seen further on in this chapter, the contributions of our volunteer actions or acts of solidarity have very different characteristics in the case of Mexico, at least in comparison with our neighbors to the north in the United States and Canada, although, on the other hand, they do occur with a relatively great intensity.

Similarly, as we shall see , the most common fields of action for volunteer action are also somewhat different from those of other countries. This is an indication of some of our clearest differences, while at the same time it indicates the kind of activities to which the socio-cultural environment gives the greatest importance.

About the Methodological Procedure

Before presenting the results of this investigation, it would seem to be important to also mention certain aspects of this work that we took into account before beginning. As has already been mentioned, we suspected that acts of solidarity by Mexican peoples were very widespread, but this was something that needed to be corroborated. This implied not only thinking about an information gathering instrument that would make possible national representation; but which would also be appropriate for capturing those aspects that seemed to us to be central in the Mexican case, such as those acts of solidarity that do not take place within institutional spheres. It seemed to us that we should try to capture not only what was taking place in regard to acts of solidarity at the moment of the interviews, but also what had occurred throughout the lives of the people interviewed since, based on what had been observed in our society with other investigation instruments, such as participant observation and unstructured interviews, we knew that at least a certain dedication to solidarity activities at times occurs during a period of people's lives that may be short or of intermediate duration since it has to do with certain characteristics of their life cycle, such as the period when their children attend elementary or secondary school. In these circumstances, it is easier for some mothers to perform volunteer work at the schools that their children attend. The circumstances of each person in this regard may vary, and hence, it was important to capture them. Similarly, it was necessary to prepare an information collection instrument capable of finding out about acts of solidarity that take place in institutions, in the typical form of what is called "volunteer work", not only because this modality has been the one most studied in other countries, but also because it is the one that most easily and directly allows for international comparisons. However, the greatest challenge consisted in preparing the questionnaire in such a way that it would lead those interviewed to think about the diversity of acts of solidarity they may have carried out or were carrying out during the period the survey was applied. As mentioned previously, at times it is not easy for people to realize or identify the type of actions they are carrying out, especially when some kind of preconception exists in this regard. For example, when a person is asked whether they do volunteer work, many say no, because they do not associate "volunteer" work with some of the actions that they have in fact carried out.

Due to prior difficulties, we decided to carry out several tests with questionnaires, which we then modified and refined based on the perceptions obtained during these first exploratory experiences. This was how we developed one that was sufficiently appropriate, although it did not completely satisfy us, as we were aware that it did not completely free us from certain limitations due to the limited time for administering the questionnaire, which would not allow for freer expression, since it would have to be applied to a national sample. In regard to the foregoing, we believe that, despite limitations, the results we present are a good sample, in which we have incorporated some of what other investigators have done, as well as exploring other veins of Mexican solidarity behavior for the first time. In this regard, some of the findings presented are surely going to surprise some people, because they go beyond the familiar stereotypes. However, the general objective of the investigation was precisely to pose some new hypotheses for well-known matters, which also lead us to other unexpected findings.

The sample was designed based on the sampling framework used by the Federal Electoral Institute (IFE, the Spanish acronym) for the Mexican Republic. Altogether, 1497 questionnaires were applied to persons of both sexes, 18 years and older. The survey is representative on both a national and regional level, as well as for both rural and urban environments. An extra sampling was done for the state of Chihuahua so as to also achieve a representative sample for that state.[2]

Actors in Solidarity

When studies have been made on volunteerism, normally actions or work done with certain regularity by people on a volunteer basis, i.e., without pay, through formal institutions, such as a hospice or disabled support center, has been included in this concept. Naturally, other kinds of actions are also included, such as helping to raise funds by means of different strategies (raffles, collections), but always considering actions or work carried out through institutions. However, in Mexico and certainly also in other Latin American countries, people carry out volunteer actions in very different situations and spheres that do not always have an institutional or formal character, although, of course, volunteer actions are also performed within the formal structure of institutions.

In this work, we propose to explore the different paths that Mexicans follow to carry out volunteer actions, i.e., unpaid actions to the benefit of others who are not their relatives and that are carried out or have been carried out with certain regularity. It may be asked why relatives are not included. One reason is that there is usually a sense of moral obligation toward them, together, at times, with an emotional situation that in some way makes it a more normal and frequent matter to perform

---

[2]The survey was applied under the direction of Dr. Miguel Basañéz (Global Quality Research, Princeton, N.J.). There is an appendix at the end with the details of the sample. Tables are included there that are somewhat different from those that are presented throughout this analysis. The readers will observe that the former correspond to multiple responses by those interviewed, and hence they are not completely compatible with what is presented here. However, we believe that the readers may find them useful.

actions for their benefit. In contrast, there is less inclination to perform support actions for people who are unknown or not close to the one acting. In this regard, we would be speaking of exercising solidarity to the benefit of others beyond the circle of one's own relatives.

Originally, different mutual aid actions served as the foundations for social organization of this activity. In primitive societies, reciprocal aid actions were indispensable for the survival of the group, but as the organization of society became more complex, money, as a means of exchange, facilitated basic interchanges that made possible an initial type of social organization. In this new context, facilitated by monetary exchange, actions in favor of others not mediated by money or blood relationship had a special value, because they helped to solve other problems, especially among those bereft of material goods or family protection. In fact, among current vulnerable groups, such as the indigenous peoples in Mexico, some acts of reciprocal support are still customarily performed through customs like the "*tequio*" or "*mano vuelta*" in relation to agricultural labor or in order to repair houses and communal property. This is a matter of mutual aid when there is a shortage of money: a situation that has undergone change with the passage of time to the degree to which communities have entered more fully into the monetary economy with a growing orientation toward the exterior. In any event, although these forms are not observed very widely in the country as a whole, some of them persist. However, in this work we will not refer to this specific type of actions within the framework of particular cultural contexts, but rather to those exercised with certain regularity in favor of others who are not relatives and without any payment whatsoever.

Volunteer Actions or Acts of Solidarity

When dealing with the subject of unpaid acts of solidarity by people to the benefit of others, we must also take into account other aspects that have to do with the modalities as well as the circumstances under which these acts are performed. Up until now, a little more was known in Mexico about those who carried out their acts of solidarity through formal institutions, but there had been little exploration of acts of solidarity carried out in informal spheres and by individuals. As was indicated earlier, prior to beginning this work, we suspected, because of our own experience, both in everyday life and by means of field observation in other types of investigations, that informal and individual acts of solidarity were perhaps very widespread among the population, but the limited information in this regard was restricted to case studies that, although they provided valuable and suggestive information, did not provide sufficient clues to determine the extent of this kind of phenomena in Mexico. On the other hand, the few available studies oriented toward broader coverage, whether at the level of a city or of the country as a whole, had sought to find out more about acts of solidarity in the sphere of formal organizations, and hence, other forms of collaboration that might be very widespread were outside their sphere of consideration.

It was also necessary to consider whether those who perform a certain type of action, for example, as catechist in a church, also help in other spheres such as work in a school or neighborhood or for some political group. To what degree does people's religious orientation help or not help to extend their volunteer actions to other fields? To what degree are people who seem not to be moved by religious motivations involved in volunteer actions? To what degree and in terms of what characteristics can we speak of a profile for those who perform volunteer actions in Mexico? And, if there is such a profile, what socioeconomic and socio-demographic characteristics define it? Or perhaps might several profiles be determined? Can regional differences be identified? Are we talking about sporadic actions or frequent actions? Do they take up several hours each time or do they have a very short duration? Are they performed through some institution or organized group or do they take place in an informal or even individual way? These characteristics are important, because they provide us with elements to be able to evaluate not only the importance of these kinds of activities; but also the possible relations that might be established with other people; depending on whether these actions are performed in an organization or group or individually. These aspects have to do with the characteristics that make up the social fabric in the Mexican context.

General Characteristics of the Survey

The questionnaire was applied at the end of the year 2005 and during the first months of 2006 with people who were over 18 years of age. The sample is representative of the country, the north, center, and south regions, the Federal District, and rural and urban sectors. An extra sample for the state of Chihuahua was also included so that it would be representative of that state.

In the country, the population of over 18 years of age is composed of 62,737,152 individuals of both genders, in accordance with the data from the 2005 Population Count (INEGI 2005).

The First Results

The first basic information that the survey offers us is that two-thirds of those interviewed (66%) answered that they have done something for others with certain regularity without pay and without those benefited being their relatives. This is a high percentage for the population of 18 years of age or older. In absolute terms, this proportion is equal to 41.4 million people. The differences between men and women, although small, favor women (see Graphic 2.1).

In terms of age groups, the variation is not very great, but the numbers slightly favor the adult population from 30 to 49 years old, since 69% of them have participated in these activities, as against 61% of young people between 18 and 29 years old.

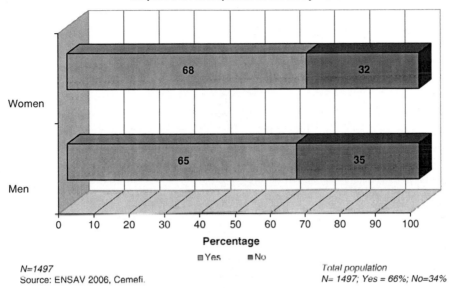

Graphic #1. Participation in solidarity work

N=1497
Source: ENSAV 2006, Cemefi.

Total population
N= 1497; Yes = 66%; No=34%

Graphic 2.1   Participation in solidarity work

As we shall see, there is a slight tendency toward greater participation at a mature age than with the youth.

The comparison between rural and urban areas favors the former with 71% of the people performing or having performed acts of solidarity, as against 65% in urban areas. Undoubtedly, the greater individualism in the cities, together with the fast pace of life and the shortage of time, produces a situation in which a larger part of the population refrains from participating in these kinds of actions.

In terms of income level, it would seem that there is slightly more participation among the low-income group, although, as already mentioned, the differences are so small that it would not make sense to take them into account. A similar situation is found with the self-employed, insofar as there is a little more participation by this group in comparison with those working on a salary or wage basis.

In reality, there are no significant differences among the volunteers in terms of demographical, educational, or income variables. *The degree of participation in these kinds of actions is very similar throughout the entire population, independent of the characteristics mentioned. This is a very clear feature, which should be taken into account and which was corroborated in several ways when analyzing the information, so that we can categorically affirm that participation in acts of solidarity by the Mexican people occurs more or less equally throughout the entire population, independently of their educational and socioeconomic situation.*

We should also add that up until now, this was not something that was understood about Mexico. Of course, some of us had the impression that this was the case, but it has been more common to think that these kinds of activities had a greater presence and intensity in some socioeconomic strata than in others. The data are now very clear in this regard in terms of the extent of this behavior.

The Most Common Acts of Solidarity

In terms of the types of actions people are most inclined to undertake, it is not surprising that they are: in first place, through church or religious groups (29%), followed by activities among neighbors or the community (20%), with school activities in third place (16%), and help or support for sick people in fourth place (10%). These four types of actions are the most common among the Mexican population (see Graphic 2.2).

Church and religious group activities that those interviewed reported are very diverse, including help with cleaning churches or washing altar cloths, some construction activities, teaching catechesis to children, preparation courses for marriage or confirmation, fundraising, personal attention to churchgoers, and other common institutional matters. It should be observed that the participation of men and women is relatively distinct. Women take part in these activities more than men do.

In regard to activities involving neighbors or the community, the actions reported have to do with organizing different activities to improve the neighborhood, whether aimed at introducing different services or adapting some installations for common use, as well as raising funds and accompanying neighbors needing company and support. In this case, there is greater participation by men than women, with a ratio of 1.7 men to each woman, while in school collaborations, two women

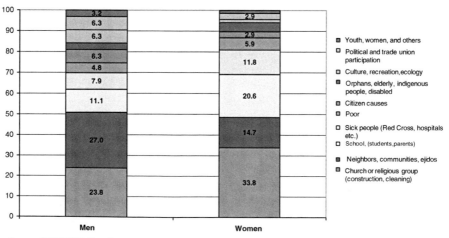

Graphic #2. Solidarity work by type of activity and gender

Source: ENSAV 2006, Cemefi.

Graphic 2.2 Solidarity work by type of activity and gender participate for every man. In activities with the sick, poor, orphans, and the disabled, there is a greater presence of women, but this is not the case with citizen causes, political groups, and projects with the government, youth, etc., where men stand out.

Activities reported for schools have to do with support for construction and improvement of the classrooms or school grounds, help with teaching itself, fundraising, and attention to students and parents.

In terms of the preferences of those interviewed, there is, of course, a clear religious orientation which, in the case of Mexico, refers almost exclusively to the Catholic Church, but we will deal more fully with this subject later on.

It is also interesting to observe that there are important variations in regard to participation in actions in favor of others and in regard to specific solidarity activities that are carried out in different regions of the country (see Tables 2.1 and 2.2).

Table 2.1 Solidarity work by region

			Region					
Total			North	West	Center	South	Federal District	Chihuahua
Yes	N=	1,497	388	309	310	330	160	300
No		66%	60%	71%	62%	78%	59%	75%
		34%	40%	29%	38%	22%	41%	25%
Total		100%	100%	100%	100%	100%	100%	100%

Source: ENSAV 2006, Cemefi

Table 2.2 Solidarity work by type of activity and region

Type of activity	Region				Federal	
	North	West	Center	South	District	Chihuahua
Church or religious group (construction, cleaning)	22.2	31.1	27.4	20.2	20.6	32.9
Neighbors, communities, ejidos	13.6	12.9	32.3	23.1	20.6	17.8
School (students, parents)	15.3	10.0	16.1	16.7	30.2	16.4
Sick people (Red Cross, hospitals, etc.)	13.6	14.3	9.7	6.4	6.3	13.7
Poor	6.8	10.0	0.0	2.6	1.6	5.5
Citizen causes	5.1	5.7	1.6	3.8	6.3	2.7
Orphans, elderly, indigenous people, disabled	1.7	4.3	4.8	6.4	3.2	5.5
Sports or recreation	1.7	2.9	1.6	2.6	4.8	2.7
Political groups or parties	6.8	1.4	0.0	2.6	1.6	0.0
Government (projects and activities)	1.7	4.3	1.6	2.6	1.6	0.0
Young people or children (boy scouts, guides, clubs)	0.0	1.4	1.6	2.6	1.6	1.4
Other (environmental, women, culture, unions)	1.7	1.4	3.2	2.6	1.6	1.4
Total	100.0	100.0	100.0	100.0	100.0	100.0

Source: ENSAV 2006, Cemefi

Regional Differences

More people have performed acts of solidarity in the south (78%) than in the north (60%) or the Federal District (59%), and more people in the rural sector have done so (71%) than in the urban sector (65%).

But the preference for the trio of actions in favor of church, school, and neighbors is maintained in all regions with some differences, and thus, this kind of majority orientation seems to be a feature that goes beyond regional differences.

However, it is worthwhile to emphasize that while preferences for actions in favor of the church are lower in the Federal District (20.6%), they are greater in the west (31.4%); orientation toward actions in favor of the "sick" was also reported to be higher in the west (14.3%), as against only 6.3% in the Federal District. The inclination toward actions to benefit neighbors or the community is also lower in the Federal District (20.6%) than in the central region (32.3%), and preferences in favor of school activities are higher in the Federal District (30.2%) than in the south. We might perhaps think that the intense urban life of the Federal District reduces real possibilities for action benefiting others and that perhaps a certain school pressure to perform actions in favor of the place where their children are educated leads more people to orient themselves in this way, especially in the Federal District. It should also be pointed out that, although actions to the benefit of others in "parties or political groups" were generally reported as very low, in the north region it is twice that for the country in general.

Given the pioneering character of this investigation, the questionnaire could not have been planned to properly explore possible regional differences in acts of solidarity. However, the variations mentioned earlier indicate that there are undoubtedly also cultural and institutional influences that in some way promote one type of solidarity work more than another in the different regions of the country. For example, in the west, where the Catholic Church has had a greater institutional presence for a long time, it is probable that this has favored a relative inclination of people toward ecclesiastical activities, as well as, perhaps, help for the sick. However, another hypothesis to explore would have to do with the greater or lesser possibility of access to public health services; if there is a greater scarcity of these services, for example, the support and solidarity people express toward the sick and needy becomes more important. Emigration to the United States would be, in the specific case of the west, another vein to explore, given the intensity of the phenomenon in that region and hence greater abandonment of the elderly population. Something similar may be happening in the case of the greater presence of solidarity work in schools in the Federal District and the southern region of the country, since institutional action may, perhaps, because of different circumstances, be stronger and better structured in the Federal District, while in the more rural and poorer south, it is more difficult to encounter this kind of presence in order to channel this kind of effort on the part of parents. In short, these are a few possibilities that we are just beginning to outline here, but they open the door to new exploration efforts for future investigations.

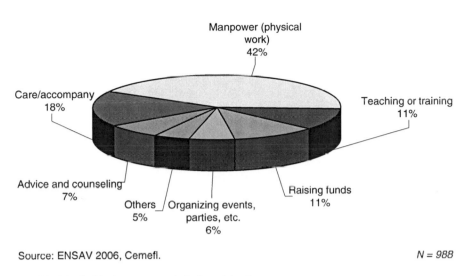

Graphic #3. Solidarity work by kind of participation

Source: ENSAV 2006, Cemefl.   N = 988

Graphic 2.3 Solidarity work by kind of participation

To return to the subject of the concrete activities undertaken, those that have to do with physical labor, handicrafts, and contributions of manpower clearly stand out. This was what 42.4% of the volunteers reported. Farther behind, we find those who have provided personal attention to those who need it (17.8%). Then, in third place come fundraising activities; in fourth place, teaching and training; and finally, activities that have to do with organizing events and parties. The participation in other kinds of activities is very low (see Graphic 2.3).

We observe that more people participate in those activities where, for different reasons, manpower is required: cleaning work, handicrafts, work contributing to construction or repairs, and similar actions.

Those who support the church or schools contribute, above all, their own physical labor, followed at a distance by teaching activities and then fundraising; in contrast, those who support neighbors or the community also do so first of all with physical labor but, unlike the foregoing case, this is followed by personal attention and care and then by fundraising. These are the most common kinds of acts of solidarity by Mexicans.

Later on we shall see to what degree these tendencies seem to go along with other characteristics of the population.

Intensity of Solidarity Activities

Half of those interviewed who said they had done something for others have only undertaken only one kind of activity: for example, they have collaborated for free with church or school, but nothing else. The other half has undertaken two or more kinds of actions: for example, they have collaborated with their neighborhood school and also with the church; others have also helped a sick neighbor. This information reveals that there is a relatively strong inclination among the Mexican population to engage in these kinds of volunteer actions, given that, altogether, considering the Mexican population of over 18 years of age, we would be talking about a third of the total population or about 20.6 million individuals. These people have undertaken at least two types of solidarity activities. We will try to go more deeply into both the modalities these actions have assumed and the characteristics of the people who have participated in them.

Trajectory of Solidarity Activities

In terms of the time dedicated to these actions, 60% of all volunteers continued to participate in at least one at the time of the interview; 8.5% had stopped participating less than 3 months before; and 8.5% had stopped participating between 3 and 12 months before. That is to say, 77% of all volunteers had undertaken at least one action in favor of others in the year prior to the interview. However, if we consider the entire population of the sample, i.e., both those who performed volunteer actions and those who did not, we find that we are talking about 50% of the total population, which, projected for the entire country, would be 31.3 million people 18 years or older. This is a high percentage that surpasses countries like Canada and the United States, where volunteer participation over a year has been 45% and 27%, respectively (Corporation for National and Community Service 2007; Hall et al. 2006).

On the other hand, those who were doing something for others at the time of the interview represented 40% of all those interviewed. This corresponds, in proportional terms, to 25 million people in the population as a whole.

The foregoing data also allow us to perceive the dynamic situation with regard to when acts of solidarity in favor of others occur, since there are moments in people's lives when the performance of these kinds of actions are facilitated by different circumstances. In this regard, it is worthwhile to remember the initial figure of 66% of the total sample who reported having engaged in some act of solidarity: 40% of the total sample said that they were doing something for others at the time of the interview and the remaining 26% of the total sample reporting that they had participated in an act of solidarity prior to the interview.

Now we are going to further analyze that initial 66% of those interviewed who reported having engaged in some act of solidarity. Half of them (33%) are engaged in only one type of act of solidarity; another 17% reported having carried out two types of actions, for example, one with the church, teaching catechism, and another with a school, collaborating with school parents. The remaining 16% performed three or more types of action. In this last group, we have those persons who have been more oriented than others toward participating in these kinds of solidarity activities. In absolute numbers for the whole population, we would have a little more than 10 million people here.

Graphic #4. Participation in solidarity activities by religious affiliation

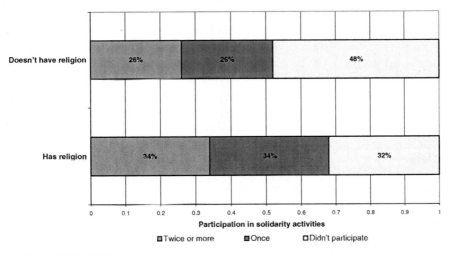

Source: ENSAV 2006, Cemefi

Graphic 2.4   Participation in solidarity activities by religious affiliation

Graphic #5. Ways of providing solidarity/volunteer work

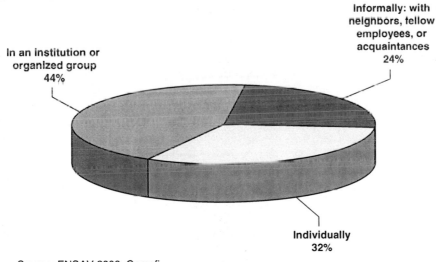

Source: ENSAV 2006, Cemefi

Graphic 2.5   Ways of providing solidarity/volunteer work

But what are the characteristics of those who have engaged in acts of solidarity in comparison with those who reported not having done so? What are the characteristics of those who have participated in more actions in comparison with those who have participated less?

Religious Affiliation and Acts of Solidarity

In the entire sample, 84% said that they were Catholic, 10% were from other religions (mainly evangelicals), and 6% without religion.[3] Among those who reported having some religious affiliation, 68% have carried out some act of solidarity with others (34% at least one action and 34% two or more), while among those who reported not having a religion, only 51% said that they had participated in these kinds of actions (26% did at least one and 26% did two or more). This difference, although it is not great, is sufficiently notable to lead us to believe that belonging to a religion leads to a slightly greater inclination toward undertaking acts of solidarity in favor of others.

Among Catholics, 30% have been principally oriented toward church activities, with neighborhood or community activities in second place (20%), school in third place (16.5%) and help for the sick in fourth (10%). Among those who belong to other religions (mainly evangelicals), the order is: the church in first place (also 30%), help for the sick in second place (13%), and school and neighbors in third and fourth places (12% each).

Those who reported having no religion were oriented, in first place, toward acts of solidarity for neighbors or the community (38%), with school activities in second place (22%), and third, sports and church activities in almost equal measure (only 6% each). It is, of course, notable that, having declared that they have no religion, there are cases of dedication to church activities, although in limited numbers. On the other hand, it is also noteworthy that actions with neighbors are very high, since actions with neighbors and with the school come to 60% for this group, which appears to be logical given their declaration of not belonging to any religion.

A greater number of those who reported that they were Catholics or belonged to other religions have engaged in acts of solidarity, and a third of those who have done so have participated in more than one type; conversely, those who reported having no religion were less oriented toward these kinds of actions and fewer people engaged in more than one act of solidarity. *In this sense, we can say that religious affiliation leads not only to a greater inclination toward acts of solidarity, but also to a relatively greater intensity of participation in these kinds of actions.*

In line with the preceding commentaries, it might also be considered that, those who claim to have a religious conviction might perform acts of solidarity more often. In this respect, however, the data do not seem to confirm this hypothesis beyond the relation already mentioned between belonging to a religion and engaging in more acts of solidarity.[4]

---

[3] The differences in this regard between our sample and the population census for the year 2000 have a lot to do with the ages considered in each source: the census includes people 5 years old and older and our sample was done among people 18 years and older.

[4] Among Catholics, 54% said that they went to church once a week or more, while 42% said that they went only occasionally, and 6% said that they never or almost never went.

Acts of Solidarity and Institutions

Another important facet has to do with the modalities in which these kinds of actions are carried out. They may be carried out through some institution or organized group or in any informal way with other people without any kind of group structure, or in a strictly individual manner. But how are these activities performed in Mexico? What types of groups or institutions are most commonly involved? Is there any relation between belonging to some group and engaging in acts of solidarity?

Of those who engage in acts of solidarity, 44% do so through some institution or organized group, 24% do so informally with neighbors, friends, or fellow workers, and 32% in an individual way. These results are in accordance with our hypothesis prior to applying the survey, since observation of what occurs in Mexican society led us to suspect that acts of solidarity developed individually or informally outside the institutional sphere were much more common than those taking place through institutions. The data now confirm this suspicion. In any event, the high percentage of people engaging in these activities either through informal groups or on their own, independently of institutions or organized groups, is noteworthy, since we are talking about more than half of them (56%). Similarly, those who engage in acts of solidarity in a completely individual way make up almost a third, which is also a high number.

The foregoing data reflect the population's preferences for participating in acts of solidarity, but they also let us see to what extent institutions and groups do or do not facilitate links among those who need help and those who wish to provide it. *Independently of the reasons and circumstances, it is clear that in Mexico these acts of solidarity are mainly carried out outside institutions and organized groups.*

Before continuing, let us also examine the types of activities volunteers carry out in accordance with the modality they have chosen in order to do so, whether that is an institution or organized group, on their own, or through some informal group of friends.

As can be seen in Graphic 2.6, the four activities that monopolize the attention of a majority of volunteers are solidarity activities in church, school, with neighbors, and with the sick, which make up two-thirds or more in any of the three cases. However, there are some interesting variations, since while the church, religious groups, and schools encourage the activities of those who participate in them through institutions, activity with neighbors takes first place among informal volunteers and also among those participating as individuals. The modality in which acts of solidarity are performed is very import, since this favors one kind of action more than another, in addition to expressing a different way of relating to the subjects or causes to be benefited. It implies a different point of view about working in each context, perhaps a different degree of commitment, and more or less interaction with other people. The modalities in which these kinds of actions are performed open several doors to analyzing this behavior: How and why are these activities begun in one of the three modalities? What circumstances facilitate this

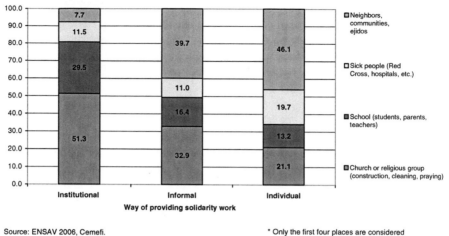

Graphic #6. Main places where solidarity work is done by way of providing it*

Source: ENSAV 2006, Cemefi.   * Only the first four places are considered

Graphic 2.6 Main modalities of solidarity work done in different sectors of activity

beginning? What kinds of motivations are there? How do they help to structure one or the other kind of social fabric? In this work, we have sought to initiate an exploration in this regard, although later another chapter will go more deeply into what happens mainly within the sphere of formal organizations.

Belonging to Organized Groups

Now we will delve into another dimension of acts of solidarity: to what extent do volunteers belong to organized groups or institutions? Does this encourage participation in acts of solidarity? It should be noted that the question of belonging to organized groups is different than the question of whether acts of solidarity are carried out through organized groups or not. The foregoing information has indicated that more people in Mexico tend to carry out acts of solidarity outside the institutional sphere, although the figure for those who do so in the context of organized groups (44%) is also considerable (see Graphic 2.7).

In terms of belonging to organized groups, the survey indicates that only 362 people or 24% said they belonged to one of them. This figure seems to be low, but it is also congruent with the results of other studies.[5] On the other hand, this information also corresponds to information from other source that indicates that the Mexican solidarity sector is small.[6] In reality, if more people belonged to these

---

[5]Layton, Michael (*op. cit.*).

[6]Verduzco, Gustavo (*op. cit.*).

Graphic #7. Membership in organized groups

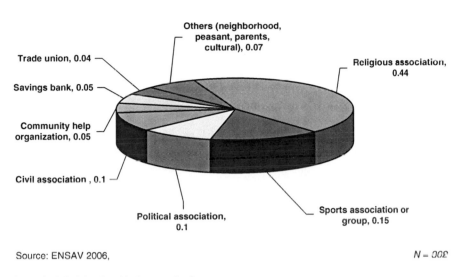

Source: ENSAV 2006,   N = 002

Graphic 2.7   Membership in organized groups

kinds of organizations, surely there would be many more organizations than the currently existing ones in Mexico.

What organized groups do they belong to? The majority said that they belonged to ecclesiastical or religious groups (44%), followed at a distance by associations or groups of a sports, political, or civil nature. Each of the last three categories accounts for 10%. Three-quarters of the people who said that they belonged to organized groups fall within these four types. Very few, 5% or less, said that they belonged to community help organizations, savings groups, or trade union associations.

In the light of the foregoing and the fact that the greatest organizational affiliation is to ecclesiastical or religious organizations, it is difficult to believe that a more or less robust civil society exists in the country. Less than half (12%) of those who said that they belonged to an organization participate in organizations other than religious and sports organizations. We reaffirm that we are talking about belonging to organized groups and therefore, due to the socio-historical processes that have occurred in the country, the low level of the foregoing figures should not be surprising, i.e., 24% belonging to some organization and the majority of those in religious or church groups. In this regard, the book by this author already cited (2003) may be consulted. However, considering this information in a broader context leads us to reaffirm that civil society in Mexico is weak, which is unfortunate for present and future democratic processes in the country.

Group Affiliation and Acts of Solidarity

Let us take a look at Graphic 2.8, and then, return to the subject of engaging in acts of solidarity. Among those who have participated in these actions, a little more than two-thirds (69%) do not belong to any organized group, but among those who belong to a group, the majority (86%) have performed some kind of act of solidarity, while only 60% of the other category have done so. *This information clearly suggests that belonging to a group implies a strong inclination toward performing some kind of action in favor of others.*

But to what degree does belonging to an organized group lead to or facilitate a situation in which people also carry out acts of solidarity through some formal institution? Clearly, the majority (62%) carried out their acts of solidarity through some institution or organized group. In contrast, among those who do not belong to any group, only a little more than a third (36%) carried out an act of solidarity through some institution. It also seems that not belonging to some group implies an inclination for people to engage in acts of solidarity on their own in an individual fashion, since 40% did so in this way, while only 16% of those who belong to a group did so in an individual way. *In this sense, although group membership is very low, it seems that it represents a certain influence, leading these people to also carry out their acts of solidarity through some institution or group.*

Now let us examine another dimension of the inclination to carry out volunteer actions: to what degree is participation in acts of solidarity related to whether another member or other members of the family do so?

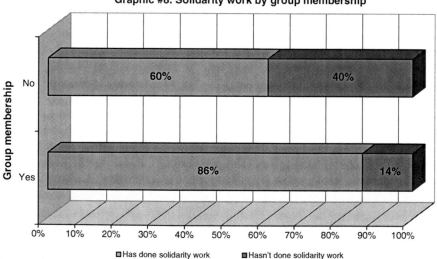

Graphic #8. Solidarity work by group membership

Source: ENSAV 2006   *N = 362*

Graphic 2.8 Solidarity work by group membership

Acts of Solidarity in the Family

In a little over half of the cases (54%), those who have engaged in these kinds of actions have other members of their families who have also participated in similar activities, while only a fourth of those who have not engaged in these kinds of practices have immediate family members who have. It would seem that in some way there is a certain influence in the home that helps or encourages other members to also engage in these types of activities. This is reinforced by the fact that, in homes where other members participate in these volunteer actions, 32% of those interviewed participate or have participated in several kinds of volunteer activity, while in cases where there are no other household members acting as volunteers, this occurs in only 18% of the cases.

This subject will be covered more extensively, later on, in a chapter about volunteers and explored indepth, based on case studies.

Frequency and Time Dedicated to Participation in Acts of Solidarity

The questionnaire also asked about the amount of time dedicated by each person to the volunteer activities they had mentioned, as well as the frequency of their participation. As will be seen, there are large variations in this regard.

A few people dedicate the entire day or every day to these activities, while others engage in them once or twice a week, or only a few times a year. Similarly, the number of hours dedicated to these activities is also quite variable.

In the information presented earlier, we have only taken into account those who said that they were participating in some kind of volunteer action at the time of the interview. This represents 40% of those interviewed which, in terms of numbers for the whole country, corresponds to a little more than 25 million people 18 years of age or older. We have limited this exercise to those who were active in solidarity work at the time of the interview. This way we were assured that they were referring with greater clarity and certainty to the facts of their current experience with regard to both the number of hours and the frequency of their volunteer activities.

Clearly, each individual dedicates different times and hours to these kinds of activities. The average for the sample as a whole shows that each person dedicated the equivalent of 27 8-h days a year. However, as we shall see presently, there is a great deal of variation.

A very few (8.3% of volunteers and 3.3% of all those interviewed) said that they were engaged in these activities every day, dedicating between half an hour and 12 h a day. On average, each one of these individuals dedicates 4.08 h to their volunteer activities. Over a period of a year, this is equivalent to 186 8-h days. In terms of the total population of the country, we would be talking about 2 million people.

Then we have those who said that they engage in these activities with a frequency of 2–3 times a week. They represent 13.2% of the volunteers and 5.2% of all those interviewed. These figures would represent about 3 million people. They dedicated 3.46 h each time, which comes to a total of 58 8-h days a year.

The next group consists of those who said that they participate in these kinds of activities once a week. They represent 15% of the volunteers and 6% of all those interviewed. On average, they dedicate 2.62 h each time, which is equivalent to 17.7 8-h days a year. In numbers, this is equivalent to 3.7 million people.

Those who dedicate some time every 2 weeks are only 3.5% of the sample volunteers and 1.6% of those interviewed. On average, each one dedicates 3.1 h each time, which would be the equivalent of 10.5 days a year. These people represent 1 million people in the whole country.

Finally, the majority are those who dedicate some of their time with a frequency lower than once every 2 weeks, making up 60% of the volunteers and 24% of all those interviewed. These people responded that they dedicate some of their time with a frequency that ranges from once a month to only once or twice a year. On average, each person in this group dedicates the equivalent of 1.7 8-h days a year. These figures would represent about 15 million people (Graphics 2.9 and 2.10).

As seen in the foregoing information, the global averages are deceptive, since they hide different nuances of reality. In this case, it is very clear, since although we can truthfully say that Mexican volunteers dedicate 27 working days a year to acts

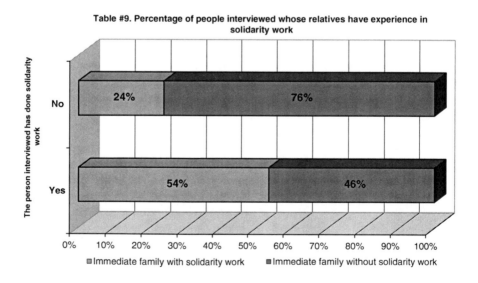

Source: ENSAV 2006   N = 635

Graphic 2.9 Percentage of people interviewed whose relatives have experience in solidarity work

Graphic #10. Frequency and average hours of participation in solidarity activities

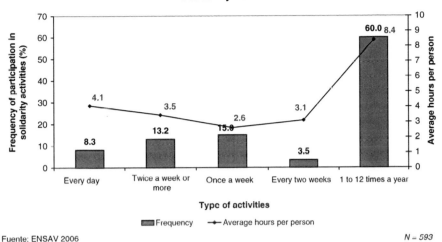

Fuente: ENSAV 2006   N = 593

Graphic 2.10 Frequency and average hours of participation in solidarity activities

of solidarity, the more detailed data indicates a contrast between the small section of only 8% in the first volunteer group, who carry out these actions every day and dedicated the equivalent of half a year or 186 days (51% of the year) and the majority of 60%, who only dedicate an average of 1.7 days a year. These are clearly two very different groups in terms of their dedication to acts of solidarity.

Similarly, we have those who, without dedicating themselves to these activities every day, do engage in them with a frequency that ranges from 2 or 3 times a week to once every two weeks, who make up 41% of total hours and represent 32% of all people engaged in acts of solidarity. We might think that these cases represent behavior more in keeping with the image we have of volunteers, people who periodically dedicate some time to solidarity activities. Considering this proportion in regard to the population of the country as a whole, it would represent almost 8 million people (7.7 million).

A careful analysis of the data led us to discover three types of actors based on their dedication to solidarity activities. This has to do with three characteristics: the first is the frequency with which they engage in these actions, since it is very different if this occurs every day or if it is a matter of occurrences distributed in different ways over the course of a year; the second is the amount of time dedicated each time they engage in these activities, from a short while to several hours, according to the availability and desires of each person; the third refers more to the degree of dedication of these people than to time and frequency, insofar as volunteers may dedicate themselves to several types of this activity, such as accompanying and helping a sick neighbor, teaching catechism at the neighborhood church, and also helping in their children's school. In this case, we are referring to those who engage in several kinds of action.

Volunteers in Mexico

Now we are going to present some information about the three kinds of volunteer actors, first segregating those who carry out acts of solidarity every day, who we have already seen are a small group representing only 8% of total volunteers (and 3.3% of the total population surveyed). In the second category, we have those volunteers who carry out actions with certain regularity, with a frequency ranging from three times a week to once every 2 weeks. This group represents 32% of the volunteers and 12.7% of the total population. Finally, the third group is made up of those who perform their actions more infrequently, ranging from once a month to a few times a year. This group makes up the majority of volunteers, with 60% (equivalent to 24% of the total population). In the preceding paragraphs, the average number of hours each group of volunteers dedicates to these activities was indicated.

Again, for this exercise, we are only considering those people in the sample who said that they were participating in some solidarity activity at the time of the interview.

As we will try to show, we have three groups of volunteers who share in certain measure a series of behavioral attributes, although there are characteristics that distinguish the members of each group from the others.

Henceforth we will call the most dedicated group "Intense volunteers", the second group "Typical volunteers", and the third "Infrequent volunteers". We believe that the members of the second group represent, in terms of their dedication, typical behavior among volunteers, since they carry out these activities with relative frequency, which ranges from one to three times a week to once every two weeks. On the other hand, the third group of "Infrequent volunteers", who make up the majority, carry out their actions less frequently, with a maximum of twelve occurrences a year.

It is also important to consider, as we shall now see, that unlike other forms of social activity, the differences in solidarity behavior in particular do not go hand in hand with demographic or socioeconomic characteristics that are distinct from those of the Mexican population as a whole. By this, we mean to say that the presence of people of different ages is more or less the same in each group, as is the presence of people from different socioeconomic segments, without there being any particular distinction for each group. This is why the observations we will make in this regard will be relatively minor and should be considered as such.

In Graphics 2.11 and 2.12, we have indicated the set of characteristics of the acts of solidarity of the three groups. It can be seen that there are important variations in several aspects, and we will indicate only those that seem most important to us. In any event, the reader will be able to see that there are also differences in other respects that we have not mentioned here. In this regard, they may find the tables themselves to be useful for further reflection.

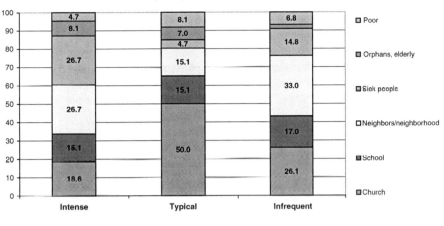

Graphic #11. Types of dedication to solidarity work according to place of participation*

Source: ENSAV 2006, Cemefi.   * Only the main activites are considered

Graphic 2.11 Types of dedication to solidarity work according to sectors of activity

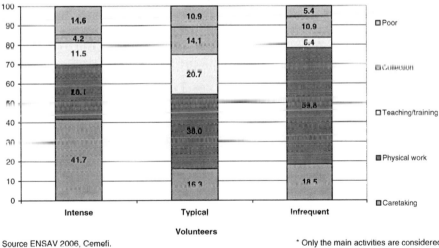

Graphic #12. Types of dedication to solidarity work by type of work done*

Source ENSAV 2006, Cemefi.   * Only the main activities are considered

Graphic 2.12 Types of dedication to solidarity work by type of work done*

Intense Volunteers

The members of the group of "Intense volunteers" are clearly differentiated from the rest by the fact that they engage in volunteer activities on a daily basis. In this sense, there is an abyss of difference in regard to the dedication to volunteer actions between this group and the third group, which engages in their activities more infrequently, during only a few days a year. We should also remember that, on average, the people in this group of "Intense volunteers" dedicate the equivalent of 186 8-h days a year to solidarity activities. They are also clearly differentiated from the other two groups in terms of gender, since 66% are women, while in the third group, the "Infrequent volunteers", women make up 50%, and among "Typical volunteers," they come to 59%.

Among "Intense volunteers", in addition to carrying out their actions on a daily basis, a little more than two-thirds were collaborating in two or more kinds of actions, in contrast to the other two groups. These attributes reinforce the intensity of these people's participation in solidarity activities, since they are people who may be collaborating every day on some community project, as well as helping some sick neighbor and visiting an elderly person, or providing their services for some church or school project.

They are also the group that carries out their acts of solidarity on their own, for the most part, without recourse to formal or informal groups. This is what 43% of them do. On the other hand, in terms of the orientation of their efforts, almost half carry out their volunteer activity with neighbors and sick people, providing "personal attention and care", as is shown in Graphic 2.11. We also present Table 2.3, which shows the whole set of data for the three types of volunteers, although we will only comment here on the data that appears most relevant.

Among those in this group who contribute their acts of solidarity through organizations (30% of the group) more than half of them teach or provide training and give administrative support. In this regard, the profile of some of these people who provide services in some third-party support organization will be seen and explored in greater detail based on case studies in the chapter on volunteers.

Almost 50% of the members of this group of "Intense volunteers" began their solidarity activities on their own initiative, although this also happened at the invitation of family members, but it seems that they were begun more because of their own design than because of some invitation (see Table 2.3). They are also the ones who contribute the least to the church (or to the parishioners), both in terms of acts of solidarity and donations of clothes or money to other people through the church. In comparison with the other two groups, they are also the ones who have received the least help from the church.

In terms of age, the people in this group are relatively concentrated between 30 and 49 years.

In terms of their religious beliefs and practices, the proportion of Catholics is higher (89%) in this group than in the others, and church attendance is also high, since 69% said that they usually attend more than once a week. On the other hand, the proportion of nonbelievers is very low, namely 2%. It is, therefore, notable that, in spite of being quite religious, they act with certain independence from ecclesiastical institutions. They are also the group with the lowest percentage among the three groups declaring that they carry out their volunteer activity because of religious beliefs.

In terms of their socioeconomic characteristics, they are situated closer to the less prosperous strata both in terms of their income and their educational level, without this representing a strong difference with other strata, as was indicated at the beginning of this section.

In comparison with the other two groups of volunteers, in this group, almost a fifth of the people work in the public sector and there are also fewer who work in the private sector than is the case for the other groups. However, in relative terms, they are the ones who have received the least help from the government.

This group includes, in relative terms, more housewives (38%) and fewer people who work full time (23%).

In general, a clear autonomy in their acts of solidarity is perceived for this group. They seem to be people concerned about those close to them, as they carry out their activities more among neighbors and sick people, trying to provide personal attention and care. In spite of being as Catholic as the rest, or a little more so, if we let ourselves be guided by external practice, they do not seem to be close to the church, at least in terms of carrying out these kinds of actions through the church.

Before continuing, we would like to draw the reader's attention to the fact that Table 2.3 is found almost at the end of this chapter and contains a concentration of important data differentiating the characteristics of the three groups of volunteers, since we will only comment on a few of these characteristics in the following pages.

Typical Volunteers

Let us look now at the group we have called "Typical volunteers". They represent a third of those who were engaged in volunteer activities at the time of the interview (31.5%). We have given them this name both because of several of the characteristics that will be mentioned in the rest of the chapter and because they coincide with the most well-known image of people who undertake volunteer activities with certain regularity.

They are the ones who work the most with the church (50%), with solidarity activities through school and with neighbors following far behind with the same low percentage for each one (15%).

Almost half (49%) carry out their acts of solidarity through some organization and fewer of them do so on their own. On the other hand, a little less than half perform their action through the church, and a third (38%) are involved in physical labor such as cleaning and arranging materials. Among the three groups, they are the one that is most engaged in teaching activities (20%), which is normally a question of catechism in preparation for first communion. If we add fundraising to the foregoing activities, altogether they account for 73% of the actions performed by this group.

On average, they dedicate the equivalent of 33.8 days a year to solidarity work.

Unlike intense volunteers, here the proportion of women is lower, although it comes to 59%.

Almost half (49%) belong to an organized group and a little more than half (59%) have been invited to participate in solidarity activities either by the members

Table 2.3 Characteristics of some acts of solidarity in the three solidarity and no solidarity groups (percentages)

	Intense volunteers %	Typical volunteers %	Infrequent volunteers %	Non-solidarity %
Age and sex				
18–29	13	22	21	29
30–49	56	45	48	39
50 and over	31	33	31	32
Proportion of women	66	59	50	50
Marital status-children				
Single	13	17	19	20
Has children	80	82	81	78
Education				
Elementary or les	39	41	44	35
Secondary or less	62	61	63	62
Basic	41	43	46	35
Middle	55	42	45	44
Higher	4	15	9	12
Work				
Housewives	38	36	28	28
Full-time work	23	24	32	32
Public sector	18	7	7	6
Private sector	9	15	18	21
Self-employed	29	29	36	27
Doesn't work	45	48	38	45
Income by household				
Less than $3000	32	31	33	22
Less than $6000	63	50	58	44
More than $6000		20	16	15
No answer		30	26	41
Income barely enough	63		59	50
Religion				
Catholic	89	84	88	81
Other	9	14	7	10
None	2	2	4	9
Church attendance				
More than once a week	69	75	53	5
Once a week	25	22	40	38
Almost never	6	3	6	56
Other socioeconomic information				
No. light bulbs 1-4	34	32	35	27
11 or more	9	17	12	15
Has telephone	52	55	49	49
Has oven	45	43	36	41
Has computer	21	24	17	18
Has internet access	5	12	11	13
Area of residence				
Urban	68	66	63	73
Rural	21	25	26	17
Mixed	11	9	11	10

(continued)

Table 2.3 (continued)

	Intense volunteers %	Typical volunteers %	Infrequent volunteers %	Non-solidarity %
Political party				
PRIPAN	2711	2117	2310	1112
PRD	9	4	7	8
Independent	34	38	50	34
Hours of TV a day				
Doesn't watch	2	4	4	4
3 or more	20	25	26	37
Regions				
North	30	25	19	32
West	29	31	19	17.5
Center	23	19	33	36
South	18	25	29	14.5
Act of donating				
Doesn't give	16	16	11	20
Money	63	56	60	53
Clothes	16	21	21	19
Food	5	6	7	7
Donating clothes				
Through church	6	19	9	7
Religious group	2	6	4	3
Non-religious organization	2	6	10	5
Group of friends	9	3	4	1
Directly	66	66	72	83
Has received help				
From the church	4	23	11	9
From the government	35	36	49	52
From a private organization	4	2	5	2
From a political organization	4	6	3	6
Other	13	3	1	4
From another person	35	26	28	23
No	59	56	59	75
Belonging to groups	34	50	30	10
Most people can't be trusted				86
How much time could devote to solidarity work a week				
More than 3 h	48	40	45	36
Not certain	4	4	4	7
Would do the following activities				
Belong to a group (regular, once in a while, did it once)	45	70	47	27
Go to group meetings	45	69	46	25
Participate in neighborhood decisions	57	74	67	40
Signing a petition	46	57	53	36
Unauthorized strike (regular, once in a while, already did so)	7	14	8	8

(continued)

Table 2.3 (continued)

	Intense volunteers %	Typical volunteers %	Infrequent volunteers %	Non-solidarity %
Social relations				
Has made friends	84	89	80	26
Someone else in the family participates	50	56	57	
Hasn't invited anyone	43	44	57	
Age when started activity				
Before 25	43	47	57	
From 30 to 39	29	24	16	
Started more than 10 years ago	43	46	53	
Reasons for engaging in activity				
Help the needy		28	31	
Desire to help		16	19	
Religious beliefs		17	7	
Way to feel useful, do something useful		15	11	
Help children		7	8.5	
Meet people		2	4	
Frequency of participation				
Once		47	51	
Two or three times		42	40	
Four or more		11	9	
Place of participation				
Church		43	23	
School		13	15	
Neighbors/neighborhood		13	29	
Sick people		4	13	
Orphans, elderly		6	2	
Poor		7	6	
Subtotal		86	88	
Type of work				
Caretaking		15	17	
Physical work		35	55	
Teaching/training		19	5	
Collection		13	10	
Advice, counseling		10	5	
How help given				
In organizations		49	40	
Informal		21	22	
Alone		30	39	
How decided to participate				
Family member invited		26	21	
Member of group		29	33	
On own		35	34	

Source: ENSAV 2006, Cemefi

of those groups or by family members. Almost all of them (89%) say that they have made friends through their volunteer work. They are the ones who, in relative terms, donate the most money, clothes, or food through the church or some religious group (25%).

They are also the ones among the three groups of volunteers that are most willing to participate in different group and collective activities and to attend group meetings, participate in neighborhood decisions of sign some petition.

They are the ones who have received more help from the main formal institutions, the church, and the government, since more than half (59%) say that they have received this kind of support. If we add help from other organizations, 70% of "Typical volunteers" have received help from the main (government and church) institutions and from other organizations.

In terms of their age, they are not different from the others, but in terms of religious practices, they are the ones who go to church most often, particularly in the category of those who go more than once a week.

In regard to their socioeconomic characteristics, without being very different from the rest, they generally tend to be situated a bit more for the middle sectors. They work less in the public sector than in the private sector and they tend more toward the average in terms of self-employment.

As we have already seen, they are the group among the three that participates most with institutions or organized groups. Also, perhaps due to these very characteristics, they have learned to receive help from institutions and at the same time they donate their time, even though they are not among the most economically disadvantaged.

Among the three groups of volunteers, the members of this one are the ones who, in relative terms, have the least philanthropic motivation to help others in need or the desire to give support to others, but rather tend to refer more to issues like "making friends" or "being recognized". On the other hand, they are the ones who most profess religious beliefs as the reason for participating. Similarly, continuing with relative comparisons, they were the ones with the smallest number who said that they performed their acts of solidarity as a form of occupational therapy. To repeat, these results and others not mentioned here can be consulted in Table 2.3, which summarizes the most important characteristics of the three types of volunteers.

Infrequent Volunteers

Once again, this group is made up of those who perform volunteer actions less frequently and who may do so once a month or only several times a year, which is why we have referred to them as "Infrequent volunteers". On average, as we saw earlier, they contribute the equivalent of 1.5 days a year. In this sense, they are clearly differentiated from the rest, and this is why we have considered them to be a distinct group.

Activities with neighbors, church, and school are the three types of activities accounting for 76% of those belonging to this group, but, in relative terms, this is the group with the highest proportion of solidarity activities with neighbors or the community.

More than half (59%) contribute physical or manual labor as their volunteer activity, and this is much higher than for the other two groups. They are also the ones who perform fewer teaching and counseling activities. Due to their more infrequent participation, it is perhaps logical that they are more involved in physical support than in teaching or training, which are activities which might, perhaps, require a more regular presence.

A little more than half (51%) have performed only one type of volunteer actions and fewer of them have been involved in more than one, in comparison with the other two groups.

They carry out their solidarity activities in both organizations and on their own with almost the same percentages in both cases, which differentiates them from typical volunteers in this regard, but they are also the ones who are least often members of organized groups.

In regard to the custom of donating money, clothes, or food, they are the group that most often does this directly, instead of through organizations or institutions. On the other hand, although more than half said that they had not received help from others, they were the group who, in relative terms, had received the most help from the government.

The proportion of people who declared that they were Catholics was almost the same as of the rest, but they have a lower rate of religious practice than the rest.

This group has exactly 50% of men and 50% of women and it is the one with the fewest housewives as well as the largest proportion of people who work full time. It is also the group with the highest proportion of self-employed people. In comparison with the other groups, these characteristics may reflect the situation of people for whom, for different reasons, it is more difficult to participate in this kind of activity.

In regard to this group which, as well have seen, has its particularities, we would like to point out that in the National Survey on Time Use (*Encuesta Nacional de Uso del Tiempo*, ENUT, INEGI, 2002), there is a section on the number of people who contribute "free labor" to the community and the number of hours they do so. We mention it here because it seems to us that, due to the characteristics of those who we have referred to here as "Infrequent volunteers" and have just examined, there may be a relatively close correspondence between these two groups in the two surveys. As we have seen, almost a third of "infrequent volunteers" (29%) said that they have participated in activities that have to do with neighbors or the community and another 15% said that they work with the sick and old people. In a way that could be similar, the ENUT indicates that 2.49 million people 12 years of age and older have contributed free labor to the community and 3.6 million have contributed free labor to "other households", for a total of 6.01 million people. In our case, the 29% of "Infrequent volunteers" who responded that they were participating in some kind of solidarity activities with neighbors or the community would be approximately

4.36 million people. The ENUT criteria do not distinguish whether the other households assisted were relatives or not, while in our case, we made that distinction, and thus it is clear that the two surveys are not directly comparable. However, it is worth noting that, considering the differences, the ENUT indicates that 6.01 million people 12 years of age and older contributed free labor to the community and other households. Having clarified these points, if we consider that the age in the ENUT (12 years or older) is lower than in our survey (18 years or older), as well as the differences in terms of whether or not help for other households includes relatives, the figures in both surveys are nevertheless relatively close to one another: 4.36 million in our survey and 6.01 million in the ENUT. We know that although it is speculation, we believe that similar populations might be involved, and we wish to make this point.

In order to have a better appreciation of these three groups of people who engage in acts of solidarity, let us take a look now at some of the characteristics of those who said that they had not participated in these kinds of activities, since this provides us with a perspective on actors who, for different reasons, have taken the opposite position (at least up until now) from those who have been the center of our interest.

Nonvolunteers

In this group, half are men and the other half are women, contrary to the situation in two of the three groups of volunteers whose characteristics were gone into above. In this case, they are the youngest group, and perhaps for that very reason they have a somewhat higher educational level than the rest since, as is well known, in Mexico the younger generations have a higher educational level. On the other hand, in relative terms, their socioeconomic level is slightly higher than that of the volunteer groups. Although there are an equal number of men and women, there are fewer housewives among the women and a few more people working full time (the data is shown in Table 2.3).

From the point of view of our main interest, which is solidarity activity, the people in this group not only have not engaged in this activity but also, compared with the other groups, there are more people who report that they do not customarily donate money either. In terms of clothes and food, they give the same amount or a little less than the others. Similarly, compared with the three groups of volunteers, they are the least willing to dedicate time to these kinds of activities.

In comparison with the other three groups, the percentage of people in this group who reported not having any religion was comparatively high, and those who said that they were believers attended church with less regularity.

In terms of group membership, the nonvolunteers are the ones who participate least in this kind of experience, given that 30% of the volunteers belong to some group, while only 10% of these groups do. They are also the ones least willing to belong to a group, attend meetings or participate in collective action.

The foregoing characteristics reveal, at least generally speaking, a set of people perceived to be less oriented toward others than the rest of the groups and, as will be seen, this would also suggest a certain individualism, closed to the outside. To the question, "What is the main reason why you have not contributed with any kind of help?", they responded as follows: more than half (57%) gave the excuse of lack of time, but a little more than a third (37%) expressed negative responses like the lack of motivation to engage in these kinds of activities, not wanting to commit themselves, having other priorities, or not believing that helping others does much good, etc. A few (6%) said they do not do so because they do not make enough money.

The foregoing responses, with the exception of the first and perhaps the last, are responses that tend to reaffirm the negative perception toward whatever is external to them as individuals.

Then again, those who, having engaged in acts of solidarity in the past, no longer continue to do so were asked a similar question, but their answers were different, except for those who also mentioned a lack of time. In these cases, the responses referred more to external circumstances, such as having moved away, the completion of the activities themselves, health problems, and similar situations, and not simply responses with negative connotations, as was the case with some of those who have never been volunteers.

Certainly these limited perceptions do not allow us to affirm something substantial yet concerning this kind of behavior, but they do clearly express a different attitude toward others, accompanied by some concrete features in terms of beliefs and behavior that at least are an indication of a road for us to follow in order to delve more deeply into these differences in the future.

A Few Conclusions

The willingness of the Mexican population to participate in acts of solidarity seems to be quite high, since this involves two-thirds of the population 18 years of age and older. In terms of the whole country, we would be talking about 41.4 million people. This tendency is also reinforced by the fact that half of all the volunteers reported having undertaken more than one type of solidarity activity, that is to say, a little more than 20 million people.

If we recall that the average number of days per volunteer was 27 a year, or 2.2 a month, and if we extrapolate that amount to include 40% of the total Mexican population over 18 years of age (the percentage of people who at the time of the survey were participating in these actions), we would have about 23 million people over 18 who would be contributing an average of 2.2 working days a month each.

If we calculate the foregoing in monetary terms and compare it with the total value of the labor done in the country, this would surely represent an economic contribution of great importance.

In order to proceed as indicated, it would be necessary to indicate that the population employed in nonagricultural activities, according to the Economic Census for
2003 (INEGI) came to 23 million people.[7] Hence, if we convert the total number of
hours contributed as volunteer or solidarity work as reported in the interviews, and
if we convert them into units of 8 h (i.e., one work day), and then calculate 260
working days a year, we would obtain the number of equivalent job positions. The
calculation would be as follows: 677,561,247 million days divided by 260 working
days a year would give us 2.6 million jobs positions, or the equivalent of 11.3% of
the employed population outside the agricultural sector: a figure that would appear
to be a truly important contribution, because we would be talking about a contribution of free labor that, in monetary terms, could be the equivalent of from 29.33 to
88.082 billion pesos.[8] The last figure would represent 1.14% of the GNP in 2004.
Or if, for the purposes of comparison, we compare this figure with total GNP for
communal, social, and personal services, which is the category that is most similar
to the one for solidarity activities, the contribution would reach 4.7%. We believe
that these figures speak for themselves and that, in monetary terms, we would be
talking about a considerable contribution by the Mexican population in terms of
unpaid actions to the benefit of third parties. However, rather than underlining the
monetary aspect, what is most important to emphasize is the social quality of these
actions, which help to maintain the social fabric for the country's inhabitants. As
was mentioned earlier, participation in these kinds of actions is quite similar
throughout the population, independent of their socioeconomic characteristics. This
is a very clear feature that should be taken into account and that was reaffirmed in
several ways when analyzing the information, so that it can be categorically
affirmed that participation in acts of solidarity by the Mexican population occurs
more or less equally among the entire population, independently of their educational and socioeconomic situation. The poor, the rich, and those in intermediate
levels engage in acts of solidarity with about the same intensity, whatever their
educational level. This conclusion is of great importance, because it allows us to
perceive an enormous contingent of volunteer actors in Mexican society whose
presence contradicts the typical view of "philanthropic volunteerism" which in
some way is commonly associated with people in medium and upper socioeconomic strata.

On the other hand, a clear preference is noted in Mexico for the trio of actions
in favor of church, school, and neighbors in all regions of the country, with some
differences, but this kind of majority orientation seems to be a common feature that
goes beyond regional differences. This has to do with the characteristics of our
idiosyncrasy: in the first place, the strong religiosity of Mexicans, as well as the
very important role schools have played in processes of social mobility for the
population and the circumstances of poverty and marginalization that perhaps

---

[7] We subtract 196,481 people included there as dedicated to fishing and aquaculture.

[8] This depends on whether a day's work is assigned the value of 1 or 3 times the daily minimum
wage.

require greater support from others. Similarly, helping neighbors and the immediate community is another feature that has to do with the difficult conditions of life for many people who, in the case of Mexico, attract the attention of those who are able to contribute through solidarity activities.

Although in the population as a whole the numbers indicate that only a limited number of people are inclined to undertake other kinds of actions more in keeping with the causes of civil society, there are areas of the country that show greater dynamism in this regard, so it would be important to explore this kind of behavior in greater depth in the future, in order to support strategies that make possible a greater development of these kinds of activities, which, as we know, are the ones that are most clearly oriented toward molding a civic attitude of concern for the improvement of democratic processes in different spheres of life.

But the best religious practices not only encourage people to undertake acts of solidarity of a religious nature; they also lead to participation in other kinds of acts of solidarity. So it would seem that new and well-structured acts of solidarity could be encouraged among these population sectors that could be oriented toward social problems that have not received enough attention up until now. These kinds of people would seem to constitute a good human contingent that could have potential for recruiting future volunteer actors that might possibly come to also foster civic causes in favor of a more defined democratic life among the population.

Although it may seem that nonreligious people are less inclined toward solidarity activities, in fact, it would be necessary to find out about their behavior in greater detail, since their solidarity contributions probably have other characteristics that have not been appropriately captured by the survey instrument used here.

Even though in Mexico, acts of solidarity mainly occur outside institutions or organized groups, almost half of all volunteers are accustomed to providing their services through these kinds of institutions, so, without minimizing what occurs outside an institutional framework, it would in any case be necessary to examine how to facilitate greater integration of volunteer actors into institutional activities.

The survey data confirm not only the low level of affiliation with organized groups, but also a very low presence of groups other than church and school organizations: a situation that has to do with the relative lack of a civic orientation among the Mexican population. This is a very entrenched problem; it does not seem that it will be easy to change, at least in short or medium term. In this sense, a strategy that would seem to be useful for the future would be to promote more actions through organized groups, since, as the data show, people participate more in acts of solidarity when they belong to some organized group, but it should also be added that we need to participate more in peer groups without the hard-and-fast hierarchies that we have become accustomed to historically, first in church and then in school. This is a great burden and has been so for a long time.

In conclusion, perhaps it could be said that although the Mexican people engage in many acts of solidarity, we still have not learned that solidarity with others can could be transformed into a civic vision, where participation with others encompasses different spheres of social life for the benefit of common goals of the civil society within which we live. This is one of our most fundamental challenges.

References

Bechtloff D (1996) Las cofradías en Michoacán durante la época de la colonia. La religión y su relación política en una sociedade intercultural. El Colegio de Michoacán-El Colegio Mexiquense, México

Corporation for National and Community Service (2007) Volunteering in America. State trends and rankings in civil life. Office of Research and Policy Development, Washington, DC

Hall M et al (2006) Caring Canadians, involved Canadians: highlights from the 2004 survey of giving, volunteering and participating. Imagine Canada-Statistics Canada, Ottawa

Instituto Nacional de Estadística, Geografía e Informática (2002) Encuesta Nacional sobre el Uso del Tiempo. INEGI, México

Layton M (2006) ¿Cómo se paga el capital social? In: Foreign Affairs en español, abril-junio

Portocarrero F et al (2004) Voluntarios donantes en Perú, Reporte de investigación. Universidad del Pacífico, Perú

Verduzco G (2003) Organizaciones no lucrativas. Visión de su trayectoria en México. El Colegio de México-Cemefi, México

Chapter 3
How to Become a Volunteer?

María Guadalupe Serna

Introduction

Chapter 2 discussed the characteristics and distribution of the volunteer population and solidarity activities in Mexico, based on an analysis of the National Survey on Solidarity and Volunteer Action (ENSAV, Spanish acronym). According to the findings of ENSAV, activities carried out by people through institutions and groups to help third parties represent 44% of the volunteer population. This implies that almost half of the population carrying out volunteering activities chooses to do so through organized groups. In addition, the ENSAV report also shows that 24% of all those participating in such an activity belong to some organized group. The percentage seems low, but corresponds with the results of other studies (Layton 2006).

Two aspects of the data that stand out call for attention (a) a significant percentage of the population carrying out volunteer or solidarity-type actions prefer to do so through organizations or institutions and (b) a fourth of the population performing these actions belongs to an organized group. Although the analysis of both aspects is relevant, we find that information about what goes on in a Mexican society is practically unavailable. In order to find out more about these aspects, the following three chapters analyze in depth what happens specifically with regard to people who belong to volunteer groups and actively participate in non-profit organizations (NPO) as a way to help others.

As a complement to the ENSAV, 15 case studies carried out in NPOs, with a total of 66 in-depth interviews, are analyzed in this chapter; the activities of volunteers are also explored in detail here. It might be mentioned that the ENSAV made it possible to develop a clear understanding of the nature of help for third parties and its different modalities in the national context. Simultaneously, the case studies will allow us to delve more deeply into an understanding of volunteers in Mexico, as well as the concerns and reasons they have for getting involved in activities to help third parties. Thus, we will have information about the behavior of the population

M. Guadalupe Serna
Instituto de Investigaciones Dr. José María Luis Mora, México D.F., México
e mail: gserna@mora.edu.mx

J. Butcher (ed.), *Mexican Solidarity: Citizen Participation and Volunteering*,
DOI 10.1007/978-1-4419-1078-3_3, © Springer Science+Business Media, LLC 2010

over 18 years of age in Mexico with regard to acts of solidarity, and also the characteristics and paths followed by actors who, in a voluntary and organized fashion, perform actions to help others.

Background

When dealing with the subject of volunteers and volunteerism, special emphasis has been placed on analyzing the nature of this non-profit sector and its relationship with the government, as well as exploring the types of services provided through these activities (Kramer 1990). These studies have contributed in a significant way to generating information about these matters. Other analyses have focused on characterizing the different types of volunteers based on their motivation levels (Cnaan et al. 1996). In certain other cases, consistent findings have been generated by means of surveys or investigation with focal groups, without looking deeply into the meanings or reasons that explain what is going on with the subject (Taylor 2005). Thus, a body of qualitative work that could provide extensive information about unpaid volunteer work and their impact on people's lives is not available (Taylor 2005).

In Mexico, the scenario poses an even greater challenge, since this is still a pending item in the research agenda. In this regard, at least the following questions need to be posed: Why do people dedicate time, effort, and knowledge to some causes? Who are the people who develop these kinds of activities? What reasons do they give for their involvement? How do they decide to join organized groups to participate in these kinds of activities? Why do some people participate individually? How do they come to have these kinds of concerns? Do their families, relatives, friends, or their own life experiences have some relation to participating in practices that may be considered beneficial for third parties? Do they expect something in exchange for what they do? The subject is complex; hence, it is necessary to develop a response to some of these questions, which will undoubtedly contribute to an understanding of volunteer activity and thus, the volunteers.

Purpose

The purpose of this chapter is to delve into the process through which people decide to get involved in volunteer groups, analyzing in depth the course of the subject's lives so as to identify the reasons that lead them to participate in NPOs and activities that entail, in different ways, support for third parties. This in effect implies expanding an analysis of the reflections of the volunteers themselves and of classifying differences among them so as to generate new research proposals on this subject in the case of Mexico.

In order to fulfill this purpose, I analyzed 66 interviews with a group of people who participated as volunteers with different organizations. They dedicated time and knowledge to help third parties, who were not necessarily members of their family group, without receiving a salary or economic remuneration. I delve deeply into the meaning this kind of volunteer work has for them, the reasons why they volunteer, and the changes noted over a period of time. To be precise, the way in which the process of giving new meaning develops that allows them to continue with these activities.

I am interested in analyzing responses that may seem socially acceptable, such as "help for others," and discussing the fact that such affirmations, and others mentioned in this text are the result of the life experiences of the subject, his or her individual trajectory, as well as the family environment in which he or she has lived.

The range of options for undertaking volunteer work includes very diverse activities, such as caring for sick people or people with diminished capabilities, attending to children who live in marginalized conditions and poverty, training others to provide education, promoting the integration of excluded groups, giving catechism courses, fostering sports or cultural activities, helping to improve the life conditions of marginalized groups, or encouraging a sense of community and integration in defense of specific causes, to mention a few.

I consider this to be an important matter since, as was noted in Chap. 2, a significant percentage of the population in Mexico is willing to undertake volunteer work. The percentages shown are relevant, given the fact that 66% of the population 18 years and older have carried out some type of volunteering activity or performed acts of solidarity in the course of their lives, and 44% of the total have done so through institutions or organized groups.

Analytical Methodology

The investigation covered in this book includes conducting a survey based on a representative national sample,[1] as well as structuring, designing, and carrying out 15 case studies in order to gain a full understanding of the processes of giving meaning and eventually an even greater meaning, to the actions undertaken by people considered to be volunteers.

One of the purposes of the investigation was to try to understand the paths followed by people who participate in volunteer groups, as well as to explore the reasons that led them to participate in these kinds of practices. In order to do so, it was necessary to generate qualitative information obtained through in-depth interviews, and come to understand how the subjects began their process of becoming involved in the world of volunteerism. This is why we chose to work based on case studies, a methodological tool that is widely used for analyzing organizations, groups within organizations, or individual subjects. Through case studies, it is possible to analyze in a detailed way the perspective of the subjects involved in some specific activity, delving into questions such as why and how the subjects do what

---

[1] The results have already been analyzed in Chap. 2.

they do in a given context, where it is possible to follow the processes involved in the phenomenon under study (Yin 1991; Meyer 2001). In addition, qualitative data provide us with a means to develop a description and a holistic understanding of the processes and activities, where it is assumed that the phenomenon under study and its complex system cannot be reduced to variables of causal relations having a linear character (Patton 1990).

For the purpose of developing and structuring the case studies,[2] one organization was considered. It was necessary to maintain contact with these kinds of non-profit entities, oriented towards different spheres of action,[3] where groups of volunteers participate. The organization was conceived as an entity in search of specific niches to offer its services that requires economic support for planning and development, and consisting of both paid and unpaid or volunteer personnel, as well as a set of social support networks. In order to analyze the subjects, the method of structuring their life histories was used, which is an analytical tool that makes it possible to examine the transitions experienced by individuals based on specific life experiences (Harris 1987). Analyzing the biography of a person brings us closer to the context in which social action takes place, not only in terms of the subject's experiences or specific conditions, but also as part of an effect of past actions in the context of present actions.

The organizations were selected based on three criteria: first, it was established that the organizations should be active in different spheres of action, based on the concerns they deal with. For this reason, documents were reviewed and some proposals were consulted (Dingle 2001; Brito Velásquez 1997). It was possible to define 12 spheres of action in which organizations were active in the case of Mexico (see Table 1, Chap. 1). The idea of including the greatest number of possible spheres of action prevailed, i.e., organizations with a diversity of purposes and niches to focus on. Secondly, the criterion was that all the organizations included should involve people acting as volunteers. Thirdly, the criterion was to include both formal (i.e., registered) organizations and informal ones, i.e., interest groups brought together by a common objective with several years of activity.

The characteristics of the organizations that would form part of the case studies were defined in accordance with the structural-operative criterion proposed by Salamon and Anheier (1996), that is to say: (1) that they had been in operation for several years; (2) that even the informal organizations had a minimal operational structure; (3) that they were active in one of the spheres of action considered; (4) that they offered support for third parties; (5) that their objective was not to

---

[2] The research design established that both a quantitative and a qualitative analysis would be performed. However, the questions included in the ENSAV were designed by the person responsible for the area and the general coordinator for the project. The design, content, and the way of carrying out these case studies were defined by the author of this text as the person responsible for the qualitative area. They were also amply discussed with other members of the group and with the general coordinator, where an interest for improving the reliability and validity of this analysis prevailed.

[3] Chapter 5 details the characteristics and particularities of the organizations about which information was gathered.

generate a profit, i.e., non-profit organizations; (6) that they included a group of people who were engaged in volunteer activities for beneficiaries of the organization; and (7) that they were distributed in different regions of Mexico.

In order to facilitate access to the organizations, we received the assistance of the Tecnológico de Monterrey: their Social Education Administration provided us with an ample number of organizations with whom they maintained relationship, either because students had carried out or were carrying out their social service with them, or because the organizations themselves had contacted the institution to request advice. Twelve organizations were suggested from this list, and three other organizations in spheres of actions, in regions that had not been covered, since the concern was that the case studies include as many regions as possible.

A total of 15 case studies were completed, consisting of 66 in-depth interviews with an equal number of people. Although this was not a representative sample, it was possible to define some general tendencies concerning the life histories of the groups of volunteers, establish specific differences among them, and investigate more deeply into certain aspects. The case studies included 13 formally constituted organizations, an informal organization, and a person who carried out volunteer-type activities in an individual way. The reason for including these three different types of classification was that in Mexico these seem to be the generally characteristic for this kind of participation (Verduzco 2003). Verduzco's analysis of the ENSAV fully corroborates this decision.

I chose to generate information from three sources to design and structure the case studies: (1) documents prepared by the organizations themselves; (2) a period of participant observations; and (3) a series of in-depth interviews within the organization. In order to facilitate coordination among the field investigators, I prepared a manual detailing the technical aspects for participant observation and in-depth interviews. For the field observation phase, I designed a set of questions oriented towards gathering information about the organization, i.e., a detailed description of the type of activities carried out, how they organized their daily activities, and who their users were. The aim was also to get closer to the subjects normally participating in order to select the staff personnel and the volunteers that would be interviewed.

When designing the in-depth interviews, the objective was to reveal the different viewpoints of the subjects making up a NPO that is focused on providing services to third parties. I thought that four different kinds of people should be interviewed for each case study based on the general characteristics of any organization: the founder, the director and/or informal leader, a coordinator or staff member, and a volunteer. It might be mentioned that, in most cases, the organizations had a structure that corresponded to the requirements established. The types of subjects to be interviewed were defined as follows:

- *Director of the organization or informal leader, who has the responsibility of fulfilling the organization's aims:* the person who, at the time of the interview, was in this position or was recognized by the members as the leader. It is possible that, in the first case, the person may receive remuneration for his/her activity. It is also possible that this person is the founder of the organization in some cases.

- *Founder, president, or volunteer advisor:* the person with the longest service in the organization or who founded it, and who participates directly in selecting a new leader. This person may or may not actively participate at the time of the interview.
- *Staff member:* a person with a specific post in the organization who directs and/ or coordinates work in specific areas. It is possible that in some cases this person may be receiving pay.
- *Volunteer:* a person voluntarily participating in the organization without pay for the activity developed. This person is also designated as a volunteer by the organization itself.

Considering the types defined above, I planned to interview the director and/or informal leader; the founder, president and/or voluntary advisor; one or two staff; and two volunteers. In this way we could find out about the perspectives of different subjects working in the organization.

In order to carry out the in-depth interviews,[4] I drew up detailed guidelines for each kind of interview, since the case studies were planned as replicas, in accordance with Yin's proposal (1991). The interviews were designed based on themes and touched on both general and specific aspects of the history of the subjects when developing activities as volunteers. The areas covered were the same in all cases, with modifications only based on the position of the person interviewed in the organization's structure. The topics were designed in order to explore the subject's socio-demographic characteristics, family, education, and work; the subject's history in support activities for third parties; mobility within organizations or outside them in activities for third parties; the reasons for being involved in these activities, with a special emphasis on volunteers; as well as the expectations, motivations, influences, types of activities undertaken, characteristics, frequency, and events reinforcing the activity or leading to distancing.

In the case of founders, the reasons that led them to start the organization and the problems associated with that were looked into more deeply. With the directors, how complicated it was to work in a non-profit organization dedicated to supporting others was explored. In the case of staff and volunteers, more attention was paid to decision-making in the structure and daily work with volunteers.

In order to select the individuals to be interviewed, the criterion defined was that the candidates be representative in terms of experience and knowledge of the subject covered by the study. For this purpose, I had the information provided by the participant observation phase on members of the organization, which allowed me to identify ideal subjects for the interviews with greater precision. In the case of founders and directors, the people interviewed were simply the people who filled these positions. In the case of staff personnel or coordinators and volunteers, people were sought who had participated in these kinds of activities over several years and who were familiar with and knew about the organization.

---

[4] See Appendix IV, Interview Guidelines.

The in-depth interviews lasted for about 45 min and in most cases two interviews were completed for each subject to cover whatever was missing or to go more deeply into specific subjects that needed to be clarified. At the time of the interview, the only people considered to be volunteers were those designated as such by the organization itself, even if there was information indicating that other people in the structure were also working as volunteers, as in fact was the case.

The set of 15 case studies consisted of a total of 66 in-depth interviews. In order to analyze the information gathered from these interviews, work was carried out on two fronts: on one hand, a classical-type manual review to answer specific questions about family history, reasons, etc., and, on the other hand, the use of the *NVivo* computer program, version 2.0. In the latter case, a series of structural conditions were established that made it possible to encounter some homogeneity in the information gathered. This was structured by means of sets of variables or attributes, and then codified based on the subjects' own enunciation context. The codification was done by means of "text search operators" and the *NVivo* program was used for this purpose. The text searches were also done with corresponding synonyms to achieve greater precision, based on an initial review of the content.

Gathering Information and Teamwork

The field work, which included a phase of participant observation, collecting documents, and in-depth interviews, was done simultaneously in different organizations between December 2005 and April 2006, with the assumption that this would make it possible to have similar conditions in the different regions of Mexico. I also chose not to do interviews after April 2006, in order to avoid having political questions affect the concerns of the investigation, since the presidential elections in July had created an agitated climate that ended up in one of the most controversial elections that has occurred in the country. This made it necessary to train a team of interviewers to carry out the interviews simultaneously in the different regions of the country.

The first team was made up of a group of 12 professionals from different areas; all of these personnel were from different campuses of the Tecnológico de Monterrey. I trained the group of field investigators, since some of them did not have previous experience with participant observation and interviewing techniques. They also received a manual with exercises, as well as advice about their concerns prior to performing the field work.

During the information gathering phase, I maintained constant contact with the team. It should be mentioned that this process turned out to be particularly work-intensive and interesting, and thanks to the support from the *Blackboard* technological platform which the Tecnológico de Monterrey placed at the project's disposal, it was possible to maintain constant and simultaneous communication with all the members of the team. There was also a technical coordinator who participated throughout the process of recruiting the team and was involved in subsequent follow-up, as well as in finding solutions to possible problems that arose.

The second team consisted of two professionals, an anthropologist and a specialist in human development, to finish up the number of required case studies. Follow-up with this team was done independently, without interaction with the first group. They used the same materials and there was constant follow-up for gathering data, although without the technological communication platform. This allowed uniformity in the type of information possible.

General Characteristics of Those Interviewed

Of all those interviewed, 74.2% (49) were committed volunteers. This means that they did not receive any pay for the activities they participated in, although some did receive support for transportation or meals when they went out to do some specific work for the organization. Another 25.8% were paid personnel, i.e., the remuneration received was pay for the work done[5] (see Table 3.1). In terms of the gender distribution, 74% (36) were women and 26% (13) were men; this gives us a 3:1 ratio in favor of the women. Thus, 75% of this group belonged to the 44% of the adult population in Mexico that participated in volunteer work and more specifically to the groups who carry out these activities every day (9%) or every other day (10%), according to the ENSAV.

As will be discussed below, this analysis is relevant for understanding the reasons given by those who participated in these kinds of activities, although they are not among the volunteers. The information gathered from the different organizations is grouped in Table 3.1, indicating the number of people interviewed, their gender, and if they were part of the paid personnel or were volunteers.

When analyzing the interviews, I found that volunteers were from all positions, such as the founder, the informal leader and/or director, as coordinators or simply as volunteers. That is to say, in the cases analyzed, the volunteers included both personnel strictly designated as volunteers as well as people who held other positions in the hierarchy of the organization.

In fact, 14.3% (7) of the total in groups of volunteers consisted of people who had been founders or advisors of the organization, and another 30% (15) were directors and/or informal leaders and coordinators. Finally, 55% (27) were volunteers, i.e., personnel who generally supported the coordinators, without having a specific position and function within the organizational structure.

Those making up the group of volunteers had a wide variety of occupations. In this category, 22.5% (11) were employees, 18.4% were business people and/or self-employed, 10.2% (5) were students, 6.1% peasants, and 6.1% worked full time in the organizations, while 4% were religious ministers. On the contrary, 32.7% (16) were housewives or retired. A higher percentage of people in this group were involved in for profit economic activity, in addition to participating in non-profit organizations.

---

[5] Although the amount they received was not considered in some cases when explicitly indicated by those interviewed, as the amount was far below what they would have received if they worked for private enterprise.

Table 3.1 Scope of volunteer actions by the organization and personnel interviewed

Sphere of volunteer action	Orientation of the organization	People remunerated	People not remunerated
Business	Aide to women in marginalized neighborhoods		4 W
Government institution	Dedicated to orphaned children	1 M 1 W	3 W
Religious	Values formed in the Catholic faith		5 W
Sports/recreation	Promoting sports among children in poorer neighborhoods	1 M 1 W	3 W
Youth/educational	Educational attention for youth in risk situations	2 W	1 M 1 W
Rural/community	Support for management of community development and labor counseling projects		3 M 1 W
Vulnerable groups	Attention to the disabled to facilitate social integration	2 W	1 M 1 W
Youth/educational	Help for abandoned and/or orphaned rural area youth	2 M	2 W
Health	Health care for women in extreme poverty	2 W	2 W 1 M
Causes	Attention for indigent sick people	1 W	4 W
Educational	Attention for street children	3 W	1 M 1 W
Cultural	Promoting and fostering culture	1 W	3 W
Individual	Contributing knowledge to improve installations		1 M
Vulnerable groups	Attention to working children in marginalized urban areas		5 W 1 M
Urban	Support for construction of housing in marginalized suburban areas		4 M 1 W

Source: Information from the case studies developed for this study

Although 75% of those interviewed were committed volunteers, when analyzing the information, I did not find significant differences in terms of their concerns and reasons for participating in these support groups between this group and those who were employees of the organizations. As a result we decided to analyze the sample as a whole. Some of the organizational employees participated in activities as volunteers in other places, and they themselves considered their participation in these NPOs as something very different from working for an institution in the government or private sectors. For the analysis in the following sections, we took the entire group of 66 subjects interviewed into consideration. The differences between the volunteers and the paid workers are only distinguished when the information gathered made such differences evident.

The majority of those involved in this activity were women, who represented 71% (47) of the total. This percentage differs from the results of the ENSAV, where 52% of those engaged in support activities were women and 48% were men. In terms of age groups, 44% of the total was between 30 and 49 years old, while 29%

were over 50, and only 2% were under 29 years old. This means that almost three-quarters of those interviewed were people in their productive stage. The ENSAV reports a similar distribution in this case. These findings places in doubt the generalized idea that the volunteers consist only of people who have free time which they fill, among other ways, by dedicating themselves to providing services to third parties, which is undoubtedly a subject which should be further explored. Perhaps this may be the case with women from more well-off sectors, but this was not the case with the ENSAV and the case studies.

In terms of the marital status of the people interviewed, 69% were married, 31% were single, and 67% of the total had children. This implies that those participating as volunteers combined their daily life and responsibilities with their family group, with a concern for contributing their personal time to third parties who required attention. We will return to this point later on, when we analyze the reasons expressed by the people interviewed. What stands out is that getting involved in volunteering demands a mature attitude toward life and the perception that others need support.

In terms of educational levels, 50% had obtained a university degree or some level of professional education, 18.2% had taken technical studies or finished high school, 12.1% had finished middle school and/or commercial schools, and 10.6% had done a graduate course. One person had a doctorate degree and only 9.1% finished elementary school or have only attended a few years. That is, a high percentage (60%) of the group consisted of people with high educational levels in comparison with the national average, which is 7.7 years. This means that the organizations amass a population with a high level of education in all cases. In fact, all of the founders and an important part of the directors and/or informal leaders had taken undergraduate or graduate studies.

This high educational level is attributed to the fact that in Mexico, multiple and difficult procedures are required to formally establish organizations that are not accessible to the entire population. In addition, procuring funds to finance the organizations and develop financially viable projects requires knowledge about various aspects. We can state that, in this case, we are dealing with a particular group in terms of its educational level, especially in comparison to the prevailing situation on a national level.

Background and Participation in Volunteer Activities

When analyzing the histories of those interviewed in relation to activities related to volunteerism, I found that 84% of the total had participated in other organizations or their immediate family had done so in an informal way. In other cases, they carried out support activities on their own after joining some organization. However, for 16% of the group, this was the first time they were involved in these activities. An interesting point is that the group of people interviewed showed no change of organization; once they join one, they stay there for several years, even decades, which imply a long-term commitment. For those who indicated that they had been in other organizations and had left them, this was generally due to moving to another city.

In terms of their experience in these activities, 24% had more than 10 years of experience of volunteerism. This group was mainly made up of founders, directors and/or informal leaders of the organizations, with a history of between one and three decades of having been involved in organizations to support specific communities. These are people with a college education who had social concerns early on, and a way of getting involved was to provide community service or advise groups in economically disadvantaged conditions. Over time they created a project and finally an organization dedicated to helping groups in poverty conditions based on specific objectives. Generally speaking, they had spent part of their lives in these kinds of activities, as indicated in the following paragraph:

> "...I've been doing this since, well, I participated in social events since I was nine years old in my community... as an altar boy I liked to sing in church... When I was 14 years old, no, 15, I started to work as a volunteer in an orphanage... at about of age 19 I did volunteer work with drug addicts... I studied and got involved with a neighborhood community, and also with volunteer work in Christian base communities and forming cooperatives and nutritional courses in poor neighborhoods. Since I returned to the [village] where I was born, I've worked on nutrition, natural medicine, people's theater, and finally we got involved in the project... where I devote most of my volunteer efforts..." (44 year-old man, founder and volunteer)

In other cases, I found women who had participated for more than a decade in different organizations to support and improve the condition of women in poorer neighborhoods, attending to sick people with few resources or with some disability. Others were professional women who contributed their knowledge and concern to attend to impoverished children or dedicated themselves to health care for women who are in poverty.

> "...before we used to live in [another city]; I was in a program supporting groups there for eight years... but, as would be the correct use of the word philanthropy, we used to support by collecting funds... Then we came here and the institution where my husband worked decided to do this on a national level. It was by invitation without any commitment... We began in a sector of poorer neighborhoods and we liked it a lot... That's where we started; we began with women in the neighborhoods..., knocking on doors where they just let us start with motivational talks and some handicrafts and learning to read, and well, in a basic way... That was in ninety-two... We've been at it for fifteen years." (46 year-old woman, founder and volunteer in the regional section of an organization)

> "I began by going with that woman [the founder], accompanying her, you see, and watching the work she did and learning... and becoming conscious of the needs there were... seeing the sick people... And then I started to get more involved, you know,... helping to get support... and I started with her in 1985, since before they did away with the old hospital, about one or two years before they inaugurated the new hospital, you see." (62 year-old woman, housewife, volunteer, and part of the staff)

Another 55% of the group had been participating in organizations for between 1 and 5 years and had undertaken similar activities on their own before that. This is a more complex universe in terms of ages where we find some young and middle-aged men as well as women, many of whom are housewives or retired. Another group was made up of young people who had supported the planning of the organization where they were now or had participated in its founding and were now directors or coordinators. Or else, people who came to the organization to provide services as part of their college education and, once there, had become involved with the project and stayed to support it.

> "No, I had never really [done volunteer work]. I came here to do my social service and I stayed... Yes, I finished in February... I don't remember... in 2003... I've been here for three and a half years. Now I'm part of the staff... I stayed, you see... It was like part of a dream; I dreamt of being a professional soccer player... and finding out about the salary, and right there I began to be concerned about forming an organization for street children... So I couldn't do the first thing, but the second one I could..." (22 year-old man, volunteer coordinator)

> "...everything began with my masters' project. I wanted to do a project and I didn't want it to be something without importance, although all the business projects were important, but that's what I'd always done... But I wanted to do something worthwhile... I thought an institution like this could help a lot... A project occurred to me, I came to see [the president] and, well, it was great, I liked it, and well, yes, it was like retaking an aspect or taking up an aspect that I had been neglecting... I said that I'm going to take advantage of what I have to do and I got more involved in this... It must be a little more than a year now; my masters' project was for three months... and now it's been the rest of the year." (26 year-old woman, volunteer)

I found many people whose family has helped in different ways, whether contributing resources or offering other types of support. When they form their own families, they find they share the concern of their spouse and they both begin to get involved with specific organizations, where they contribute their time to develop some activity.

> "...look, in my family there has always been a great concern for others... but here... [in the organization], through my wife's family... and really it was due to them. One day we were at a family dinner... They started to talk politics and... the social action projects he had been supporting came out in the discussion and, well, this woman [one of the people from the board of trustees] began to tell us about the work they did here, and I got interested... She invited me to be a child's godfather and I came here to the offices, and I remember very clearly that they were passing out care packages and I helped them... And now I'll have been here for two years this August." (32 year-old man, volunteer)

Twenty-one percent of the group has not had any experience as volunteers, since they are people who have worked in the organizations and receive a salary for doing so. Young men and women who have decided to have a personal experience of this kind and have sought out the way to do so for the first time are also located here.

Time Devoted and Kinds of Activities Performed by Volunteers

In this section, several variants in terms of dedication and type of activities undertaken by different groups of volunteers are discussed. I encountered two very distinct groups in this regard: "intense volunteers," i.e., people who devoted between

7 and 10 h a day to volunteer work in organizations, and a variable group whose participation varied from 1½ to 10 h per week.

The people who worked a full day as volunteers were mostly young people still living with their families and, therefore, it was their parents who were supporting them, although some faced certain economic problems. Others were women between the ages of 45 and 50 years who were housewives or who provided auxiliary assistance for their husbands in their business activities, with a great deal of their time devoted to the organization they had promoted or that they led. With regard to the young volunteers, I found that they had made the decision to dedicate a few years of their lives to working in an organization, thinking they were contributing to help others, and at the same time acquiring experience.

The second group devoted between 1½ and 10 h a week to volunteer work. I found that they were people who planned and devoted precise amounts of time to their economic activity and combined this with work as volunteers, which they did once to three times per week. In other cases, they were women who were housewives or employees who distributed their time among their household responsibilities, the activity that provided them with economic income, and their volunteer work.

Those who devoted themselves to volunteer work on a full-time basis had made the decision to commit themselves to a project they had also initiated. That is to say, some of the members made the decision in agreement with the group to commit themselves to assuming leadership and taking responsibility for fulfilling the objectives of what they had created over a period of time of 2–3 years. This was with the expectation that someone else would later replace them, which has happened in some cases. This has led these volunteers to practically dedicate their lives to guaranteeing the permanence of the project, even at the cost of not entering the labor market, which has caused problems for some. Although these volunteers were aware of the amount of time they devoted to what they were doing, they were also conscious of the difficulties in trying to reduce the work load and even to find someone to replace them, given the commitment that taking responsibility for the organization implied.

> "How long... let's see, if I get there at eight and I leave at five, that's... eight, nine hours. Subtracting lunch, that's eight hours a day: a hypothesis, because yesterday, for example, I left at six-thirty, so... Not for the last week... let's see... last week I was working until seven, from eight to seven, more or less, or 11 hours a day... But, the truth is I really try to leave. For example, it's four o'clock and if somebody comes in who can stay, I leave." (32 year-old woman, founder and volunteer)

Assuming the responsibility to carry the project forward implies undertaking multiple activities and tasks of a very diverse nature, from tending to daily chores to generating fund-raising projects for the organization.

> "...Well, for example, I got here today, I prayed, and then at eight or eight fifteen, the children start to arrive. So I receive them, etc., and they go directly in to have breakfast. I hardly even go into the kitchen. Then I check my mail, what I have to do. Since the cleaning girl came late, I went up to the hall. When she finished, I was coordinating like... I opened the silkscreen workshop. I had some things to do, so I spent some time checking a project that I'm finishing up. I started to talk about movies, we're going to show a movie, and well... At one-thirty I went up to help the young people who work here bring the

children down to eat and all that. I was checking the kitchen to make sure everything was OK and all that. Then I went to see an accountant who does the report for the institution, to see if we are in time, when we're going to do it and everything. I came back, I ate... what else did I do? ... Well, as always, I prepared some things for some activities, what we're going to do, recreation, what had to be sent off. Then I checked my mail again... and that's all." (28-year old woman, volunteer director of an organization)

In the case of young people from other countries with a commitment they understand for a specific period of time, which is in fact the case, will be in dedicating time and help with the organization's activities. They will work together on a daily basis with the personnel and the users, usually children or young people in poverty; these are the people they are to help, carrying out the activities they are told to do. In this case, there is a personal decision to devote a specific amount of time to this experience, and they prefer to look for organizations in developing countries.

"I'm committed for about two months. I'm working intensely... I'm like a monitor in a neighborhood for children who have experienced and suffered a lot... I live in a house they call 'the community'... I help with the daily work in the house and in the afternoon I help the kids with their school work... I don't just watch but do some things. It's not about sitting around with your arms crossed. On the other hand, I work helping the resident to get the groceries and have everything ready for when the kids come. Sometimes I go with him to look for things at the supermarket, and in the afternoon, if it's necessary, we go with some kid to buy things for their homework. [The town] is close by, and we buy the things there in some stationary store." (21 year-old student volunteer)

For other young people, helping others is an activity that is part of what they do in their everyday lives for the community where they live. Therefore, they have to coordinate this with their work schedule, where they get the resources to live and be able to fulfill their personal commitment. Some of them even help during their free time and on the weekends...

"Well, I work here every afternoon. My work there is from eight to four. Then I go home to take a bath, eat, and then I come here... It's about two hours in the afternoon... It's close to here... They tell me to lead the workshop, to provide training... I'm already a promoter... I also prepare my work. I write about my subjects and I have to get information about it..." (21 year-old man, employee, volunteer)

"Well, look, the fact is, it's on a monthly basis, every month I go see them [the organization]. Sometimes it's on Friday, Saturdays and Sundays. On Friday it's from two-thirty or three in the afternoon until seven, eight, nine at night. On Saturday from nine-thirty to ten in the morning or until four or five in the afternoon. If it's on Sunday, we also go at nine, ten in the morning until four, five in the afternoon... So it's almost a marathon. You end up physically tired, but mentally rested." (26 year-old man, volunteer)

There are also cases of women with household responsibilities who, on their own or because of invitations from other people, made the decision to participate in specific organizations as volunteers, so they have a very precise idea of the time they devote to these support activities.

"Well, here doing volunteer work about eight hours a week, or just when it's necessary to do some procedure or other things, it's a little more time, a little extra, or when you have to buy things like stationary, you know, those kinds of things." (45 year-old woman, volunteer founder)

"In the case of the NGOs [referring to others in which she also participates], well, they're, ah, let's say every month on the board, since it's once a month, say, about three hours for the meeting. And here, as committee members, it's once a month for two hours. So that's five hours altogether." (45 year-old woman, volunteer founder)

There is variety in terms of the amount of time devoted to helping others, but in a high percentage of cases, there is a relatively clear idea of the amount of time dedicated to volunteer work, while a minority has a certain lack of clarity in this regard. In the latter case, we are talking about people who have assumed a commitment to carry forward the project they have initiated or to which they have been invited.

Individual and Family Background and Participation in Non-profit Organizations

In order to understand why people became interested in participating in activities to help others and become volunteers, I analyzed the life histories of the subjects in order to find elements that would make it possible to explain this practice. That is, I examined the question of whether there was something in their background in terms of their family, their personal interests, or some kind of event that would explain their participation in these activities.

I found that 57% of all those interviewed had been influenced by their immediate and/or extended family, to be concerned about others. Another 23% had been influenced by their spouse, siblings, or family friends. In 20% of the cases, I did not find a specific prior influence, but rather an event that had occurred in their lives that unleashed this interest. In other cases, a personal commitment had arisen during the process of their education, in relation to evident social inequality when working with different groups.

These findings make it possible for me to affirm that, in accordance with the information collected, a key element with certain pre-eminence that leads subject to be concerned about others is the family group. Specifically, the family is the place for interaction where learning takes place and among other things, about what reciprocity means, the performance of specific activities, as well as processes of transmitting values and principles that will be put into practice in adult life.

Let's qualify this affirmation now. Although it was evident in some cases that those interviewed had been taught by their families, through practice, to be concerned about others beyond the group of their relatives, it did not seem so evident to some of them that this was indeed the case. Rather, when examining their life history, the family came out as a key element. When reflecting on the question, the role played by their father, mother, grandparents, or an aunt and uncle in learning this became evident.

"I grew up with an uncle. I love him a lot, since I lived with him since I was about eight years old... My uncle had a neighborhood pharmacy in Spain... He kind of had the idea that if he, as the pharmacist, left the employee to prepare the medicines, and then he wasn't going to do it. He also watched the pharmacy at night... The point is, my uncle felt responsible for the health of the people in the neighborhood. They were taking care of him, his mother, and his sister, and in exchange, he had to give them something back... In the mornings he went over the prescriptions and then went out for a walk on the street to see the people he knew were sick or whatever... Then he'd give them medicine on credit. I don't think they ever paid him, but it was understood as something of value... So I grew up seeing that, his responsibility to the people he felt depended on him. It wasn't true, but, well, he thought it was... I grew up with that, which was the opposite from my aunt..." (63 year-old man, performing acts of solidarity on an individual basis)

Among family members, participation in volunteer work is often due to the influence of the mother, especially for women. This fact was confirmed by 32% of women through what they said and considered in this regard, while the influence was much less for men. Only 10.5% of the men explicitly mentioned the influence of their mothers on their participation in volunteer work. Here, however, the subject of values, ethics, and religion was included as an element explaining this kind of orientation. This leads us to affirm that the socialization process is the time when a complex process takes place in which values inculcated by the mother are combined with specific practices that will have a determining influence for those people who will become involved in support activities for third parties in their adult life.

"In the case of my mother... She always used to say that you have to sow in order to reap... I don't remember her belonging to any club... She was with Catholic action with the neighbors. I remember that if someone needed something, my mother was always ready to help. And that's like something that always stayed with me, that saying of hers." (52 year-old woman, volunteer and director)

In other cases, it was a complex mix of religious values promoted by the family group combined with their education and some event in the person's life that influenced them and unleashed a process that led them onto the path of volunteerism.

"I think that the education I received, both from my parents and especially the academic education I received, has a lot to do with it. I remember that ever since I was a little girl we would go to the outlying neighborhoods in the city... I participated there since I was very young. We had a school; we created a school, right there in the garbage dump... I've always wanted to be God's instrument... Before my son was born, I prayed that I might be His instrument at the same time I was pregnant, when I didn't have any idea I was going to have a son with a disability. He sent me a son with a disability... So the message from Him was very clear..." (54 year-old woman, volunteer founder).

It should be added that this complex mix of elements has led a person to consider that their vocation or calling was something beyond just a personal or family problem, and she has focused on helping others in similar situations. According to the information collected, for some people, commitment is expressed in the concern for resolving or contributing in some way to the solution of a problem affecting their community, a decision that is undoubtedly not very common, even when this may be of a philanthropic nature.[6] This kind of decision is made especially by women, and this has been documented for other similar cases, especially by the media.

This kind of situation was not present in all cases. For one group it is a matter of concern about social affairs, in the sense of doing something about the abysmal social differentiation that broad sectors of the population suffer, which has played a fundamental role in promoting participation in activities to help or give advice to third parties. In this case, it is a matter of ideas formed in specific contexts or key moments in people's lives, which resulted in them having a different perspective at a very early point in their lives. It might be thought that inclinations toward this kind of participation are not related to the family, but rather to the subject's specific experiences and interaction with peers.

"[When I was a student] I came up in a context I think was very interesting: '68. Many things made an impact on me: the French '68 movement, the whole movement against the Vietnam War, Martin Luther King's civil rights movement, and 1968 in Mexico... I was one of the few that were into that trip at that time... The whole question of social justice... The whole more conscious, more committed change, shall we say, at that time... All that in an environment that invited you to do something. And then I found myself, I found myself through friends and acquaintances and since then..." (58 year-old man, volunteer).

For other people this process occurs during their adult life, after having formed a family, with the interaction with friends who invite them to get involved and they do it "because they enjoy it" or due to a special interest, for example, in children. In these cases the process began in order to share things with friends, which led them to get more involved than what they originally expected.

"[When already married with kids], some friends [from where the husband worked] invited me to participate. I liked going to the neighborhoods a lot, being in contact with the children, with the mothers, all of that... And I always used to say 'God, send me a job where I can make a little money and I'll devote myself to something with children'. That's what I used to say, and he sent me here, which doesn't pay anything, and it's a whole bunch of coordination things, but it's very satisfying. I'm happy. Really, you believe there's a need around you, but you don't get it and you don't see it until you're here. I love the children. I'm getting to know all of them little by little. So here we are." (47 year-old woman, volunteer president)

In reviewing the histories of these subjects who are volunteers, the role played by family and relatives in volunteer activities is evident. However, the process of socialization that takes place within the family stands out due to its importance, and particularly the practice and communication on the part of the mother figure. Friendships made in the course of the subject's life also influence this participation, most of which begin in adult life.

Although less relevant, at least for the group analyzed, events or occurrences affecting the subject's life are often a trigger leading to practical action that may even lead to the promotion or creation of organized forms of support transcending

---

[6] I say that it is not common, since in Mexico we have thousands of people with some kind of disability and, consequently, thousands of families who have helped people in this condition, yet there are not thousands of associations dedicated to this as a result.

personal problems. However, everything is not a matter of learning or of reproducing certain practices, since there are other elements, such as social commitment, that also hold a predominant position, as will be discussed when analyzing the organizations. This leads to a different kind of participation in organizations that is necessarily distinct from philanthropy or assistance organizations, and more directed towards social commitment and responsibility.

The Context and Reasons for Participating in Volunteer Groups

In the preceding sections, I have presented a general profile for volunteer workers, and at the same time, the diversity of situations and contexts that have influenced the subjects' decision to make a commitment to these kinds of activities has been explored. Now I am interested in examining concrete examples where it is possible to observe how the subject's life history is interwoven with societal elements that, in the end, lead to specific practices. For this purpose, I have selected four cases – three women and one man – where it is possible to observe who these volunteers are, what they have been like during different stages of their lives, and how their actions are interwoven until a subject concerned about helping others, and at times having links of solidarity with their community, emerges.

Aurelia: Acts of Solidarity Among Equals

Aurelia is a 43 year-old woman born into a peasant family in the north, like many others in Mexico. She was the oldest of five siblings, and when she remembers her childhood, she considers it to have been sad, difficult, and full of precariousness, with a constant struggle to make the arid land where they lived produce, although with little success. They had to migrate from one community to another, which led to her father becoming a wage worker for a while, which was a difficult time, since one of her brothers and her mother got sick. Like many peasant families in our country, they were completely attached to the land, so, after a while, they once again obtained a small piece of land.

In terms of education, she only studied, with interruptions, up to fourth grade in elementary school, since her mother was constantly sick and the family was also always moving. When Aurelia was 12 years old, she began to work washing and ironing other people's clothes and helping her father with work in the country, since her mother was still sick, it was necessary for her to contribute to the family's survival. When she was 20 years old, she got married to another peasant like herself. From her point of view, her life improved. Both of them started to work, they had four children, which they were able to send to school, although "they didn't give them the education they would have wanted" due to a lack of sufficient resources to do so.

Aurelia was always active. She tried to help her husband, learned how to make bread, and sold it to help.

When analyzing her life and identifying when and why she began to get interested in helping others in some way, we found that at age 23 she began to organize women in her community to receive supports and improve their homes. . She took up the task of organizing a committee of women poorer than her, since she has always been interested in helping "the poorest of the poor." This was at a time when government projects were focusing on providing privies and other construction materials. She actively participated for her group to receive these resources, although she was not always successful.

In the 1990s, she and her group of women heard about the organization which she belongs to now and joined it. With that, there was a small improvement. She was able to get cement and sheet metal to fix up their houses, and she made sure that debts for the materials provided were paid. Some years later, they had to deal with the fact that the Conasupo warehouses were closed and they were left at the mercy of the "coyotes," to whom they had to sell their products at whatever price were demanded. She participated more actively in the face of this difficult situation. She took courses and learned to apply for supports. She dedicated herself to promoting production projects, and the group of women left the problems of marketing to the men.

The main activities Aurelia has carried out in the organization have been helping women in her community apply for projects aimed at improving the situation of poverty in which they live. For this purpose, she sought information about the characteristics of the proposals available and once she had found it, she dedicated herself to visiting the communities to promote and get specific projects started. This has been something urgent for her, since the migration of men leaving the zone has increased in recent years, and the communities now consist of women heading the household and caring for the children, while their husbands work "in the North" to be able to send resources, which do not always arrive.

She is part of this group and despite the efforts to promote the establishment of production projects; these have not always been successful, especially in recent years. Two years ago, her two oldest children migrated to the United States and a year ago her husband decided to do the same thing, due to the precariousness of their situation. Currently, she divides her time between caring for their small piece of land, making bread, taking care of her two youngest daughters, and doing the housework. She also works to support women in nearby communities as a coordinator in the organization in which she has gained respect from others. She thinks that it is important to continue working in that organization, since she has been able to develop, little by little, a small patrimony for her children. The work she does is exhaustive, with long days and constant travel to apply for support for their communities. Nevertheless, she has not thought of abandoning the work she does of helping the poorest of the poor, the peasant women like her, not due to an altruistic concern but out of a social consciousness that corresponds to the organization where she participates.

Martha: The Need to Help

Martha is a young, 28 year-old woman born into a middle-class family. She is the eldest of two children and lives with her parents and grandmother in the family house. Her father is a self-employed professional and her mother worked as a secretary until she retired. She came to the area when she was little, since her family, who lived in the Federal District, decided to move after the 1985 earthquake.

Her education was in private schools and she received her bachelor's degree in education. After graduating, she had several jobs, interim positions, where she substituted for other teachers. She worked like this for 2 years, which allowed her to get to know other communities apart from where she lived. Finally, she had to decide between looking for work outside the area and staying there. She decided to do the latter, since she had become involved, together with other young people, in forming an organization.

When trying to establish the reasons she decided to help others with her time and knowledge, we found that her family had a certain tradition of helping others *as much as they could.* She remembers her trips to the north-east of Mexico from when she was a little girl, to visit her parents' families with the car full of clothes, toys, and groceries that they took in order to contribute in some way. Her mother did this as well, since she was not very attached to material goods, and if someone needed something, she would lend it to them and not necessarily get it back. In this family group in which there is a constant concern for others, the subject who most stands out is the grandmother, who, at her advanced age, has been going for 10 years, every Tuesday and Thursday, to an orphanage to prepare the food.

So she has been brought up and formed based on a tradition of helping. When she was 11, Martha actively participated with a group of scouts. In her opinion, this reinforced her service orientation, and starting at that time she began to work with children at risk due to living in conflictive places. During her college years, she continued to seek out organizations or people to be able to help in some way, at the same time she was learning from other professionals. She completed her social service in a community center where a group of psychologists provided professional help for minors, and once she finished, she decided to stay for another 2 years.

Six years ago, she met a group of four young people who helped street children. They invited her to participate and she accepted. At the beginning she did not have much time, since she worked in the mornings. Eventually, she decided to stay in the new organization. Analyzing the reasons she decided to stay, she considers it to be a matter of faith: *"God goes about arranging things and they happen."* Her parents supported her in this decision, providing her with what was necessary to live. Participating in this group has been very important for her, since she has had the chance to see that these children, who live in very difficult circumstances, have access to education, food, workshops, entertainment, and attention from people willing to do this.

The last 3 years of her life have been particularly difficult because she lost the person who was going to be her life partner after a long period of illness. He was someone with whom she shared a help project, the mover and creator of the organization. After a long process of mourning, she says "*I've started to live from day to day*," and plans to continue because it's "*God's will*" and because she has made the decision to make Christianity the guiding principle of her life, not simply a religion, and "*God has placed me at the head of the project, so that it can continue.*" This is why, over the past 2 years, she has taken the reins of the process of consolidating the organization where she is a full-time volunteer.

In terms of her everyday activities, at first she helped the children directly so they would receive their meals on time and so the teachers would start their classes and the children would be ready. Or when some children did not come, she would go to see them to find out what was happening. Later, her activities changed because she was able to organize the everyday activities so that they could develop without her. As a result, she now concentrates on designing projects so that the organization can develop more resources to continue to develop, collecting donations for daily expenses and involving more people as collaborators. In this case, there is a complex mix of values and personal events interwoven with a family tradition that has kept her on the path of volunteerism.

Ernestina: In the Face of Need, a Good Orientation and Support

Ernestina is a 45 year-old woman born into a middle-class family and the older of two sisters. Her father is a rural businessman and her mother is a housewife. She studied in private schools and finished high school. She did not go to college, but instead decided to get married. Her husband used to be a salaried professional who has devoted himself to business activities over the last few years. They have two older children who are still studying.

When analyzing her life history in order to determine how long she has been carrying out these kinds of activities and the reasons for doing so, we found out that during her childhood she helped her grandmother who had devoted herself to teaching the children of the day laborers how to read and write. They were not always successful, but since some did learn, they continued doing it. In school, she also liked to participate in activities that had to do with collecting clothes or money for others, as was also the case in church, where she taught catechism classes.

However, once she was married, she concentrated completely on her new household duties, and caring for and raising the children and attending to her husband. Six years ago, now that her children were grown, one of the other mothers at the school invited her to sell tickets to collect funds. It seemed to her to be a good idea and she accepted. In the beginning she sold tickets for raffles or sold clothes, but she did not know about the kind of activities that were being financed this way.

Finally, she had the opportunity to find out about the work the organization accomplished. She was invited by the promoter to visit the sick that they helped and accompanied her on her rounds for some time. As a result when she was invited again to become part of the group, she accepted at once, since, from her point of view, she had always been concerned about sick people getting well.

When she started participating, she only received support from her younger son, while her daughter and husband had some reservations. Her husband thought it meant neglecting her duties as wife and mother, and her daughter thought she would neglect her. On the other hand, Ernestina's mother was sick and she frequently traveled to help her. She established a schedule for the obligations she had acquired, trying to keep them from interfering with her previous duties.

To her the reasons she participated in this organization that helps sick people with severe economic difficulties, is "*a moral commitment, like everything in life.*" In practical terms, she explains, it is based on having had the chance to see for herself that with the right orientation and support, people who are in a difficult situation at some point can get back on their feet.

So what is involved is a commitment, a decision to help based on recognizing the existence of needs that have to do with precarious economic circumstances, together with a lack of institutional knowledge and a lack of information on the part of the people, which can be remedied by someone's help, or with the help of people, like her, who have voluntarily decided to do so.[7]

Her first actions were to get information about how the institutions related to the health sector operate, who to contact when something happens, and information about certain kinds of diseases, so as to have an idea of what the patient might need and for how long. She has also given the organization a new drive by posing the need for developing a structure that makes it possible for each person in charge of an area to have a clear idea of their responsibility. She has been at the organization as a volunteer for several years, from Monday to Friday, from 9 in the morning until 3 in the afternoon. Two years ago, she was named coordinator of one of the areas.

In terms of the kinds of activities she was involved in, these basically consist of helping people with few resources, many of them speakers of indigenous languages, who come with sick family members, so it is necessary to help them with processes and requirements they need to fulfill, or with studies they need, and even, in the case of a death, with the whole process of transferring the deceased.

Her other activities also included identifying people's problems and finding a solution, in accordance with the organization's resources, and taking part in the area of relations with other institutions to get temporary support from young people doing social service. This is due to the difficulty faced in recruiting volunteers. Her main concern is to be able to recruit volunteers, which is not an easy task, since they only stay for short periods of time because of the types of problems they attend to.

In Ernestina's case, her altruistic concerns stand out as a reason for helping those who, because of their precarious conditions, have few tools to solve the serious problems they face.

---

[7]The consistency she shows in why she engages in these kinds of activities should be noted, insofar as they are basically the same reasons that can attributed to the work she did as an adolescent when she taught workers' children to read and write.

Francisco: Commitment to Others

Francisco is a 32 year-old man born into a middle-class family in the north of Mexico who has five siblings. His father is a businessman and his mother a housewife. In terms of his education, he studied and went to college and then studied for his master's. He worked for a few years as a salaried professional, and 2 years ago, after marrying, moved to a city in the west where his wife lives. They are currently the owners of a small business which they both run.

When trying to determine the history of volunteer-type activities and the reasons he has been involved in them, it is evident that his family has always been concerned about others. His father made donations to an orphanage on a regular basis, which Francisco found one day when he found the receipts. Also the family received a kind of crumpet known as *"buñuelos de viento"* every Christmas from the nuns at the orphanage. His father and his brothers all participated in social work with scout groups, such as going to an orphanage to play with the children, or participating in collections for a senior care home and taking them for dinner on Saturdays. His mother also had a way in which she helped, which consisted of organizing the collection of used clothes with her friends, which they would take and distribute in nearby rural communities.

However, he says that it was not always this way, and that there was a time when he forgot about others. When he was about to finish high school and during a large part of his college life, his interests had changed and he went out with friends, he liked to have girl friends and have fun with them. In other words, he liked to do what people of his age usually do, if they are in conditions to do so. In his last year of college, a student association invited him to develop social help project, which he accepted immediately. The result of his participation in this activity was that he realized that it was possible to help others in an organized way. He developed some projects which he later took charge of. That was the time when he met the person who would be his wife, who also participated in similar activities. When he started to work, he had to suspend his relationship with these groups again. Two years ago he became involved again, when he received an invitation from the person in charge of an organization dedicated to taking care of children who work on the streets.

When analyzing the reasons that have led him to participate in these types of projects, he confessed that he had not thought about this. However, after thinking about it, he suggested that it is *"something that comes to you, he couldn't be indifferent if someone required his help."* It is a question of learning which led him to undertake actions to help others for personal satisfaction. When relating it to his background, this seems to indicate that he does not look for recognition for what he does, but rather that it has been an everyday thing in his life. Over and over in the conversations, he reiterated that he is a person convinced of the "butterfly effect" which, to him, means that *"a small action can have an impact on consequences for a person, group, or society, not like in the movie, but in real life."*

In relation to the kind of activities that he participates in as a volunteer in the organization, he says he does everything, including providing support in the office, helping to repair computers, carrying groceries, or talking with the children's parents. This last activity is particularly interesting to him, especially understanding that for some parents it is more important to continue receiving money in the household from the work of their children in the streets than if those children were to study. In cases like this his work then, is to try to convince them to receive the support that the organization provides them with and that things will work out better for everyone in the long run if their children go to school and to the workshops. Although he is aware that it is not something easy. The part he likes the most about his work is helping children catch up with their studies and designing computer courses for the older children, as a future employment option. This is the activity he has been involved in for the last 2 years, and he devotes two afternoons a week to it, and occasionally weekends when needed, while his wife takes care of their business.

A Brief Review

In these four case extracts, it can be seen how subjects, who are concerned about others develop, in the course of their lives. The complexity of the elements that come into play in different ways to characterize the subjects' orientation is clear, as well as how they give meaning to their actions and revalue them in each context. In this sense, there is not a single type of volunteer, but rather several types of volunteers, where their life history plays a fundamental role.

In some cases, like that of Aurelia, a life of precarious conditions transforms a person into someone with a clear idea of solidarity with their community, even when they may not know the term, they express it with their actions. It is an awareness that one is living in a world where their precarious conditions are not so bad compared to those of others, and this implies the need to help them and to educate oneself to do so.

In other cases, like Martha's, it is derived from aspects interwoven with social environments, religion in her case, and a certain kind of altruistic attitude which leads to helping the needy, living in a Christian way to serve them, to alleviate in some way the situation of those living in difficult circumstances, in this case children who have had to take to the streets to help their families. In this case too, a truncated process of transition to forming her own family leads her to the path of fulfilling everything the two of them had planned before.

There are other cases like Ernestina's, whose concern for others beyond her immediate family waited until she completed an important part of her life cycle. When her children had grown and just before they formed their own families, she decided to embark into a new service, establishing a moral commitment that links her past and future, where what will become the other part of her life begins to take shape. But she not only established a moral commitment, she also educated herself to fulfill it and rationalized the details of why she was doing so, at the same time giving meaning to her actions.

Even the determinant role played by the biological families' positive influence, as in Francisco's case, can be observed to lead the subject to try to replicate what educated him at an earlier moment and acquire a long-term commitment. Here it seems to have to do with how the subject conceives society and himself as part of a framework in which specific actions can lead to greater well-being.

So far, I have analyzed the characteristics of the population interviewed, as well as their life histories, where we observe different ways in which the subjects become concerned about others and the multiplicity of reasons that explain this kind of orientation. The following section will be devoted to a different kind of exercise in which we try to explore how the subjects interviewed define their activities and assign them specific terms when referring to them. The purpose is to analyze the terms with which they themselves define their activities, so as to develop a semantic field providing certain homogeneity to their diversity and defining the context in which the terms are employed. The intention is to quantify the sentences of the actors involved in order to construct specific hypotheses about their volunteer activity and thereby develop a general profile.

This kind of analysis shows that the members of the organization, both volunteers and employees, share similar codes regarding what they do and why they do it. Based on this, it is posited that being an employee or volunteer in these nonprofit organizations is perceived, by the group as a whole, as an activity that is different from activities carried out in the governmental or private sectors.

Conceptual Map of Volunteer Activities

The purpose of this analysis is to structure the information generated by the interviews based on sets of variables or attributes in order to "code" the information based on the expressive context of the subjects interviewed. In spite of the fact that, within the overall information, the individual characteristics of the subjects are very heterogeneous, it is possible to note outstanding similarities among men and women that make it possible to propose a prototype volunteer profile for the Mexican case.[8]

The *NVivo* program[9] was used for this analysis, which makes it possible to examine the subjects' codes based on text patterns in the responses derived from the interviews. For this purpose, patterns were sought which expressed volunteer

---

[8] We hope that new investigations on this subject will be generated in the near future and that this volunteer prototype is used to either reinforce these findings or criticize what is indicated here.

[9] In order to carry out the analysis with the *NVivo* program, we were assisted by José Sánchez and Soledad de León, both of whom are experts on this program, and whose valuable findings helped to explore new analytical territory in this field. The conceptual map that they designed makes it possible for the reader to understand how the relationships in what was expressed in the interviews were established.

acts, representations, ideas, and feelings, which led to a group of semantic categories recurring in the interviews.

Of the total of 66 interviews, those that had between 98.5 and 75.7% similar
responses[10] were compared, which resulted in the following semantic field regarding volunteer actions: "Giving," "support/help," "I think," "what is needed," "deficiencies," "what should be done," "satisfaction/like it," and "I feel." By taking into
consideration the range of greater frequencies, the following conceptual map (see
Fig. 3.1) was established, which constitutes the central nucleus of what was clearly
shown in the interviews as a whole.

In order to construct hypotheses or implication relations between codes, intersections are established between two general conditions: men + code versus women +
code. In each case, the code contrasted is indicated and a comparative analysis
between both groups is derived.

Based on this conceptual map, it is possible to affirm that the activities of those
interviewed, both volunteers and other members of the organization, are defined by
them as the act of giving, helping, and supporting others, believing in what they do
and in what is lacking or needs to be done. When the participants in volunteer
activities evaluate their own actions, they assume a prospective position, i.e., in
most cases, they believe that what still needs to be done and is necessary to do is a
task of great scope, and therefore there is a need to promote these kinds of activi-

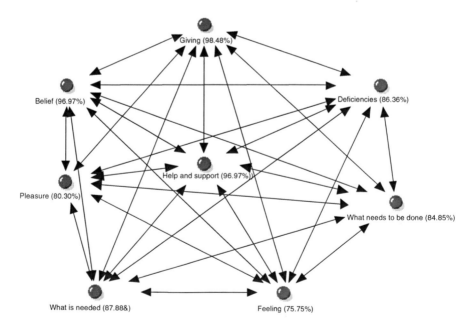

Fig. 3.1 Conceptual Map of Volunteer Activities

---

[10] Between 65 and 50 similar responses.

ties. Similarly, the group of people interviewed expressed the satisfaction they feel because of what they do, so this return is more important than the possibility of receiving economic payment for doing it. When referring to the activity, those interviewed describe it in a subjective way, i.e., that it is done because of the satisfaction and gratification that comes from supporting others.

Giving, Helping, and Believing as Frequent Terms

In order to develop a detailed vision of what the conceptual map shows, a group of eight hypotheses were proposed to interpret the selected codes. The hypotheses establish the correspondence among the structural aspects and the most influential semantic field elements, in the definition that the people interviewed provide us for what a volunteer is. Extracts are also included from some of the paragraphs to substantiate the hypotheses formulated.

When analyzing the information with *NVivo*, it was found that it was homogeneous if the results of the codification were compared when distinguishing between men and women. On the other hand, it is important to reiterate that the position held by the different actors interviewed in the organizations is not determinate in the semantic composition, so their responses are not compared.

Hypothesis 1: Men Conceive of Giving Differently than Women Do

Men and women express the idea of promoting social advancement and economic well-being for others through volunteer activities. However, when dealing with sharing these ideals of giving, there are important differences in the way they are perceived: for men, donations have a social character referring to the community, social networks, commitment, and institutions. For women, giving is also a form of personal redemption since, by favoring the growth of others, the person who undertakes the specific activity or actions perceives a growth of her own person.

> **Man:** I'm going to be sincere, well, I didn't used to believe in this, that you have to "give to receive", but with the passage of time, you begin to find out what the movement is like. I liked participating, working, collaborating in the community, because it's the only way somebody who's in a screwed up situation can get ahead and get some benefit, something for the family. Because otherwise, it's difficult; no, it's impossible. It can't be done. (50 years old, volunteer coordinator)

> **Woman:** This group of volunteers was founded in Mexico twenty years ago with the idea of helping people of limited resources to get ahead and **give** them the means, as we say between quotation marks, the means for them to be able to have an economic income and hence a better quality of life... Well, I really feel that God has blessed me a great deal... and I feel that, well, we should give a little, **give** of our time, to benefit others. It's a great sat-

isfaction... Since, look, it's also a way for you yourself to grow, because dealing with these people is very enriching. (44 years old, volunteer founder)

Hypothesis 2: Men and Women Conceive of Concern for Helping Differently

Apparently, women conceive helping in a more disinterested way than men do. In keeping with Hypothesis 1, men see helping as something useful for the growth of others and for strengthening interpersonal relations. For women, it is a moral concern, a commitment toward others.

> **Man:** helping others is something I've always liked. I think that that is also part of why I fell in love with my wife, since she is also someone who likes to help others... I've never thought that there has to be a special reason for helping others, it's something that comes to you... I think it might be something that's already in your blood... Maybe what motivates me to stop and help others is, well, that I've always had an example at home... To me, this has always been something natural that I learned to live with since I was a boy... Both my parents and my brothers and sisters have always helped others, whether, as I said, through the scouts or with my mother's group... or by your own volition. (32 years old, volunteer)

> **Woman:** Well, in my mother's house, she always said that you have to sow to reap and, although at that time, no, I don't remember her belonging to any club, but there she was with Catholic action with the neighbors. I remember that if someone needed something, my mother was always ready to help. And that's like something that always stayed with me, that saying of hers. (46 years old, volunteer founder)

Hypothesis 3: Volunteer Participation Is Clearly Defined as a Function of Beliefs

Working for others for the good of others is a value shared by both men and women. Finding out about what people lack and their needs is translated into motivation and commitment for the person participating in volunteer activities, who gives his or her work an ethical sense that is vaguely located on the threshold between religiosity and lay principles. It is a conviction rooted in principles where what one should be is disinterested and generous, and that is what allows for the growth of others and of oneself.

> **Man:** Although I heard a lot about missions and missionaries when I was little, I think that today we are all missionaries in some way, even if we aren't religious, which I don't think has anything to do with this. I think that if we all help, we can live helping others to better themselves and I think you yourself also grow when you help others grow. (47 years old, volunteer)

Woman: Look, personally I feel fulfilled, because I realize the needs that exist in our society, and you become more human and try to solve or minimize those problems to the degree possible. I think we should all participate for society, because there's a great deficiency, a great deal of selfless cooperation is needed. We should not just work when we get paid, but work giving whatever time we have, whether a little or a lot, for our society, that has so many needs. It's the only way we can meet these needs. (53 years old, volunteer)

Hypothesis 4: Men and Women Conceive of Their Commitment Based on Recognizing the Needs of Others

Recognizing the needs of others by individuals generates a sense of commitment among men and women in the same way that identifying the existence of different kinds of needy sectors of the population becomes a stimulus for active participation. At the same time, there is a certain concern about people's indifference in the face of something that is evident to the person who helps. Hence, even though the participants in volunteer activities devote time and material resources to these tasks, they insist that this is insufficient, given the magnitude of the problems detected.

Men: ...it commits me more, as well as when I'm at home sitting in the armchair watching TV, since I imagine that there are needy people and that the work we do is important... and that we can't give up... And if other do it... can't we? (34 years old, volunteer)

...I think it's with us from birth, for most of my brothers and sisters and me, helping people who need it; that's mainly the passion for soccer, the passion for helping others, and the passion for teaching people. (43 years old, volunteer director)

Women: I haven't dedicated myself to a single cause as such; I've always tried to help where it's needed, in homes, orphanages, the church, the DIF, etc. (53 years old, director)

...it makes you feel impotent, because you don't have enough time to do everything you want to do and everything you see needs to be done, and you don't have enough money to cover all the needs either, so all of that weighs on you a lot and it's very exasperating. (34 years old, coordinator and volunteer)

Hypothesis 5: Men and Women Define the Deficiencies that Promote Volunteer Participation Differently

When the participants in volunteer activities define the deficiencies faced by others, they do so in contrast with how they perceive themselves. In the case of men, a concern and social responsibility to attenuate social differences through commitment and participation in different actions is observed. In the case of women, this seems to be focused on a moral responsibility that everyone should assume.

Men: ... I think that a deficiency in what is most needed in this country is to support people without resources. People do not have anything and, well, try to awaken in them a little the idea that they should play sports and study, because that is the only way the situation in this country is going to change. This is something that I am convinced of, that the only way to change the situation in this country is through education and sports. There is no other way, is there? That is the situation. (43 years old, director and founder)

It makes me, uh... like that... sad to see that they can't and I feel that I'm complete... and if I don't help them, there's no one who will, you know? I'm a complete person and I help people who face **deficiencies...** (21 years old, volunteer)

Woman: I think we should all participate for society, because there's a great deficiency, a great deal of selfless cooperation is needed. We should not just work when we get paid, but work giving whatever time we have, whether a little or a lot, for our society, that has so many needs. It's the only way we can meet these needs... (52 years old, volunteer)

Hypothesis 6: The Ethical Vision of the Objectives Pursued by Volunteer Activities Is Shared by Men and Women

The influence of religious values is evident in the participant's representations of the actions they develop in regard to what must be done to affect and transform the inequalities and needs of others. The desire to improve the situation of those in difficulty is often linked to the religious conviction that a better world is possible and desirable. However, it should be pointed out that this is more often the case with women than with men.

Man: Knowing that Jesus Christ had always, had always, uh, distinguished himself as being on the side of the poor, of the needy, of the sick, of those who needed something from Him, well, then I come to the parish with the idea of, well, helping the most needy. (58 years old, volunteer founder)

Woman: Look, I think we're just passing through this life and that we have to do something with our lives, something meaningful, something for others, something [that] makes our lives worth living, and what better than loving one's neighbor. Especially when you consider that you're in a position where you have been very privileged and have received many blessings, and that is when I most feel the commitment that I have to share with others. (45 year-old woman, volunteer founder)

Hypothesis 7: Participation in Volunteer Activities Is Valued in Subjective and Not Economic Terms Among Men and Women

Participants in volunteer activities establish subjective parameters for evaluating what they do, such as personal satisfaction, the pleasure of doing it, without expecting any type of economic compensation. For the group interviewed, this is, again, an ethical and emotional matter.

Men: I'm very happy with what I do; it is very fulfilling, because I know it has a big impact. There are definitely people for each thing. (32 years old, volunteer)

Well, I like it, because it makes me feel very good personally, not because of what they'll say. I don't expect to receive a prize or payment. It's a personal satisfaction for me. (56 years old, volunteer coordinator)

Woman: Why do you do it? Not for anything in particular, just for the pleasure of doing it. I love children. (53 years old, volunteer)

Hypothesis 8: Those Interviewed "Feel" Differently About Belonging to a Group of Volunteers Based on Their Gender

There are significant differences between men and women in the expressions about belonging or being part of a group. Women tend to explicitly define their participation as something ingrained, as religious-type beliefs, while among men there is constant reference to social responsibility and commitment.

Men: I feel that my role has been as a symbol of unity or of calling on others to resolve conflicts or develop more organized work. It's like my role has been to make sure the process isn't interrupted. I invite the others to be tolerant, although we all make mistakes, including me. (45 years old, volunteer founder)

First I came to do tasks, one, two, three, as a volunteer and then as an associate. I started to enjoy the work and saw that it was nice thing to work in the community. (73 years old, volunteer)

Women: So, I don't know why other people don't like it, that is to say, I like it, because I feel I'm serving God, you understand? That's why I like it. And I don't know, I mean, I don't know why, you know? But I like it! ...They say that people don't thank me, and that's true! I mean, I see that, but I say: I don't care about the people; I do it with love for God and as a service to God. And it's the only thing I tell him, you know? (41 years old, volunteer organizer)

Some work was started with these kids, why not continue? And on the other hand, I had something in me, like... in my relationship with God, for example, that I've been trying to have, it was like something that God was telling me, talking to me, about your mission in life. Those kinds of things... Well, I don't know. At the beginning it was like... hmmm, I don't know. I can tell you in one word and I can explain it to you. I think that it is God's will for my life, that's it, definitely. (49 years old, volunteer)

The hypotheses for each group of statements in this breakdown let us see very clearly how volunteers define their activities: an act of giving, helping, and supporting others due to a personal and subjective interest, due to the pleasure of doing it and the satisfaction the person doing it receives. It is equally clear that social and moral responsibility is always present. Men are inclined more towards the social aspect, while women relate themselves above all in terms of a moral and ethical commitment. All of this is within an evident framework of recognition, on the part of participants, of the profound inequalities for broad groups of the population and of the severe challenges that we as a society face in Mexico.

Conclusions

In this text, the process followed by both the members of volunteer groups and those who work for non-profit organizations has been analyzed, in order to examine activities involving help for third parties. It was clear that, when entering into these kinds of activities, they acquired a commitment to the organizations where they participate and that this is due, in large measure, to previous experiences in their family of origin. It is also related to specific events that occur at different points during their lives. The reasons their commitment remains active and the type of activities they undertake as volunteers was also analyzed. It was possible to observe that, for the set of 66 in-depth interviews conducted; women devote themselves to volunteer activities more than men, with a ratio of 3:1.

It was also possible to discover that those who become involved as volunteers include both retired women and housewives, as well as other people, both men and women, who are also engaged in economic activity, which is where their income comes from, and dedicate part of their time to helping third parties that are not necessarily related to their family or group of relatives. They are people at a productive age who coordinate and divide their responsibilities between work, volunteer activity, and their families. This finding demystifies the popular misconception that volunteers are essentially women from the middle classes who devote themselves to works of charity to fill their idle moments.

We are dealing here with people that have a commitment to others, expressed in the continuity of their actions, the time dedicated to this kind of activity, and the expectation that they will continue on the same path. When going deeper into the general characteristics of those interviewed, I found that they could be separated into two large groups or types. One is the group of full-time volunteers over a specific period, which we can call "intense volunteers," as Verduzco indicates in this book, and the second group is made up of people with a definite and specific commitment in terms of the time dedicated to these activities, that we can call "systematic volunteers."

With regard to the reasons why people join in these kinds of activities, we find that the family plays a predominate role, since it is at home where the subject receives the values and principles that will be put into practice in adult life. In other cases, social concerns are also an important element for dedication to these activities. Therefore, a single pattern does not exist, but rather a framework of different elements is in play in the course of a subject's life that leads to showing concern to help others and that finally takes the form of joining a volunteer group among the organizations designed for this purpose. Motivations range from the convictions regarding the social differentiation that places an enormous contingent of people in a needy situation without the possibility of getting ahead on their own to those that have to do with moral issues, like protecting the helpless.

References

Brito Velásquez E (1997) Sociedad civil en México: Análisis y debates. In: Sociedad Civil, no. I, vol. II, pp 185–204

Cnaan R, et al. (1996) Defining who is a volunteer: conceptual and empirical considerations. In: Nonprofit and voluntary sector quarterly, no. 3, vol. 25, pp 364–383

Dingle Alan, 2001, MEASURING VOLUNTEERING: A Practical Toolkit, Independent Sector-United Nations Volunteers, Washington, DC

Harris C (1987) The individual and society: a processual approach. In: Bryman A et al (eds) Rethinking the life cycle. Macmillian, London, pp 17–29

Kramer R (1990) Voluntary organizations in the welfare state: on the threshold of the 90s. Centre for Voluntary Organizations, LSE, London

Layton M (2006) Cómo se paga el capital social. In: Foreign Affairs en Español, no. 2, vol. 6 http://www.foreignaffairs-esp.org/

Meyer C (2001) A case in case study methodology. In: Field Methods, no. 4, vol. 13, pp 329–352

Patton MQ (1990) Qualitative evaluation and research methods. SAGE, Newbury Park, CA

Rehnborg SJ (2003) A US perspective on volunteerism. In: Butcher J, Serna G (eds) El Tercer Sector en México: perspectivas de investigación. Cemefi-Instituto de Investigaciones Dr. José Luis María Mora, México, pp 372–388

Salamon L, Anheier H (1996) The emerging sector. The Johns Hopkins University, Institute for Policy Studies, Baltimore, MD

Taylor FR (2005) Rethinking voluntary work, In: The Sociological Review, no. 2, vol. 53, December, pp 119–135

Verduzco G (2003) Organizaciones del sector no lucrativo: visión de su trayectoria en México. Cemefi-El Colegio de México, México

Yin RK (1991) Case study research. SAGE, Newbury Park, CA

Chapter 4
The Concept of Giving in Mexico

Jacqueline Butcher

Introduction

The preceding chapter considered the motivations and reasons why most of those interviewed engage in volunteer work and solidarity activities, many of them without receiving any remuneration for this work. It explains in detail the processes that people involved in volunteer groups have followed and explores their life histories so as to develop an analysis of the thoughts expressed by these subjects.

The purpose of this chapter is to go more deeply into the data and informational cross references obtained from the interviews for the qualitative part of the study, and in particular examines the semantic expression most often mentioned by them: giving.

Social investigation delving into the subject of citizen participation, solidarity, altruism, prosocial behavior, social responsibility, and related themes is the point of reference for examining these activities. A description of the semantic links in the discourse of those interviewed is developed here, and their work is analyzed from the standpoint of different theoretical and conceptual frameworks, based on the perceptions of the actors themselves and the way they understand and conceptualize their own actions.

Giving in the Conceptual Map of Volunteer Actions and Acts of Solidarity[1]

In 65 of the 66 interviews completed for this study 98.48% of the subjects interviewed most frequently mentioned "giving." This is the semantic category that recurs most often in the perception of those interviewed in our universe, together

J. Butcher
Centro Mexicano para la Filantropía (Cemefi), México D. F., México
e-mail: rivasjb@prodigy.net.mx

[1] We would like to take this opportunity to thank José Sánchez from the Centro de Investigaciones Sociales, Universidad de Guanajuato, and Soledad León from the Universidad de Guanajuato for their work. Both are experts in the *NVivo* program.

J. Butcher (ed.), *Mexican Solidarity: Citizen Participation and Volunteering*,
DOI 10.1007/978-1-4419-1078-3_4, © Springer Science+Business Media, LLC 2010

with the semantic categories of "support and help" (96.97%), "I think" (96.97%), "what is needed" (87.88%), "deficiencies" (86.36%), "what should be done" (84.85%), "satisfaction/like it" (80.30%), and "I feel" (75.75%), which represent the central core of the expressions analyzed in the preceding chapter. It should be remembered here that 74.2% of the people interviewed (49 individuals) were considered to be committed volunteers, i.e., they did not receive remuneration for their work. The remaining 25.8% (17 individuals) were paid personnel or lived from what the organization paid them (including the directors and staff members). All of those interviewed participate in either formal or informal civil society groups in Mexico. We reiterate here that the position held by the different actors interviewed in the organizations does not have any impact on the semantic composition, so their responses are not compared.

The conceptual map of acts of solidarity/volunteer action presented in Chap. 3 indicates that the eight semantic categories are interlinked and represent a concentration of the greatest number of verbal expressions regarding the logic of volunteer action. The set of volunteer actions is conceptually identified here with volunteerism. This means that those interviewed share a sociocultural representation of all volunteer actions, i.e., of volunteerism.

Figure 4.1 is a conceptual map of volunteer actions and acts of solidarity that complements the one presented previously. It is the result of the comments made by the informants during the interviews performed as part of the 15 case studies, and it shows the 22 most common expressions used by the people interviewed.[2] The semantic networks allow us to observe how the plexus of meaning is constructed in regards to the qualitative information. In order to identify this network, a matrix was developed – with the help of the *NVivo* program – of the intersections of all the codes used. Each intersection is the equivalent of how one concept is related to another. When a network of relationships is constructed by using this method, the result is a conceptual map that in itself demonstrates a hierarchy among these relationships, as the product of selection and identification.

The network of blue lines linking the categories indicated in red represents the most relevant relationships, defining what the associations studied conceive to be volunteer actions. The code "giving" articulates all of the codified documents (65 out of 66), while the categories "conflict," "pay," and "solidarity," among others, play a marginal role, as can be seen in the diagram. That is to say, volunteer action and acts of solidarity are defined by the Mexican people as the act of giving to others in an unselfish way, without receiving anything in return (see Fig. 4.1).

Based on the data obtained, in summary, we can affirm that:

- Giving to others is an unselfish act from which "satisfaction" is obtained.
- The "need" to "support and help" others is observed not only as a "duty/what should be done" but as a "satisfaction/like it."

---

[2] See Chap. 5 of this volume, which refers to the organizational structure aspects of the associations and groups having volunteers and explains the different roles played in them by volunteers.

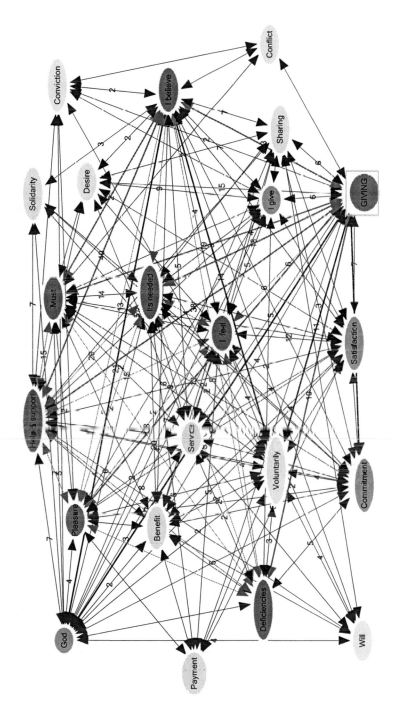

Fig. 4.1 "Giving" as the source of solidarity and volunteering

- Those who participate in the associations studied recognize that there are "deficiencies" and a need for more support to continue with their activities.
- The recurring use of "I think" is used by those interviewed for self-evaluation of their actions and also to evaluate needs and requirements, which are generally mentioned as demands for "support and/or help."
- "I feel" is often used by women to express how they evaluate their participation in associations.

It is important to note that, as determined in the preceding chapter, the words used by these individuals to express their motivations are discursive elements that give meaning to their activities and build up their own sense of fulfillment in their daily lives.

It has been said that volunteer actions are defined by those participating in them as the act of giving, helping and supporting others, as well as believing in what they are doing and in what remains to be done. Different conceptual categories with a differential semantic weight are articulated around the act of giving time, resources, or sociocultural abilities to others: (a) cognitive, (b) symbolic-affective, (c) moral, and (d) pragmatic.

(a) *Cognitive categories:* Giving cannot be reduced to an act with practical meaning. Also, "giving" demands knowledge of the needs it is based on. For this reason, "deficiencies" and "needs" are cognitive categories that make the giver an expert who recognizes what is needed and lacking, both on the part of those who participate in volunteer programs and those the programs are meant to serve.
(b) *Symbolic categories:* Giving is a symbolic gesture in which the giver extends recognition to those who need it through his or her acts, rather than recognition being given to the giver. For this reason, giving is a "satisfaction" and a "feeling." The dimension of these categories is symbolic, because it is intangible and depends on imagining the volunteer actions. The use of categories like "I think" expresses a system of ideas or beliefs regarding the relationship of the volunteer to those benefiting from acts of solidarity.
(c) *Moral categories:* "Giving" is a duty, an ethical obligation. It does not demand any payment whatsoever, but, rather expresses an ethical principle of recognition in which "I give others what they do not have." The logic of the gift corresponds in ethical terms to what we ourselves would like to have, develop, or learn, if we were in a situation of limited resources and sociocultural abilities.
(d) *Pragmatic categories:* "supporting and/or helping" concentrate on the practical meaning of acts of solidarity. To support others, it is necessary to evaluate what is needed and take a position in regard to the subjects of volunteer actions and acts of solidarity.

Later on, other investigations might explore the question of whether giving demands some type of reciprocity and how this takes place. This is not expressed in the information in this study and might become a mechanism for evaluating volunteer actions, where we could ask ourselves: How can the efficiency of giving be measured? What happens in the act of giving? What is the relationship between the giver and the receiver? Theoretically speaking, we might say that reciprocity is found in receiving and returning the gesture in many ways, such as may be the case with learning, growth, and personal development. However, the relational structures between those interviewed and the beneficiaries are not established here, and no judgment is proffered, in and of itself, about whether the action of giving is positive or negative for the society the solidarity actors say they are serving. We consider that it is through the information provided by descriptive studies such as this one that elements for evaluating these activities may later be developed.

Intersections Among Codes: Conceptual Interrelations in Giving

This section explores the interrelation between the concept of "giving" and the main codes articulating the bulk of the information provided by the investigation. As part of the study, those interviewed established priorities in terms of the order of importance they attach to their actions. The information emerges from the total conglomerate of interviews with volunteers, and individuals collaborating in different ways in the organizations studied. However, insofar as we are exploring connections among the categories in terms of meaning, and since the information is very homogeneous, it was not necessary to divide it into groups or by associations.

Satisfaction and Giving

Satisfaction due to volunteer actions is closely linked to giving to others, as this gives rise to feelings of happiness and satisfaction. It belongs to the conceptual symbolic category, because it reflects feelings on the part of the volunteers. They say that giving is something that they like and enjoy and that is pleasurable and satisfying. When analyzing the discourse of those interviewed, it is possible to detect that these individuals are oriented toward giving to others, that they feel capable of supporting and helping through their activities to serve others, and that they do so willingly, based on the conviction that their efforts will make a contribution to transforming their reality. In a parallel fashion, those who participate in the organizations studied mention different forms of compensation, satisfaction, and personal growth that they perceive when they carry out these activities. The fact that the majority of those interviewed in this study have declared that they experience satisfaction when giving to others, seems to be a primordial factor for understanding the phenomenon of volunteer actions and acts of solidarity.

Personal satisfaction during the act of giving is emphasized. This is an essential element, insofar as one of the characteristics of volunteer activities is precisely the feeling of pleasure, achievement, or satisfaction when performing them (Luks 1988, 39).[3] At times, this sensation is perceived to be a personal benefit in some way. In fact, it is. When the participants observe that their acts have an impact on others and obtain a satisfactory response, the logic of "giving" is fulfilled: the only reciprocity is found in seeing the growth of the other (Godbout 1992).[4] The following statements are representative of this characteristic:

> "First I came to do tasks, one, two, three, as a volunteer and then as an associate. I started to enjoy the work and saw that it was nice thing" (73 year-old man)

> "...so that's it, to me it's giving a little of the time he dedicates to us. Then I feel satisfied doing it..." (49 year-old woman)

The expressions of people acting in the organizations draw our attention repeatedly with expressions and phrases like: "satisfaction," "I like it," "gratification," "I felt useful," "security," "it gives me meaning."

> "...well, then, I like to, well, give my time, put in my hour and a half for what they probably need... listen to advice, help... listen, help me with this..." (23 year-old woman)

> "... because it gives me confidence, it gives me security, it gives me love to give to the little ones, to give them the attention they deserve and should get, the care they should receive, see how they come and go..." (56 year-old woman)

There are different theoretical tools that are useful for understanding volunteer actions and acts of solidarity in terms of the subjective and collective process dimensions involved. Humanism,[5] for example, provides a basis for evaluating human action and behavior from its point of view and emphasizes the relevance of interpersonal relations,[6] life experience, and phenomenological experience.

---

[3] This study, carried out with 1,700 volunteers (A), together with a survey of 1,500 more volunteers (B) reported that 68% of the women in study A and 88% in study B experienced a physical sensation of pleasure during volunteer action as well as greater peace of mind and sense of self-esteem, in addition to the sensation of pleasure. Luks calls this a *Helpers High*, since the biochemical result in the organism is the secretion of endorphins that help the organism to reduce stress and which are released in the same way as after intense physical exercise. What is interesting is that when the experience is remembered, this stimulates the secretion of endorphins once again. It produces a double effect, when giving and when it is remembered. This only occurs when the action is voluntary and there is personal interaction. It does not happen when making a donation, no matter what the amount or the importance of the cause.

[4] Godbout incorporates ideas like those of Mauss and Douglas and argues in his book, *La esencia del don*, that giving is considered to be a social relation in which giving cannot be considered to be " ...a series of unilateral and discontinous acts, but is rather a relationship." Giving constitutes "a system of specifically social relationships, insofar as they are not reducible to economic interests or power."

[5] Authors representing this tendency go back to Aristotle, Plato, Saint Thomas Aquinas, Saint Augustine, Brentano, Heidegger, Wertheimer, Dilthey, Rousseau, Claparede, and J. Dewey, to mention the most relevant ones. Their contributions were later taken up by the phenomenological and existential tendencies and have provided basic principles for this tendency in psychology. Other authors considered to be humanists include: Allport, C. Rogers, A. Maslow, Angyal, Ash, Combs, Lecky, Kelly, Jourard, Buhler, Moustakas, Contril, Horney, Goldstein, as well as Rollo May, Martin Buber, Erich Fromm, Victor Frankl, and A. Sutich, among others.

[6] Rogers' theories (1980) center on the subjective quality of interrelations between two individuals and propose environments that facilitate the natural growth of man through interpersonal relations, which is what occurs with the act of giving.

An essential part of volunteer actions and acts of solidarity – based on our definition for this study – has to do with the individual's capacity to decide to give based on choice and free will. With an emphasis on the meaning of life and responsibility, in which man possesses an innate power of self-determination in deciding his own destiny, this potential is renewed and grows based on freely chosen values. If people give, it is because they choose to do so, and if they do, it is because they consider it to represent a value to them. When choosing freely among these possibilities, man forges his existence: *Human existence is to be responsible because it is to be free* (Frankl 1992, 130.)

In regards to our analysis of the act of giving, this perspective proposes that the way of giving will depend both on the person's circumstances and the level of intellectual, emotional, and cognitive development of the individual performing this action. In other words, the activity of giving itself has the potential to produce personal changes and it is possible that it may have an effect on the individuals' emotional and cognitive maturity.[7]

The development of a person's character is manifest to the degree to which we have these parts of our personality resolved. Thus, a person who has not developed their character beyond the merely receptive aspect ,will interpret the act of giving as renouncing or being deprived of something. Alternatively, for a person with a productive character, giving acquires "the highest expression of strength. In the act of giving itself, I experience my force, my wealth, my power. This experience... fills me with happiness" (Fromm 1990, 32). Among the volunteers interviewed, many express their satisfaction about giving their time and energy and do not relate it to any economic benefit. On the contrary, they experience it as pleasure. The following expressions by volunteers talk about their perceptions related to the satisfaction they receive:

"The gratification or satisfaction, the pleasure, is something that isn't in the salary, it's in seeing, for example, a child's smiling face" (53 year-old woman)

"Yes, in a certain way, but not economic payment. But yes, compensation..." (24 year-old woman)

Not in terms of money, but in terms of satisfaction, quite a lot, because I have become more and more well-known... (25 year-old man)

---

[7] There have been advances since the decade of the 1980s in social psychology investigations in regards to altruism, prosocial behavior, social responsibility, and related subjects. See Piliavin and Charng (1990), researchers from the University of Wisconsin, regarding 183 studies and investigations that indicate changes in mentality regarding altruism. Other studies to be consulted include Batson (1991), who presents a theory of empathy-altruism, and Eisenberg (1986), who studies the cognitive development of individuals and help relations that occur in children and concludes that: "it seems that the cognition associated with prosocial actions in children becomes more internal and less related to external profit as they develop." The studies of Staub (1978), Aronoff and Wilson (1984), Piliavin et al. (1981), and Rushton (1981) may also be consulted. Studies on voluntary donation of kidneys (Simmons et al. 1977) and blood (Condie et al. 1976; Heshka 1983; Reddy 1980; Drake et al. 1982), consider these actions to be altruistic, since the donors do not know who the receiver will be.

From a different theoretical viewpoint, we can also select the relational standpoint to analyze our subjects' commentaries, where it is observed that, in addition to the satisfaction of giving, an interchange of equivalents is not spoken of in relation to giving, but rather relations of reciprocity.

> Giving has no commercial equivalent. The debt from giving is never paid. While results are what count in the market, in the case of giving, everything resides in the gesture, in the way in which something is given. Giving has no price. Price implies an unequivocal commercial equivalent for another object of the same value, while giving calls forth the counterpart of giving which depends on the relationship that has been established between the two people, the sequence, etc. The value of the relationship does not have any monetary equivalent (Mocchi and Girado 1999, 20).

From the analytical angle of the relational perspective, it is observed that reciprocity,[8] which is postulated as an equilibrium between what is given and what is expected to be obtained, cannot be explained from the paradigms of self-interest (Mansbridge 1990), since this practice is based on motivational and relational aspects. In this sense, reciprocity constitutes a system of interpersonal relations and becomes a system of support, of reciprocal help.

Giving and Believing

The commentaries analyzed reflect the current state of Mexican society, in which giving to others is not a generalized practice, although the people working in the non-profit organizations considered in this investigation think this should be the case. Belief establishes the decision to give something to the receiver of the action and, therefore, belongs to a symbolic category or dimension, because it represents the position of the one who gives, the way of giving. Those interviewed expressed that giving support to their fellow Mexicans is an urgent matter, especially to those who are in vulnerable circumstances. Similarly, they have assumed a responsibility when they offer and provide support for others in the belief that their contribution is important. Belief also expresses a potential, a possibility. In order to create a different culture with regard to giving, it is first essential to believe that this is possible. Structures begin to change when the mentalities of those sustaining them are changed first.

In the analysis in the preceding chapter, different ways of giving are evident when comparing the men and women who are part of our study. It is mentioned that men assume more of an attitude of social responsibility when giving, while an important section of women have motives of charity and assistance, expressing

---

[8]Traditionally, the analysis of reciprocity has been delved into from different anthropological, sociological, philosophical, and psychological fields of knowledge and schools of thought. However, providing a complete panorama of the subject goes beyond the scope of this work.

greater moral concern. Those interviewed have assumed a commitment and a new responsibility even though they cannot guarantee – other than through their attitudes and actions – the results of their efforts. They do this because they are convinced that their action is valid and necessary. This leads them to assume a proactive role, where their attitude of commitment leads them away from dependency. When this does not happen, there is a risk of adopting attitudes of charity. Freire (1990, 50) warns about this with these words:

> [T]he great danger of charity is in the violence of the anti-dialogue that imposes silence and passivity on man, does not offer him special conditions for development or "opening" of consciousness and, in authentic democracies, it must be a form to be ever more criticized... charity is a form of action that robs man of the conditions of achieving one of the fundamental needs of his soul: responsibility.

Those interviewed in this study expressed that the ways of "giving" should change, since everyone does not know how to do it:

> "...we should help and, especially, give... I think that we often face a society that is not really used to giving, don't we?" (47 year-old man)
> "Well, in the first place, not everybody knows how to give. I think [that] giving is a value and that it's more difficult for people as human beings " (57 year-old woman)

For some individuals, giving comes to be a way of being, a "value," as this volunteer expresses it. For some people, giving cannot be disconnected from receiving; for others, it is tiring activity. Others experience it as a continual source of energy and growth. Our volunteer also reminds us that "not everybody knows how to give." We may indicate here that giving is something that is discovered and learned. If giving is something learned, this learning requires consciousness in order to have meaning for daily life.

If we were to go through the stages of giving in terms of an individual's physiological, psychological, and spiritual development, we would see that there are stages in life when man is essentially egotistical, and that this attitude gradually evolves and changes to the degree he matures. Both in terms of moral development and the field of individuals' cognitive evolution, Kohlberg (1984) and Piaget (1974), respectively, develop steps or facets that explain what happens in these terms as a human being grows and develops. Villanueva (1985) presents an informative table of different theoretical sources which includes the three psychological tendencies: psychoanalysis, behaviorism, and humanist existentialism. Each one of them expresses a theory of development, changes, and growth, but taken as a whole, they are complementary and allow us a glimpse of the enormous complexity of the process of human self-discovery.

For the purposes of our analysis, we can establish that in the first stages of life, children begin to discover who they are, to relate to the people surrounding them, forming a basis for their personalities in this way. In terms of giving, it could be said that it is the moment when a human being receives from others. In fact, the ability to give is not yet developed, but rather latent. In these early stages of life, children begin to realize that in order to be accepted and loved; they have to cede some of their independence and freedom of action. They imitate the examples they have around them. And that is when the model of giving takes on importance. In many ways, adults have "given" them a lot: life, protection, food, and, in most cases, love and acceptance. If the actions of these adults benefit others, the child learns this.

In early adolescence, the scope of relations extends beyond the immediate family nucleus toward peer groups. Adolescents learn that they will not receive if they do not give. This is when they begin to leave aside their egotism in order to relate to others, although still harboring feelings of jealousy and envy. Development is still incomplete in this stage. Late adolescence corresponds to an attitude of rejecting society, accompanied by individual questioning and existential awakening. Adolescents have not yet achieved maturity, but little by little they realize, through encounters and interactions with other human beings, that they will have to take responsibility for their actions. To the degree to which they develop the ability to give, they continue along the path to complete maturity.

This stage is not related to physical aging, but rather to maturity and both psychic and spiritual plenitude. Some individuals never mature, although they grow older, since they do not learn to give or to give of themselves. An indication of having reached the stage of adulthood is learning precisely this. Those people who have not had the experience of giving in the first stages of development have the option of experiencing it during the adult phase. Emotional maturity is reached when this ability to give is demonstrated in daily life, where this may go to the extreme, -to giving the most prized value – one's life – for another, if the person considers this to be necessary.

Here those interviewed explain how their acts coincide with what they think and believe is important...

> "I think that all that has been lost. That's why there's so much aggression, so much violence, because giving yourself to others doesn't exist anymore" (49 year-old woman)

> "...helping, because in the end, it benefits our children, and the act of helping, I think it comes back to the same thing, giving our children an example so that they turn out the same way..." (43 year-old woman)

> "I think that realizing that you can work and do something for other people's lives is very important..." (34 year-old woman)

A dynamic experience of giving to others within human relationships allows individuals to discover new aspects of others when the act of giving evolves as a process. In the last commentary above, the volunteer mentions that "realizing" that she can work for others has been important for her. Everyone has experienced giving, and giving of oneself at some time. If the experience has been significant, it is possible for this to become more conscious, and it may be incorporated into a system of personal values to then be repeated in the construction of a commitment. The action in and of itself, the "lived" experience is what leads to forging a commitment to a cause. It is at the individual level that change is experienced. However, mostly organized groups of individuals that commit to a cause obtain major social change.

Giving, Support, and Help

It is relevant to mention that in the national sample for the ENSAV used in this investigation, the subjects' main motivation in acts of solidarity was to *assist those who need help*. It should be remembered that the survey is statistically valid, and that 309 Mexicans out of the sample of 1,497 (21%) mention help as the answer to the open question: "There are many reasons to do something to benefit others. What are yours?" The second most common response to the question, by 164 people (11%) was the *desire to help others*, followed by the comment that *it's necessary to repay the community*, in the case of 120 people (8%) who made this comment. It is interesting to observe that 6%, i.e., 93 people in the sample, mention that their reason for doing something for others are their *religious beliefs*. The numbers show us that among Mexicans, these are the most powerful reasons for engaging in acts of solidarity.

In the qualitative part of the investigation, when studying people who work in NPOs, the data was buttressed by means of in-depth interviews and analysis of their discourse. The words "support" and "help" are closely related to evaluations like "I think it's necessary" or "I think we do things well." They belong to the pragmatic conceptual category about the practical meaning of these actions and indicate that the problems for which a solution is offered have been differentiated. They also have to do with the original purposes that motivated the creation of the social organizations, generally speaking, to help people with limited resources or to respond to different community needs.

Another level of discourse shows us that occasionally they demand or ask help from others. Helping reinforces the logic of giving (Schrift 1997): the idea of giving is socialized through practice. From this viewpoint, in personal terms, "helping" is intrinsically related to what the people interviewed are in a position to offer the other, knowing that they have knowledge or resources to place at the disposal of others. That is to say, support is an act of generosity. As a consequence, the relation between "support" and "giving" defines the logic of volunteer actions: one supports someone who needs it, giving something of oneself. The following excerpts illustrate this analysis:

> "This group of volunteers was founded in Mexico twenty years ago with the idea of helping people with limited resources to get ahead and give them the means, as we say between quotation marks, the means for them to be able to..." (42 year-old woman)

> "The motto is: "A helping hand so the street isn't the only thing in their lives." And yes, it's like giving them a hand, just to help them, as well as to motivate and encourage them. And that was what meant the most for the children..." (33 year-old woman)

When people willingly devote themselves to this work, they make a commitment to volunteer work. Their willingness to do so is related to their commitment. Assagioli (1990) presents different forms in which the will manifests itself, examining the different facets of this concept. Certain strength is necessary to develop a commitment. This author calls a facet of the will that demands constant work, as well as conscious and adequate development, a "strong will," as this is the aspect that provides the drive and energy to carry an action through to fulfillment. It becomes translated into not only realizing what we "are" and that we have a will but also to understanding that there is also "being able to do," which indicates that we have the ability to achieve it. When the two women volunteers comment that they "have" to help, they are referring to the fact that they are committed to these activities and this is related to a commitment that they have established for themselves.

> "If they could just finish elementary or middle school. If not, there were also other things we had to help them with. Their health, providing some workshops, dealing with drug addiction, sexuality, for them to see some dentist, or get involved with sports..." (26 year-old woman)

> "Right now, there isn't anybody else who can help out, and since we have a shortage of volunteers, we have to choose where to focus our work other..." (42 year-old woman)

The collective leadership with whom we wish to invest time and commit our actions will imply "being able to do" together, solving something – in the best-case scenario – for the common good. Achieving a consensus of wills is not an easy task; here Assagioli reminds us that will, now a collective will, also needs to be "good" in a collective ethical sense.

Giving and Deficiencies, What Is Needed, and What Should Be Done

The last three semantic interrelations are also related to giving and to one another, because in some ways they go beyond individual action toward collective action. They are: "deficiencies," "what is needed," and "what should be done."

The comments by those interviewed are related to what they see and think is needed or lacking in terms of evaluation within the cognitive category. These individuals are aware of their actions and of the needs that arise from the community around them. They try to develop a good understanding of the activities they have to undertake in order to see to the needs of others and evaluate the path to be followed in order to be able to get the necessary resources and support to guarantee the effective operation of their organizations. At the same time, they recognize not only what they themselves achieve, but also what is necessary to do together to produce an impact that would achieve the results desired for everyone. That is what those interviewed express:

> "...from when you're little it's inculcated and from your experience, you evaluate what you have, what you lack, and what you can give" (39 year-old woman)

> "...a bunch of things to do here, which we've already started to do, but we're short of hands and we lack resources to give a course in this area. I don't have anyone in fundraising now, and I don't have people in administration..." (53 year-old woman)

Among the Mexicans interviewed, the idea persists that "we all need each other" to invite others to get involved in the efforts undertaken by volunteer organizations.

When they talk about "what should be done," we should remember that conceptually this belongs to a moral category where the possibility of offering others what they do not have is recognized. At the same time, recognition of the needs of others becomes an inducement to make the greatest possible effort.

> "Well, I imagine there are needy people and that the work we do is important... and that we can't give up" (32 year-old man)

> "...if you need something some day and if I have the means... right away, I'll help you, because I like to give more..." (37 year-old woman)

> "Well, look, for me it's really important to give yourself to others. I always have said that we all need everybody else..." (61 year-old woman)

Abraham Maslow (1982), an expert on human motivation, emphasizes the importance of obtaining satisfaction through social interaction.

> In fact, I can say more firmly than ever and for many empirical reasons, that basic human needs can only be satisfied by means of and through other human beings, i.e., society. The need for community (belonging, contact, association) is a basic need in and of itself (*Ibid*, 333).

These comments point towards a collective consciousness of the act of giving, since a human being is a being-in-relation. Self-fulfillment and individual development are achieved through others.

> For him [Fromm], man is a social and political being that can only develop through the collective and historical process of exchange with the environment. The self-fulfillment of human beings in their singularity is only imaginable, for Fromm, in the framework of a historical and collective process in which human beings are linked to their environment through activity and love (Quitman 1989, 292).

Those interviewed emphasize that giving to others is an ethical responsibility that Mexican society is losing or has not acquired. One should give to the needy as a question of duty and empathy, placing oneself in the others' shoes. This leads to evaluating and understanding the importance the act of giving has for them:

> "I think one should give of one's time, place oneself in the other's shoes, I mean, the needy person..." (46 year-old man)

> "...because the answer they give is "I don't have time"; and if not, one must look for the time to give to others. For example, I could tell you "Yes", if you tell me, "You know what? I want you to help me sell some tickets..." (28 year-old woman)

This last interrelation underscores the solidarity that underlies the act of giving.[9] Those interviewed consider that it is necessary to develop opportunities for encounters and create more situations so that volunteer actions can increase in terms of the number and frequency of hours involved, "you should give of your time," both individually and as a group. In terms of understanding social needs: "place oneself in the other's shoes, I mean, the needy person..." It's clear what "should" be done, since it is received to be given again: "it gives me love to give," says one volunteer.

---

[9] See Komter (2005).

The volunteers in this study comment that it is important for them not only to give to others but also to give of themselves in solidarity with others. This is what three of the people interviewed say:

"It was very nice; I like it like that... Since I saw a response from the people, and now I want to give the people a response from me" (42 year-old woman)

"Well, I think it's being with people, knowing that you can give something of the little you know to someone else and see how they grow..." (34 year-old woman)

"I feel that, well, we should give a little, give of ourselves, you know, give some of our time to benefit others, it's a great satisfaction" (35 year-old woman)

When giving, and giving of oneself to others, there can be a process of existential discovery. This means intentionally going outside oneself to find the other, as Buber says, or fulfilling oneself in others, as Coreth[10] indicates, where one's own essence is affirmed when giving of oneself to others. Commitment is then achieved in a relationship of encounter that elicits full participation by the participants: "he who commits himself cannot set aside a portion of himself" (Buber 1970, 60).

We can refer the commentaries of people expressing solidarity through Mexican volunteer groups to the words of the American philosopher Rorty (1991), who presents the idea of human solidarity considering, in his judgment, what should be done: take into account the suffering of others and the importance of expressing solidarity in the future. Expressed a different way, it is a matter of giving fundamental importance to the perception of the needs of the other, since some of us have what others lack. He defines it in these terms:

The conception of what I am presenting sustains the existence of something like moral progress, and that that progress is oriented in reality in the direction of greater human solidarity. But it does not consider that solidarity to consist of the recognition of a nuclear self – the human essence – in all human beings. Instead of that, it is conceived as the ability to perceive with ever greater clarity that traditional differences (of tribe, religion, race, customs, and other similar ones) lack importance when compared with the similarities having to do with pain and humiliation; it is conceived, then, as the ability to consider people who are very different from us as included in the category of "us" (*Ibid*, 210).

Finally, to complete these comments that I have provided by way of analysis, we come to an investigator of volunteer and solidarity activities, Robert Wuthnow (1991, 83–85), a professor of sociology at Princeton University, who presents his ideas about actions by volunteers through what he calls "acts of compassion." He has interviewed a large number of volunteers and has invited them to tell their stories. What these histories end up revealing, the same as our universe of 66 interviews, is that although the intention of this investigation is to encounter the explicit motivations that would explain why a person does one thing and not another, we

---

[10] Coreth (1985, 178) explains it as transcendence: Man is transcendence. Only when overcoming himself or going outside himself, in giving of himself to the other, does man realize his own authentic self. The more he transcends himself, the more he fulfills his own essence. The more he gives of himself, without looking for himself, the better he finds himself in the realization of his supreme possibility.

find that in reality we cannot talk about a single motivation, since there is a complex mix of motivations underlying what we do.

Our research task is to try to delve into and find in the narrative of our interviewees the particularities that give us a way to both understand the general tendencies involved in these activities in Mexico and to discover in them universal concepts. We find simple stories that express personal values in the explanations given by our interviewees, which do not provide a hierarchy of motivations, with some being more pertinent or relevant than others. However, on the table for discussion in future studies, it will be necessary to find out in greater depth what are ideally the values that should be promoted in Mexican society, as well as the motivations – like those that have been considered in the case of giving – that are found behind them.

This author explains that, in general, volunteers are not naïve people. They do not even believe, as some of their critics suggest, that all society's problems will be solved with all the time they dedicate to volunteer work. It simply seems to be that "there is a value to one person helping another," as one of the people interviewed comments. Professor Wuthnow (*Ibid*, 234) provides this evaluation of this activity:

> Volunteer work will not, like a vaccination against polio, save us from evil. We will not have a better society because all the homeless people will eventually be housed and all the illiterate people taught to read. No. Volunteer work will save us because it implies hope. It gives a sense of efficacy, of being able to make a difference. It inspires confidence in the human condition in the goodness of those who are truly needy and deserve our help. To participate in voluntary organizations means we are making a choice for the better, siding with the good, doing something, rather than sitting idly by while the specter of chaos and corruption advances...

> This, as I say, is a hope that lies in the realm of symbolism and myth. But it is no different than many of our other dreams as a society... It is not really the belief that a cure for cancer will give us eternal life that inspires our hope. It is the image of people like us that inspires us. The one person who learns to read may in the larger scheme of things make very little difference to the health of our society...But teaching that person to read does have a demonstration effect. It reminds us – those who hear about it – of the importance of reading... So it is with volunteer work. Helping others may not lead to a better society, but it allows us to envision a better society.[11]

By way of a conclusion, in this chapter – which has reflected upon the different ways in which giving is shown to be the main expression of the Mexican people interviewed – it can be observed that in the same way individuals verbalize their belief systems, it is through concrete and committed action that they express their interest toward their fellow Mexicans in conditions generally more precarious than their own. It is necessary to find more paths to understanding the "logic of giving" and expand the comments expressed. Here we have tried to analyze this phenomenon, adding some theoretical-conceptual perspectives, with full awareness that other conceptual angles still remain to be considered and that there is much yet to be done to come to understand this phenomenon in order to construct theories concerning

---

[11] The author of this chapter changed the order of the paragraphs in this quotation to make the idea clearer.

solidarity activities. These comments may serve to stimulate investigation and the search for new motivations that affect and stimulate volunteer actions and acts of solidarity by the Mexican people.

References

Aronoff J, Wilson JP (1984) Personality in the social process. Erlbaum, Hillsdale, NY
Assagioli R (1990) The act of will. Mackays of Chatam, UK
Bandura A (1977) Social learning theory. Prentice Hall, Englewood Cliffs, NJ
Batson CD (1991) The altruism question: toward a social-psychological answer. Erlbaum, Hillsdale, NY
Buber M (1970) I and thou. Scribners, New York
Condie SJ et al (1976) Getting blood from collective turnips: volunteer donation in mass blood drives. J Appl Psychol 61:290–294
Coreth E (1985) ¿Qué es el Hombre?. Herder, Barcelona
Drake AW et al (1982) The American blood supply. MIT Press, Cambridge, MA
Dovidio JF (1984) Helping behavior and altruism: an empirical and conceptual overview. Adv Exp Soc Psychol 17 pp 361–427, Academy press
Eisenberg N (1986) Altruistic emotion, cognition and behavior. Erlbaum, Hillsdale, NY
Frankl V (1992) Psicoanálisis y existencialismo. Fondo de Cultura Económica, México
Freire P (1990) La Educación como práctica de la libertad, 40th edn. Siglo XXI, México
Fromm E (1990) El Arte de Amar. Paidós, México
Godbout J (1992) La esencia del don. Siglo XXI, México
Habermas J (1996) Conciencia moral y acción comunicativa. Península, Barcelona
Heshka S (1983) Situational variables affecting participation in voluntary associations. In: Smith DH (ed) International perspectives on voluntary action research. University Press of America, Washington, DC
Kohlberg L (1984) The psychology of moral development. The nature and validity of moral stages. Harper & Row, San Francisco, CA
Komter A (2005) Social solidarity and the gift. Cambridge University Press, UK
Luks, A (1988) Helper's High. Psychology Today, October, pp 39–42
Luks A, Payne P (1991) The healing power of doing good: the health and spiritual benefits of helping others. Fawcett, New York
Mansbridge JJ (1990) Beyond self-interest. University of Chicago Press, Chicago
Margolis H (1984) Selfishness, altruism & rationality: a theory of social choice. University of Chicago Press, Chicago
Maslow A (1982) La amplitud potencial de la naturaleza humana. Trillas, Mexico
Mochi P, Girado MC (1999) El Voluntariado: Una Elección de Solidaridad y Reciprocidad. In: Sociedad Civil, no. 9, vol. III, pp 9–26
Piaget J (1974) El juicio moral en el niño. EMECE, Buenos Aires
Piliavin JA, Charng HW (1990) Altruism A review of recent theory and research. Ann Rev Sociol 16:27–65
Piliavin JA et al (1981) Emergency intervention. Academic, New York
Quitman H (1989) Psicología humanística. Herder, Barcelona
Reddy RD (1980) Individual Philanthropy and Giving Behavior. In: Smith DH, Macaulay J (eds) Participation in social and political activities. Jossey-Bass, San Francisco
Rogers CR (1978) Terapia, personalidad y relaciones interpersonales. Nueva Visión, Buenos Aires
Rogers CR (1980) El poder de la persona. El Manual Moderno, México
Rorty R (1991) Contingencia, ironía y solidaridad. Paidós, Barcelona

Rushton JP (1981) The altruistic personality. In: Rushton JP, Sorrentino RM (eds) Altruism and helping behavior: social personality, and developmental perspectives. Erlbaum, Hillsdale, NJ

Schrift A (ed) (1997) The logic of the gift: towards an ethic of generosity. Routledge, New York

Simmons RG et al (1977) The gift of life: the social and psychological impact of organ transplantation. Wiley, New York

Staub E (1978) Positive social behavior and morality, vol. I. Academic, New York

Staub E (1979) Positive social behavior and morality: socialization and development, vol. II. Academic, New York

Wuthnow R (1991) Acts of compassion. Princeton University Press, Princeton, NJ

Villanueva M (1985) Hacia un modelo integral de la personalidad. El Manual Moderno, México

Chapter 5
Nonprofit Organizations in Mexico: Case Studies

María Guadalupe Serna

Introduction

Volunteer groups were analyzed in the two previous chapters, including their different facets, their relation to individual life experience, as well as the reasons for which people participate in them. The fundamental role played by the family group was also discussed among other elements that encourage a subject to take the path of activities to help third parties. Semantic categories related to volunteer action were also examined and the volunteer's perceptions were discussed, as well as the terms they assign to the type of activity performed. In this chapter, I will focus on exploring what happens in the organizations. Given the richness of the qualitative information gathered, it is possible to develop a framework in which volunteer group actions occur in order to achieve a complete scenario that also includes the type of organizations in which these volunteers participate.

Background

There is little information about nonprofit organizations (NPOs) in Mexico and so there is a broad field of study yet to be explored from the standpoint of different perspectives. According to Verduzco (2006), NPOs are the most common form of organization in Mexico, and they also constitute a particularly heterogeneous universe, as other studies have already noted (Méndez 1998; Brody 2003.) These organizations direct their attention and concerns toward a very diverse range of fields of action. Among them, some of the most important include: helping the sick; caring for children, women, the elderly, or indigenous people in marginalized circumstances; educating specific groups; promoting sports or cultural activities; encouraging a sense of community; and the defense of specific causes, to mention a few. In addition to this multiplicity of fields and forms of actions, there are

M. Guadalupe Serna
Instituto de Investigaciones Dr. José María Luis Mora, México D.F., México
e-mail: gserna@mora.edu.mx

J. Butcher (ed.), *Mexican Solidarity: Citizen Participation and Volunteering*,
DOI 10.1007/978-1-4419-1078-3_5, © Springer Science+Business Media, LLC 2010

different organizational models and alternative practices, and, therefore, it is important to examine concrete cases of NPOs operating today.

In the bibliography on the subject, the complexity of establishing the position of NPOs as part of civil society stands out. There are few detailed studies in Mexico of organizations of this type that analyze the purposes, internal structure, operational mechanisms, and decision-making process, as well as the way they raise funds and the sources from which their funding comes from (see study by Gordon 1998). This is why it is pertinent, once we have analyzed the subjects who participate in NPOs in different ways, to undertake the analysis of the organizations themselves and deal with questions like those noted and which will contribute to the discussion about the difficulties in defining this subject of study.

Purpose

This chapter analyzes the characteristics of 14 NPOs[1] that function in Mexico. The study is organized in terms of four main themes for each organization: (1) the origin of the organization and its objectives; (2) the goals it pursues and its achievements; (3) its operational structure and the way in which decision-making process is carried out; and (4) its sources of financing. From my perspective, the detailed analysis of these elements makes it possible to structure a first inventory of different types of NPOs in Mexico. For this purpose, I use the information derived from 14 case studies that included a total of 65 in-depth interviews[2] with different participants in the organizations, including the founder, the director or informal leader, the coordinators, and the personnel considered to be volunteers by the organizations themselves, as well as some materials generated by the organizations.

The Problem of Defining the Organizations

NPOs are a particularly complex and heterogeneous universe, mainly because they participate in a wide variety of areas, which have very diverse characteristics. From the U.S. perspective, this group forms part of the third sector, as a way of establishing the difference with governmental organizations – which seek control – and business organizations – which pursue profits. Other authors prefer to speak of the volunteer sector, placing their emphasis on the unpaid, volunteer work that people provide through these organizations. In spite of this dispute, there is some agreement

---

[1] A total of 15 cases studies were done, but only 14 of these were concerned with specific organizations. The remaining study was done about a person who was independently engaged in volunteer-type activity. So this last case is not discussed in this chapter.

[2] In this case, 14 organizations about which information was gathered are analyzed, with a total of 65 interviews. The person who is engaged on an individual basis in helping third parties is not taken into consideration in this regard.

that stable groups of people are involved. That is to say, they have been operating for several years, they have an operational structure and specific operational rules, they were initiated with an objective in mind, they have some concern for professionalizing their activities, and in many cases they have become formally established, and so they exist as legal entities (Canto 1998, 79).

So what is involved are citizen organizations that identify a field in which they are interested in carrying out collective actions and activities to support specific groups of the population that they have previously identified. This makes them different from labor or trade organizations, organizations having political representation, and those that produce commodities (Canto 1998).

If we take the foregoing points as a reference to group the organizations about which information was obtained, we find that Salamon and Anheier's proposal (1996), based on operational-structural type criteria, to be pertinent to analyze these kinds of entities. The definition proposed by these authors includes five characteristics: they must be organized, i.e., be institutionalized to a certain degree; they must be self-governed; they must be designed to control their own activities; they must be nonprofit organizations; and they must include volunteer activities or at least a certain degree of collaboration of this type by some of their participants.[3]

The Organizations Selected

The organizations analyzed[4] are located in the following regions: the north, northeast, center, west, and southwest of Mexico. The gulf, northwest, and southeast regions were not covered, since it was not possible to include organizations from those places due to a lack of appropriate links. Table 5.1 shows the general characteristics of the organizations selected, their fields of action, their legal designation, and how long they have existed.[5]

As can be seen, the NPOs selected include an informal organization with almost 8 years of activity, two private assistance institutions (I.A.P., Spanish acronym),[6] ten civil associations (A.C., Spanish acronym),[7] and a governmental-type organization. This last

---

[3] Authors like Verduzco (2006) and Gordon (1998) also use this definition for their analyses.

[4] The way the organizations were selected and how the case studies were structured was discussed in Chap. 3 of this book.

[5] The exact name and location of the organizations is kept confidential, since this requirement was established by some of their directors or founders. This does not affect the analysis to be performed, however.

[6] In Mexico, some federative entities and the Federal District government have Private Assistance Institution laws. The following is a link to the law for the state of Mexico that may be consulted to understand the character of these organizations in the case of Mexico. http://www.edomex.gob.mx/legistel/cnt/LeyEst_099.html

[7] For information about what a civil association is and how to organize one, see www.senado.gob.mx/comisiones/directorio/relextorg/Content/como_construir%20ONG/COMO_CONSTIUIRUNAONG.pdf

Table 5.1 Organizations by field of action, orientation, type of registration, and age

Sphere of volunteer action	Orientation of the organization	Type of registration	Year founded
Business	Aid to women in marginalized neighborhoods	A.C.	1990
Government institution	Dedicated to orphaned children	Governmental	1985
Religious	Values formed in the Catholic faith	Informal	1998
Sports/recreation	Promoting sports among children in poorer neighborhoods	A.C.	1999
Youth/educational	Educational attention for youth in risk situations	A.C.	1997
Rural/community	Support for management of community development and labor counseling projects	A.C.	1987
Urban	Support for construction of housing for populations in marginalized suburban areas	A.C.	1988
Vulnerable groups	Attention to the disabled to facilitate social integration	A.C.	1990
Vulnerable groups	Attention to working children in marginalized urban areas	I.A.P.	2004
Youth/educational	Help for abandoned and/or orphaned rural area youth	A.C.	1966
Health	Health care for women in extreme poverty	A.C.	1999
Causes	Attention for indigent sick people	A.C.	1988
Educational	Attention for street children	I.A.P.	1995
Cultural	Encouraging and promoting knowledge of our cultural heritage	A.C.	

organization is not self-governed and receives direct financing, although it fulfills the other three characteristics noted by Salamon and Anheier (1996). It is included because it is a very common organizational form in Mexico, usually generated by a government entity to take care of orphans, where it is common to find volunteers, and an operation that is formally separated from the structure of the government. Including it in this study has been a way of establishing differences and similarities with the rest of the organizations and emphasizing its particular characteristics.

A broad variety of organizational forms are found within the spectrum of civil associations in Mexico, both among those about which information was gathered and an endless number of private schools, not necessarily for people with limited resources,institutions of higher education, or organizations oriented toward promoting the political participation of the citizens, to mention only the most common. Therefore, the findings presented here are limited to the organizations studied.

Origins, Characteristics and Objectives of the Organizations

The organizations were motivated by five different types of initiatives: (a) those that are part of a larger entity, either an international or nation-wide organization; (b) those that have been promoted by one or several people united by a common concern; (c) those that arose from an initiative on the part of a group of neighbors due to a specific problem; (d) those initiated by people related to the church; and (e) those promoted by a governmental entity. In this regard, the fields of action of the different organizations are diverse, even when the way in which they arose may be similar. The users or beneficiaries of most of the organizations are groups in conditions of poverty in urban, suburban, rural, or indigenous areas. Only in one case central objective was to resolve a problem cutting across different strata like disability.

Organizations that are Part of a Larger Entity

Two organizations fall into this first group. The first of them is a local office of a larger entity that began its activities more than three decades ago, encouraged by a business foundation and run by the wives of company officials. The purpose was to support housewives with limited resources who live in marginalized areas, by means of different courses that have to do with their households, as a way of taking better advantage of their resources, as well as training them for employment. This project was reproduced in 1990 in the northeast by a group of 13 volunteer wives of officials and/or employees in the company, who took up the task of getting the project started. They were supported by the organization's headquarters with some economic resources and knowledge about how to develop the project.

By 2006 the organization had a total of ten people, six of whom were volunteers – four participants from the original group who continued working on the project even when their spouses no longer worked for the company – two retired teachers who received support for their travel expenses, three students doing their social service who provided support with computer and English classes, and a cleaning woman who was paid for her work. The volunteers, all of them housewives, gave dressmaking, cooking, and beauty care classes and took care of the children with a game center while their mothers attended the classes.

The second organization began activities in Mexico in 1999 in the south of the country as part of an international organization that had been engaged in activity over several decades and had offices in several countries. Its central purpose is health care for women in extreme poverty conditions. When it was established in this country, they decided to locate a region with severe marginalization problems, in accordance with the purpose of their headquarters. Seven years after establishing themselves in Mexico, they had two small health units that offered medical visit and gynecological attention services to both marginalized and limited resource groups. They had professional personnel to attend to their patients: a doctor, nurses, and personnel trained in gynecology. A total of 22 people were working in the organization, 13 of whom were personnel hired for specific activities, four were on scholarship, three were students doing their social service, and two were volunteers.

Organizations Promoted by One or Several People

Six more of these organizations were promoted by one or several people to achieve a common purpose. Of these, two organizations attended to vulnerable groups, specifically children, as a response to the lack of continuity of a project previously promoted by a governmental entity. The oldest group, which brought together a group of private individuals who collaborated with the DIF,[8] began in 1995 in a municipality of the western region, and arose as a response to a report prepared by UNICEF-DIF where an evident social problem was explicitly indicated: a large number of children were dropping out of school to work in the streets. In the face of this problem, the municipality took up the task of promoting the organization, the purpose of which was to help the children. They were divided into two groups: those who still maintained ties with their families and those who had broken these ties. Within this framework, the DIF tried to get the children off the streets and the organization tried to get scholarships. In addition to giving out a monthly package of groceries, cost studies to estimate the cost involved in maintaining a child in school were performed, and a donor program for private individuals interested in supporting the program was designed.

In 2002, they decided to become independent, since the support from the municipal government declined and limited to paying the rent and delivering the groceries. For this reason, they modified their purpose, devoting themselves exclusively to caring for working children with family ties. Four years later, a total of 18 people were working in the organization, 10 of the paid personnel distributed were among administrative personnel, social workers, and psychologists, five social service students, and three people who systematically supported different organization activities as volunteers.

Another organization, located in an urban area with important rural migration in the central region, was also established based on a report similar to the foregoing one and more or less during the same period. In this case, the DIF in the area established a project based on the report where the objective was to defend the children's rights by providing education and recreation for minors who remained on the streets and in the markets begging or selling gum while their parents worked, also generally, on the street. A group of promoters was formed for this purpose and they worked on the project for 3 years. In 2000, at the end of that administration, the project was closed, and in mid-2001, four of the promoters (all young people) who had participated in the project, decided to continue it as a way to respond to the demands of the children. Since they did not have a place to operate, they began to

---

[8] *Desarrollo Integral de la Familia* (DIF), Integral Family Development.

give classes in public places, such as the park, the main square, and the market, until they were awarded some funds through a project from the Mexican Youth Institute, in 2002, and were able to pay rent and operate independently. In 2004, they decided to formalize the organization.

The organization's purpose is to provide support, attention, basic education, recreation, and the development of Christian values for children and young people who are socially vulnerable and apt to suffer from street situations. They have focused their attention on small children in day care, preschool, and elementary school, who are picked up from their homes every day to take classes, play, and be fed while their mothers work. By 2006, there were 17 people in the organization, 15 of whom were volunteers. Of this total, ten were young people committed to the organization's progress, five were teachers from the CONAFE and INEA system[9] who received minimal support for travel and meal expenses, and two were paid personnel, an accountant and a cleaning woman, although their pay was very meager, given the precarious nature of the resources available.

A third organization, the oldest of the group being analyzed, with 40 years of activity, is located in a small rural/urban population in the central region of Mexico and was promoted by two women who decided to contribute something to their community. They began by offering support and advice to people who had committed some offense. In their conversations, they found that many of them came from broken homes, had suffered some kind of child abuse, and/or had been abandoned by their parents. This was when they decided to create an organization whose purpose was to provide support for children and young people of age between 5 and 18 years old, who were in vulnerable circumstances. Their concern has been to accompany them during the process of growing up, offering them a "home life". They have installations for this purpose where the children and young people live, and they provide them with an education in the local schools. As part of their integral development, they also receive job training. This takes place through their participation in specific productive projects and human development and spiritual life practices, so that they become socially responsible and productive adults.

The organization has developed an integral and integrating educational proposal that has included important efforts to make possible human development and personal attention for the children and young people who live in the installations voluntarily. The organization had about 40 workers in 2006. One of the people in charge was a relative of one of the founders. The organization also included the participation of young people doing their social service and a small group of volunteers, mostly foreigners who participated over short periods and were carefully selected.

The fourth organization is located in the northeast region in an important urban area that receives members of the indigenous population coming from neighboring states. This organization is the result of intense activity begun almost 40 years ago by a woman concerned about sick people with limited resources and severe or

---

[9] CONAFE: *Consejo Nacional de Fomento Educativo* (National Educational Promotion Council) and INEA: *Instituto Nacional de Educación para los Adultos* (National Adult Education Institute).

terminal health problems. It was formally established in 1998 as an organization of volunteers. The promoter, an active woman, began to personally help sick people in a hospital that received low-income people in the city where she lived. A short time later, her friends also got involved as volunteers and they helped her with the activities of getting both economic support and medicine.

Many years later, the organization was formally constituted with the idea of continuing the project that the founder had promoted. Similar work was continued with the goal of supporting sick people in precarious economic circumstances by providing specialized medical care and medicine, as well as burial services when necessary. The organization is made up of 18 volunteers, although only seven of them participate actively, because of their age.

The fifth organization, constituted as a foundation for a group of organizations, was formally established in 1990 in an important urban area in the northern region with the purpose of providing support and services for people with some kind of disability. The idea came from a woman with experience in organizations and management, who came in as an official of the municipal government and opened up the possibility of posing the need to promote a project that would coordinate the organizations devoted to helping the disabled. She received support from several people for this purpose, some of whom had family members with some type of disability.

When getting the project started, she identified the organizations that would participate and held several discussion meetings over a period of 2 years to outline the general proposal and method of operating. Once it was formed, the purpose of the foundation has been to work with organizations that provide awareness for certain types of disabilities, with the aim of achieving more efficient resource use, avoiding duplicate efforts, as well as sensitizing and educating society about disabilities, since it is a field that has received little attention, despite its impact on all sectors of society. Their efforts have been focused on promoting ways of getting close to disabled people in order to develop their human potential. From the beginning the project received support from a number of people in the business sector who made important voluntary donations. The organizations that have been part of this effort continue to operate their own programs.

Currently, 14 people work in the guiding organization, including professionals and administrative personnel, as well as some social service students. In terms of the volunteers, the patients' mothers participate directly as volunteers, even though the directors only have two people who are formally considered as such, since they think that some professionalism is necessary to care for their users. They carry out an annual fund drive 1 day per year in which different groups of the population participate in a voluntary way.

The sixth and last organization began its activities in the 1980s, through the efforts of a group of people who were working to promote a museum located in an urban area in central Mexico, and they were interested in making this resource known. At the beginning, they focused on contributing through donations, to care for, preserve, and popularize works of art, and to do so, they visited people who could make monetary contributions. As it became a solid organization, its objectives were strengthened, and a fundamental concern has been to promote knowledge of the cultural heritage available through the museum, promoting visits and helping to consolidate and maintain this cultural patrimony by means of fundraising. The person in charge of the volunteers in the organization is a paid employee who has the assistance of five volunteers for specific periods of time for guided tours and cataloging.

Organizations Promoted Through Neighborhood Initiatives

Two other organizations arose due to the initiative of neighborhood groups interested in solving a problem where they lived. The first of them began informally and sporadically in 1985, in a densely populated urban area of central Mexico, when a group of neighbors began to organize soccer as a way of providing possibilities for interaction, and use of free time for young people and children in a lower-income neighborhood in an at-risk situation (drug addiction and gangs). One of the neighbors participating was a coach who decided to actively collaborate with the project to contribute to alleviating the problems where they lived. To begin with, they practiced in the afternoon. Later, the coach suggested creating an organization to provide continuity for the neighbors' concerns. However, he was not able to interest them in the proposal, and the practices were constantly interrupted over several years.

Finally, in 1999, with the help of an administration student, the coach was able to formally establish an organization whose purpose has been to help limited-resource children and young people who live in low-income neighborhoods by means of promoting sports activities as a way of preventing a high index of delinquency in the area. In order to attract people interested in soccer, he had to look for the institutional coverage of a recognized team. By 2006, the organization had a small office in a space provided by the founder's family, and the sports activities were carried out on some fields in the same neighborhood area, although it was necessary to pay for their use. The coach, and founder, is concerned about supporting the community, so he also gives classes to help children and young people catch up in school. In terms of the number of members, the organization consisted of nine people, five of whom were paid for their work and four who were volunteers, who are mothers of some of the children who receive grants to be able to participate in the soccer classes.

The second organization, located in a suburban area of northeast Mexico, has been active since 1998, although it has not yet been formally established. The idea arose from a group of neighbors interested in building a small chapel for the local residents, who had settled two decades before on nonpatented land. The area has been home to poor families, some of whom are squatting, especially those who are living along the river. Others have been able to obtain a deed for their lots and build houses, although these are made from temporary materials.

The group of women who promoted the idea began collecting funds to build a chapel, and they have been able to do so little by little, but at the same time, they have also been structuring a project where part of them work in the chapel giving catechism classes and others have chosen to provide support through church social action, helping adults with greater economic problems. So far, the assistance has basically consisted of helping people with the procedures for getting their election identification cards and telling them about their rights and the possibilities for different types of help. At times they have gotten support from merchants in the urban area and they have given some food packages to the neediest people. The priest assigned to the chapel under construction has served as a normative figure and there is no interest in formalizing his activities. The group is made up of 11 people, all volunteers, although only eight of them participate actively in the organization, while the other three do so sporadically.

Organizations Promoted by People Related to the Church

Three organizations have been promoted by people related to the church, two of which operate as community base units, one in a rural area and the other in a rural/urban area. The first one began, thanks to the concerns of a priest who came to work in a very poor peasant area of northern Mexico at the beginning of the 1980s. Inspired by the spiritual principles of the ecclesiastical communities, he got involved in understanding peasant life and needs, which were very extensive at that time. Little by little they began to act in other areas, particularly in achieving a guaranteed price for the products harvested in the region. Gradually, other concerned individuals, including a municipal official, also became involved because of the situation the peasants in the area were experiencing. Later, other professionals with organizational experience arrived and they supported different producers' groups in the process of forming an organization that was formally established in 1987.

The purpose of the organization has been to promote fair prices for agricultural products and promote production, community development, and resource management projects. The organization has increased its presence in a third of the municipalities of the entity and has about 6,000 members. There are about 100 volunteers in this group who are the people who provide some service for the organization in the municipal councils. There are 11 people working on a daily basis in the main offices: four state coordinators with 2-year terms of service who receive living support from the members, two advisors, two technicians, a secretary, an administrator, and a field supervisor; these last seven people are paid organizational personnel.

The other organization is located in a low-income rural/urban area in the western region. It was created based on a movement led by a person with social concerns and who had participated in ecclesiastical communities and the urban people's movement due to his religious education. When he returned to the area where he was born, he became involved in community activities, where he found that one of the greatest needs was suitable housing and the difficulty of obtaining it. He took up the task of holding meetings among the people he knew. The idea he had was to work in dynamic communities with the aim of opening viable paths to developing residential areas. Over 3 years of discussions in meetings, the conditions arose to be able to obtain some land where the members of the group could begin to build their houses. Finally, they took possession of the land, established a neighborhood, and formalized their organization in 1988.

The purpose has been to promote processes among low-income groups to advance community life, and build housing and areas for social interaction. So, from the beginning, they have worked together to design housing areas, streets, sidewalks, green areas, an area for community meetings, and the necessary water, drainage, and electrical services. Currently, the group has 15 active volunteers, although there are a total of about 100 families in the organization, and about 50 people who collaborate occasionally.

The third organization was promoted by a person who was the vicar for several years in a conflictive area of central Mexico, and had the opportunity to get to know and work closely with young people who were having problems with drug addiction, gangs, and violence. He found that one of the possible causes contributing to the problem was school dropout, precarious economic situation, and that, consequently, the interaction of these factors left these groups without options for a better future. A scholarship program was developed in an informal way in the community for several years so that young people could remain in school. The scholarship money made it possible to cover the costs of transport and school materials.

However, the complex situation required help. So he designed a project that was formally established in 1997 with the support of members of the community, particularly business people, who served as benefactors and began to participate actively and voluntarily in what they considered to be a viable project.

The main objective of this organization, which operates as a foundation, is to help low-income youth to continue with their studies by providing them with the economic resources for their basic necessities and for developing their abilities. They have opened another program in a different community which also seeks to work on community development problems. Currently, the foundation provides free elementary and middle school education and scholarships. At the high school level, a minimal contribution is requested. At-risk youth are admitted between the ages of six and 18, although the most important group is in the 13–18 year range. Language courses and workshops are also provided to prepare the young people for a productive life. They also have agreements with higher education institutions in the area, where some of the interested students have been able to receive complete scholarships for their professional education. There are 80 people currently working in the organization, including administrative, teaching, and maintenance personnel. The students themselves participate as volunteers and receive compensation for their activities. There are also three volunteers who are mothers of scholarship students, as well as teachers who instruct some workshops without pay.

Organization Promoted by a Government Initiative

In this last group, we find an organization that also operates as a foundation and was initiated by a government entity in 1985 in an urban area in central Mexico. It was begun as a social welfare project for orphaned or abandoned children dependent on the state government. A council was established for this purpose as a decentralized public entity with its own legal status and resources, although it has been administered by a board of directors selected by the state governor. Its purpose has been to provide quality, friendly housing and protection, 24 h a day during the entire year, for 6-year-old children who are sent to this home. Its concern has been to provide a welfare rescue alternative for these minors and improve their physical and emotional circumstances, strengthening and preparing them for integration into a family or society. In 2006, 41 people collaborated with the institution, including administrative personnel, nurses, pig-farming personnel, cooks, washerwomen, and security guards. There were, also, five volunteers and some social service students.

Goals and Achievements

The organizations analyzed vary from 2 to 50 years of existence from the time they were created, which implies important differences in their processes of consolidation and their achievements. In order to analyze the fulfillment of their goals, their activities are focused on the following three important criteria (a) a clearly defined and delimited project related to the niche where the organization will operate; (b) the support of a group with a clear idea of the project, and of how to transform it from a personal concern to a well-defined and institutionalized organization; and (c) a support network, in terms of social capital, from the beginning and throughout its process of development.

Organizations that can Establish Themselves

Half of the organizations analyzed, seven of the total, had the proposed elements, in spite of important differences in their longevity, which ranged from 10 to 40 years of operation. In this case, the goals they set and their achievements are evident: the projects were well formulated, the area in which they would operate was chosen, and the type of contribution expected was determined when setting up the organization. In some of the interviews, poorly organized beginnings were mentioned. However, it was possible for them to develop a project having a detailed proposal. In other cases, the project matured through discussion sessions and meetings with the group interested until it took shape. It is worth mentioning that, in most cases, the promoters of the idea were professionals with experience in organizations and an understanding of development processes. When the organization did not have this kind of profile, they looked for professionals in these fields. The beginnings were difficult, since this implied convincing possible participants and establishing viability networks. The process was facilitated, in part, when it was possible to show the first achievements.

In four of the seven cases, there were people who contributed part of the economic funds by means of creating a foundation or trust as a way of supporting a project considered to be viable. They even participated actively in raising funds, relying on networks of friends and acquaintances. One of the organizations in this group was created based on combined action by private individuals and the municipal government then in office. In another case, government funds were received through a foundation, which guaranteed its permanence. In yet another case, initial funds and solid institutional prestige were put into action to look for financing based on generating projects. The last case was a community project that, due to its design and support, achieved a broad base of supporters who were directly benefitted by its operation.

All the foregoing, combined with a structured project, led to a process of institutionalization that implied the design of specific projects for foundations and national and/or international foundations and organizations that financed them. This made it possible for them to expand their resource options and fulfill different programs in progress. This also implied the growth of the organizations and even the possibility of opening new service areas and expanding the assistance, as well as recruiting more personnel. All the organizations in this group have prepared and submitted reports indicating their achievements and their maturity as organizations. Only three organizations in this group are in the process of becoming self-sustaining.

Organizations with Difficulties in Establishing Themselves

The other seven organizations were not able to achieve these three elements when required, for different reasons. This could have been due to the project being formulated with a very short-term perspective, without necessarily having expectations for growth, and/or a lack of support networks to help them on other fronts with the completion of the project. In this group, one of the community-based organizations was structured by a leader and a group of collaborators who established guidelines for the operation of the new entity. For some time, the direct users and beneficiaries actively participated in fulfilling some of the goals that had been set. Nevertheless, some years later, they began to experience difficulties in consolidating a constant network of external support to help with the negotiations they required. This generated, in part, a situation in which the advance was not as rapid as expected, and there were also disagreements between the members and the leader that caused greater delays in some activities than had been planned.

A second organization began as part of a project with very concrete objectives. Its members, organized as a group of volunteers, have carried out activities that are an extension of what they used to do in their homes. Even though they had institutional support to achieve their goals, they have had to deal with difficulties in trying to become integrated into the community they are interested in serving, which has required investments of time and multiple activities to develop the organization. They have had to dedicate time to building networks in the area where they carry out their activities, and they have lost members from the original core. In addition to this, over the years they have practically lost the employment connection between the company and the participants, who were formerly officials' wives. In spite of this, they have continued to support the organization because they consider it to be a priority project. However, it now seems unlikely that they will be able to again increase the number of volunteers needed to push the project forward, notwithstanding the efforts of the members. Despite constant work, for the time being, the organization has begun a phase of adjustment with the aim of defining the path to be followed.

Two other organizations, also composed of volunteers, have achieved a well-defined project and established the niche where they operate, although they did not carry out careful planning about how they would develop and they also lack social networks to support the project. This is why it has been difficult for them to fulfill their goals, since the lack of a support network of acquaintances seems to have a negative impact on designing a viable long-term project. In both cases, although they have been able to carry out part of what they planned to do, this has led to important costs in terms of operational time for the members and leaders of the organization.

Two other volunteer organizations seem not to have planned how to maintain their operations. This meant that, although they have had a support network and have advanced in maintaining their operations, in recent years those responsible have devoted part of their time to establishing medium and long-term goals. Recently, they have been planning how to consolidate the project and expectations have been modified that, in large part, were derived from personal concerns, and therefore their transformation into an institution guaranteeing the continuity of the work is still a pending task. In terms of their achievements, there has been a slow advance, due in large part to the lack of expectations for the future on the part of the members.

Finally, the last organization, of an informal character and also made up of volunteers, has operated on a personal basis, planning short-term actions without a well-defined project. This is due to a lack of knowledge about management, as well as the lack of financial support and social support networks to be able to serve the small core of users. Their achievements have been expressed in terms of activities and actions planned over a very short-term, without any growth or consolidation in this respect.

Operational Structure and Decision-making Process

According to the information gathered, there are at least three different kinds of operational structures in these organizations: (a) structures where horizontal decision-making predominates; (b) those with a well-defined command structure with specific functions; and (c) those operating based on consensus where the community base has an important presence.

Horizontality and Consensus

The first group consists of six organizations that, from their beginnings up until now, have been made up of volunteers without economic remuneration for their activity and have undertaken the most diverse activities to keep the unit active. The commitment they have had to the project's development and the commitment established among all the participants seems to be an element that has guaranteed permanence. These are small organizations, with five to fifteen members. They have a certain structure, i.e., there is a person at the head of the organization, the director, and others fulfill specific coordination responsibilities. There is a consensus among the members interviewed that the decisions are made in a horizontal way. They meet and discuss the activities and listen to the opinions of the director, and then the group decides what to do. According to the information, there is a good relationship among all involved, since they are interested in advancing and fulfilling the objectives established and they have maintained the idea that everyone can participate in decision making. Only in one case did the foundation that provides support, in terms of both how to do things and some economic support, decide on some activities.

Well-defined Authorities with Specific Functions

The second group consists of organizations that have a command structure made up of a general director, who in several cases responds to a board of directors or foundation as the entity that decides and plans what to do in the long-term, as well as administrative personnel and coordinators. In this case, the people considered to be volunteers represent a minority percentage of the whole. The operational structure varies in complexity according to the scope of the project. However, in all cases, I found there is a director who is in charge, reports to a board or council, and manages subordinates who coordinate the different areas of the organization. These coordinators, in turn, have a group of people who are directly responsible and have personnel who help them regularly, who are simply called volunteers. In all cases, the members of the structure are people who receive remuneration for their work, although, according to the information obtained, their salaries are not competitive with what they could make in other sectors in the same positions. That is to say, there is a profile of people interested in and committed to the project, who receive modest remuneration and are willing to work extra hours without any extra pay.

Four of these organizations have a foundation and/or trust made up of several members who perform their activities and responsibilities on a volunteer basis. This trust and/or foundation is headed up by a President who does not receive remuneration for his or her activities and to whom the management reports. Decisions are made by members of the foundation and/or trust and the directors can submit their proposals. In the case of organizations with only one director, this person is responsible for annual planning, and listens in the evaluation meetings to the coordinators, and in some cases, may include his or her own suggestions.

Volunteers are at the bottom of the structure in all the organizations in this group. I also found that in most of the organizations analyzed, this label is assigned due to the lack of another or to emphasize that they do not carry out a specific activity, which also implies that they have few possibilities of professionalization in this field; the directors are not even clear about the kinds of activity these people can perform. This complicates the scenario for those interested in participating in these nonprofit organizations.

From the perspective of the volunteers, they do not have the possibility of making decisions, but just of carrying them out. This volunteer sector only has specific positions and responsibilities in two of the organizations in this group, where they consider themselves to be part of the structure. This fact seems to imply a relationship of commitment that also implies the professionalization of their activities in the middle term. In the other cases, the idea is to help however much one can, not necessarily in relation to some specific task, but rather to help the organization's workers with whatever is needed.

Operation by Consensus Among the Base

The third group consists of two community-based organizations that have a different structure and membership from the types already described. Designed by professionals, the participants are inhabitants of the communities where the organizations develop their activities. All of them share similar living situations and do the same type of work to make a living. Among those interviewed, a sense of belonging and solidarity prevails, and the leader and founder receives recognition, although in one case he no longer participates in the project.

The organization with the largest number of members out of all the organizations analyzed has a board of directors made up of three people who are elected by the community and receive subsistence support from all members of the organization during their two year term in office. This structure is reproduced in committees that operate at the municipal level in the area where the organization has influence, although in this case they receive no subsistence support. These positions are renewed every 2 years. The peasants are responsible for leadership positions and the advisors are located outside the command structure, which has led to a more active participation on the part of the members. Both the advisors and the technical support team are paid personnel.

In this organization, everyone who participates in specific tasks in the different committees is a volunteer. In relation to decision-making, there is a consensus among the members about the kind of decisions they can make and the difference with regard to the governing entity, which decides about activities over the long-term. There have been ups and downs since, during certain periods, the members have viewed the directors as individuals who are distant from their concerns.

In the case of the second organization, the leader is the same person who founded it, although there are conflicting opinions about the role he has played among different members of the group. All the members of the organization are part of the general assembly, which has a coordinating commission elected by them and consists of five people. One person, at the head of the administrative council, is responsible for funds, and the other four people coordinate areas of interest for the community project. The members of the commission are changed periodically, although there is no specific term of office, but rather the assembly decides according to the "need for renovation". In no case is any compensation received for these positions. Currently, they have problems with the commission elected recently, where the founder was reelected, which has partially blocked the development of activities, since it is thought that some goals have not been fulfilled and the way decisions are made has not been clearly identified.

Sources of Funding

The organizations analyzed, in order to get started with their projects, require a group of people to manage them and make decisions in the field of action involved, as well as people interested in providing support to generate the economic resources that make development and consolidation possible. This implies putting multiple strategies into effect on different levels, among them the way daily expenses will be covered and the way the planned services will be guaranteed over the long run.

It is evident that it is important to obtain everyday and long-term financing, since this means the continuation of the project and even the possibility of expanding it, reproducing it, and making it self-sustaining in the middle term. The information collected indicates that three broad groups can be identified in terms of the characteristics of their organizational fundraising sources: (a) those that have enjoyed a constant source of economic resources from the beginning; (b) those that begin and diversify their possibilities at the same time they show concern for becoming self-sustaining; and (c) those that operate with uncertain economic funding.

Constant Source of Financing

This group includes organizations that have taken up the task of forming a trust made up of people from the community, usually business people, who devote time, make donations, and use networks of acquaintances and convince them of the viability of the project and the need to support it. In these cases, they began with a fund that is sometimes supplemented periodically with annual fundraising programs among the general population, as well as specific donor programs. In other cases, there have been problems with donors, due to the way the resources have been distributed, since the amount dedicated to administrative expenses and paying salaries is considered to be excessive, leaving less than half of the funds for the scholarships. Organizations that have delineated a well-structured long-term project are found in this group.

Diversified and Self-sustaining Financing

The second group includes organizations that have obtained financing from different sources over time. At times these entities began with a group of donors who provided funds in a more or less systematic, although limited, way, which made it possible to begin the project. Their possibilities have been expanded over time by developing specific projects aimed at carrying out certain action. In other cases, they have received specific support to pay the rent or other needs. In other cases, they began with limited support from the larger entity they belong to with the aim of later developing their own financing, and have structured projects that, at the same time, have been planned out in order to develop their ability to sustain themselves in the long-term. In these cases, we are also dealing with organizations with a well-planned initial project and expectations of growth in the middle term.

Uncertain Financing

This group consists of organizations that were started, for the most part, based on the good will of some individuals but with very limited initial financing, and so they face financial problems on a daily basis. In fact, sometimes it is the people involved themselves who have provided the funds to cover eventualities and organized events, bazaars, raffles, food sales, and collections of minor donations among acquaintances whose support is irregular, or have even sought support from some businesses, which has also been temporary. This means that the organizations have to be constantly looking for funds to carry out their day to day activities . Some of the organizations in this group have a project and long-term objectives that have not been defined with precision.

When the organizations analyzed have achieved funding in addition to a trust, when there is one, it is noted that this usually comes from international foundations, or from federal funds (especially programs like INDESOL or SEDESOL), and by way of exception, support from state and/or municipal governments. In some organizations, where the need to become self-sustaining has been posed, funds from projects or services they offer, or the sale of products are also very important.

Among the financing problems found, what stand out are the difficulties with structuring financially viable projects. In some cases, as already noted, the organizations do not have trained personnel to design projects and submit them for consideration for funding to different possible entities on a national or international level. This seems to be a severe limitation about which there is no discussion. It is possible that this is due to the ignorance of the participants themselves about the need to professionalize this aspect. In other cases, if somebody among the participants has the tools to be able to develop a project, it is usually the same person who leads the organization. For this reason, the flow of daily commitments limits the possibilities of attending to these matters, even when they are urgent. This problem is evident in organizations where the director is a volunteer and is also occupied with a multiplicity of daily matters.

Finally, another problem discussed in some organizations has to do with the amount dedicated to administration and paying salaries. At times, the donors that receive the monthly and annual reports consider the percentage dedicated to these items to be excessive in comparison with what goes to scholarships and direct services to the users. Although this is a problem detected in some organizations, it indicates the need for them to develop a more efficient administration, so as to avoid these kinds of complaints.

Conclusions

We have discussed the characteristics of the NPOs involved in the study based on four concrete aspects: how they began and the kind of objectives posed when they started; the goals proposed and accomplished during their efforts; the characteristics of the structure with which they have operated and their decision-making process, as well as the mode of financing developed by the organization.

We found that the organizations analyzed make up a particularly complex and heterogeneous universe, due, in part, to the fields of action they are involved in, the way they were formed, and the length of time they have been in operation. For the most part, they are concerned with problems associated with poverty, with special emphasis on a very vulnerable sector, i.e., children. We found that the group of organizations analyzed arose due to four different kinds of initiatives that include: units formed as a replica of other larger units whose concern is to expand their field of action to other regions to meet different needs. Here the nodal point has been serving women in two different ways: through courses on better money management and maternal health care in areas with severe problems in this regard.

However, the largest number of organizations were formed by private individuals, i.e., by people whose concern has been to contribute, in the degree possible, to solving some problem through education. In these cases, attention has centered on children and groups of adolescents to have an impact on their educational process and provide tools and preparation to allow them to enter the labor market. Other important fields of action have been support for health care for the population in poverty conditions or trying to contribute with professional attention for problems that cut across social strata like different forms of disability. Neighborhood initiatives have also been a way of providing support for solving problems that the community considers to be important, such as gangs and drug addiction. In other cases, what concerns the local inhabitants is building a chapel, and helping alleviate marginalized conditions, which require information about matters that, in another context, may involve things that have already been resolved.

The activity of people related to the church, whose concern has been to improve areas where the members of their church live, has led to organizations where the community has played a central role. In this case, church ministers or people with social concerns have taken up the task of attending to different problems. Some problems that stand out include the education of children and adolescents, access to decent housing, defense of guaranteed prices for their products, and the creation of production projects to improve their precarious economic situation.

In the case of Mexico, government entities are a familiar form of organization concerned with providing assistance to orphans, since they seem to be the appropriate entities for providing this kind of help, due to the characteristics of our legislative process.

In terms of the goals set, these units observed a correspondence between the objectives posed and the goals. In this case, we find enormous variations in the organizations in relation to their achievements, which seem to have to do with adequate structuring of the initial project. In this regard, it seems to be important to carry out prior discussions in order to plan a project with short, medium, and long-term objectives since, in the cases in which this was reported, there seems to be a certain guarantee that they will be able to maintain themselves in the niche they have opened to provide assistance services to third parties.

In relation to their operational structure, we found that some organizations, especially very small organizations made up of volunteers, have operated at times in somewhat precarious circumstances in financial terms. The reason for this has been that they have not enjoyed systematic support and do not have trained personnel in these areas. Larger organizations generally operate with long-term plans and projects and also seem to have their financing problems partially solved.

In the latter case, the few volunteers involved in the daily work do not form part of the structure, which blocks any increase in their activity, except in cases when they are assigned specific activities. For community-type organizations, it was observed that there is a difference in what is understood as such in daily practice. These are undoubtedly particularly interesting, since they require specific forms of interaction to establish solid relationships of mutual confidence among their members.

To conclude, it is relevant to emphasize that the group analyzed is diverse in terms of its composition, and so it may be supposed that this heterogeneity is in fact one of the characteristics of nonprofit organizations in Mexico, and it is, therefore, necessary to continue with this line of investigation in order to develop a more profound knowledge of these units.

References

Brito Velásquez E (1997) Sociedad civil en México: Análisis y debates. In: Sociedad Civil, no. I, vol II. pp 185–204

Brody E (2003) Are nonprofit organizations different? In: Anheier Helmut K, Ben-Ner Avner (eds) The study of the nonprofit enterprise. Kluwer Academic/Plenum Publishers, New York, NY, pp 239–246

Canto M (1998) La participación de las organizaciones civiles en las políticas públicas. In: José Luis Méndez (coord.) Organizaciones civiles y políticas públicas en México y Centroamérica. Academia Mexicana de Investigación en Políticas Públicas, A. C.-I.S.T.R-Miguel Ángel Porrúa, México, pp 77–100

Dingle A (compiler and ed) (2001) Measuring volunteering: a practical toolkit, 2001. International Year of Volunteers, Independent Sector, and United Nations Volunteers

Gordon S (1998) Entre la filantropía y el mercado: La Fundación Mexicana para el Desarrollo Rural. In: José Luis Méndez (coord.) Organizaciones civiles y políticas públicas en México y Centroamérica. Academia Mexicana de Investigación en Políticas Públicas A. C.-I.S.T.R-Miguel Ángel Porrúa, México, pp 293–319

Méndez JL (coord.) (1998) Organizaciones civiles y políticas públicas en México y Centroamérica. Academia Mexicana de Investigación en Políticas Públicas, A. C.-I.S.T.R-Miguel Ángel Porrúa, México

Patton MQ (1990) Qualitative evaluation and research methods. SAGE Publications, Newbury Park, CA

Salamon L, Anheier H (1996) The emerging sector. Johns Hopkins University, Institute for Policy Studies, Baltimore

Verduzco G (2006) Dilemas de un encuentro difuso entre el sector no lucrativo, la sociedad civil y la economía social. Reflexiones a partir del caso de México. In: Butcher J, Serna MG (coords.) El Tercer Sector en México: Perspectivas de Investigación. Cemefi-Instituto de Investigaciones Dr. José María Luis Mora, México, pp 64–84

Chapter 6
Findings, Challenges, and Implications

Jacqueline Butcher, Gustavo Verduzco, María Guadalupe Serna,
and Ernesto Benavides

This volume contains information of interest about volunteer actions and acts of solidarity in Mexico, and represents one of the first investigations of its kind in the country. Due to its methodology and scope, it is a pioneering work offering information at a national level. The intention is to validate these activities, quantify the number of volunteers and people expressing solidarity, as well as the hours worked, and, particularly, to understand, as far as possible, not only the nature of volunteer work, but also its geographical distribution in the country, its characteristics and principal motivations, the insertion and participation of volunteers in social organizations, and to provide a closer approximation of the role played in these organizations by those we have identified as volunteers, and people expressing solidarity in three ways: intense, typical, and sporadic volunteers, in accordance with our own classification.

This chapter brings together what we think are the main contributions of the study presented in *Mexican Solidarity* and also brings together the two main complementary components of this study, i.e., the results of the ENSAV[1] and the findings of the 15 completed case studies. It also poses some suggestions and indicates certain implications for engaging in these activities in the Mexican context. We considered that all solidarity and volunteer activities and actions by the Mexican people were valid and pertinent for inclusion in this investigation, and the study and methodology were designed based on this reasoning, which was considered to be appropriate for the work presented.

J. Butcher
Centro Mexicano para la Filantropía (Cemefi), México D.F., México

[1] *Encuesta Nacional de Solidaridad y Acción Voluntaria* (National Survey on Solidarity and Volunteer Action),

J. Butcher (ed.), *Mexican Solidarity: Citizen Participation and Volunteering*,
DOI 10.1007/978-1-4419-1078-3_6, © Springer Science+Business Media, LLC 2010

Main Findings and Contributions

Survey

As previously mentioned in this book, it is common to hear the opinion that those who contribute the most volunteer work are people from middle and high income brackets since they may perhaps be able to dedicate more time to these kinds of activities due to their relatively secure situation. Our study shows that this not the case. *People from different socioeconomic sectors in the country contribute in equal measure to acts of solidarity. This means that neither high- nor low-income individuals engage in more acts of solidarity; neither do those with lower educational levels contribute more or less time and effort than those who are more educated.* This is one of the most important general findings of our work. In regard to this kind of behavior, like others, expressions of solidarity in Mexican society take place with a similar intensity across all social strata.

However, *preferences for the trio of acts of solidarity in favor of church, school, and neighbors in that order, reveal and reflect the importance that Mexican society as a whole accords these two institutions (church and school), as well as to other actors, one's neighbors, who are part of daily life due to their proximity.* We should not forget that most Mexicans declare themselves to be Catholic, and that the undiluted Catholic tradition that has been inculcated in the country's inhabitants throughout its history, through acts of piety and worship, as well as through commemorations of patron saints, most often plays a central role in both urban neighborhoods and rural communities. Alternatively, school has come to represent a symbol of social mobility, which, together with the objective processes of learning, has given it great prestige. This is why Mexicans perform an important part of their solidarity activities in favor of schools that are educating or have educated their children. Also, *the degree of dedication to solidarity in these three categories is basically similar in all regions of the country*, with only a few minor differences. This kind of orientation on the part of the majority seems to be a clear characteristic that is expressed among Mexicans in all parts of the country.

In terms of the *different kinds of acts of solidarity performed by Mexicans, we find that those who carry them out, whether it is through the church or school, provide physical labor above all, followed at a distance by teaching and then fundraising activities.* These are three very necessary kinds of activity, especially in the conditions of a country like Mexico, where even minimal resources are often scarce. This is why help is frequently requested for cleaning in churches and schools, as well as for certain basic maintenance work for classrooms and offices. Fundraising is another important activity, perhaps more used in churches than in schools, but even in schools this is done to supplement academic materials in poorer schools of the country, and many of which are public schools.

For their part, *those who support neighbors or their community also do so, first, by engaging in physical labor, and what follows in second and third place are direct personal care or attention, and then fundraising, which is different from the previous cases.* It should be recalled that, different types of work are performed in many small towns and neighborhoods to improve them, like introducing potable water, improving streets and roads, or repairing public works.

In the aspect of religious beliefs, we have also found that 68% of those who said they were religious have carried out some act of solidarity with others (34% at least one action and 34% two or more), while among those who reported not having a religion, only 51% said they had participated in these kinds of actions (26% at least one action and 26% carried out two or more). This difference, although it is not great, is sufficiently notable to lead us to believe that *belonging to a religion leads to a slightly greater inclination toward undertaking acts of solidarity in favor of others.* Likewise, we can also say that religious affiliation not only leads to a greater inclination toward acts of solidarity, but also facilitates a relatively greater intensity in performing these kinds of actions. However, we should take into account that we are talking about a population in which almost everyone (94%) says they believe in some religion, at the same time, as has already been mentioned, one of the main contexts through which acts of solidarity occur is through the church.

In this same context, it is appropriate to recall that *among the group of those who answered our survey saying they have no religion but do engage in acts of solidarity, the types of activities they engage in the most have to do first, with their neighbors and community, and secondly with school.*

In answer to the question of whether acts of solidarity take place through organized groups or not, *it is clear that in Mexico these kinds of actions mostly occur outside of institutions and organized groups.* This is another finding of our investigation, and as mentioned in the corresponding chapter, has now been supported by data indicating that engaging in acts of solidarity and belonging to organized groups are not necessarily the same for Mexicans. On the contrary, most of these kinds of activities are carried out individually or through informal groups with a structure that is probably quite weak.

However, we also found that *belonging to a group tends to imply a greater disposition toward engaging in some kind of action to benefit others.* This is a characteristic that is related in some way to group membership, so, although group membership is low, it seems that when present this has a certain impact, encouraging these people to perform their actions through an institution or group.

A more careful analysis of the information led us to identify *three profiles of solidarity actors:*

First, there is the small group of what we call *"intense volunteers"*: the 8% of solidarity actors who said they work every day in these kinds of activities, although with differences in the number of hours each one dedicates to this. They provide an average equivalent to 186 eight-hour working days a year. *This group is made up of almost two-thirds women, in contrast with the sample as a whole in which the proportion between the genders is very similar (46% men and 53% women).* We think that this is probably due to the intense nature of these kinds of activities, insofar as women being more dedicated to household duties may have some affect on this kind of behavior, in part, perhaps, because of having a little more free time. However, this would be a subject to explore more thoroughly in the future.

On the other hand, in the northern and central regions of the country, there are a few more of these kinds of actors (30% and 29%, respectively), while in the southern region they only represent 18%. This is a notable difference, especially because there are more deficiencies in the southern states. However, this is another point it would be good to explore further in the future: What other factors in the Mexican sociocultural and economic situation impact solidarity action behavior? We shall leave this question open for the moment, since the data gathered here does not allow us to pose any solid, plausible hypothesis at this time.

We have called the second profile that was identified the *"typical volunteers"*. They have a constant dedication to solidarity activities that ranges from 2 to 3 times a week to once every 2 weeks. They represent 32% of volunteer actors and dedicate an average of 34 eight-hour days a year to this activity. *There are a few slightly more women (59%) than men in this group. However, in contrast with the two other profiles, they are the ones who work the most in the church. They are also the ones who engage in most activities through organized groups (49%). Similarly, they are the ones who are most likely to belong to an organized group.*

Finally, the third profile of solidarity actors corresponds to those whom we call *"infrequent volunteers"*. Their dedication to these labors ranges from once a month to several times a year. They dedicate an average of 1.7 working days a year.

In summary, the average number of days per solidarity actor was 27 per year, which is equivalent to 2.2 days a month, and if we extend that amount to the 40% of the Mexican population over 18, we would have about 23 million people, each providing an average of 2.2 days of work per month or 27 days per year.

All together, these working days would amount to 2.6 million jobs, *equivalent to 11.3% of the employed population outside the agricultural sector* for the Mexican population over 18 years old during a year. Calculating this based on the minimum wage, we are talking about between 20.33 billion and 88.082 billion pesos.[2] This figure would represent 1.14% of the GNP in 2004. If we compare this figure to the total GNP for community, social, and personal services, it would come to 4.7%. That figure would represent, in monetary terms, the contribution of free labor that the Mexican population provides the country in expressions of solidarity.

Case Studies

As a complement to the 2005 ENSAV survey, the case studies have provided an indispensable qualitative dimension for understanding volunteer action and acts of solidarity. It was decided to do these studies in the structured environment represented by nonprofit organizations, where it was easier to contact and interview volunteers. Similarly, it was thought that a possibility would open up within these organizational

---

[2] Depending on whether 1 working day of free labor is assigned a value of one or three daily minimum wages.

structures to observe and delve more deeply into different activities and actions carried out by volunteers, based on their own reflections and comments.

Three of the chapters in this volume deal with analyzing and discussing the material gathered based on structuring 15 case studies with a total of 66 in-depth interviews with volunteers, including people designated as such by the organizations, staff personnel or coordinators, the director or informal leader, and the founder in each case, when possible.

The general characteristics of the organizations were analyzed, as well as the family and personal background of the subjects and the reasons and motivations expressed by them for engaging in volunteer and solidarity-type work. Finally, the discussion went more deeply into "giving" as the main motivation of the people interviewed.

In terms of the most relevant findings concerning the themes dealt with, and the way in which nonprofit organizations are developing in Mexico, this analysis *revealed that personal initiative or initiative by a group of people is a fundamental element in the creation and structure of both formal and informal organizations.* Specifically, in order for a concern to have meaning and become an institutional project with the possibility of becoming consolidated, and reproducing itself over the long run, common people with certain particular characteristics and have an interest in doing something for others are required.

In addition, *it was found that the possibilities for the success of a project depend on several different factors and that there is a definite risk that it may not become consolidated.* But there is less risk of this to the degree that the project's promoters take the necessary time to structure a good proposal, as well as to develop a support network making it possible to continue functioning during the first years, which seem to be the most uncertain ones. This implies that the founder plays a key role in the process, as does all economic and social support that may be attained.

In the cases analyzed, some of the founders were professionals with the tools and experience necessary to undertake the task of attracting other interested parties, as well as developing a series of support links. They understood that both economic resources and a framework of social networks were required to support and maintain a structured project. *That is to say, in order to achieve a more solid organization, the professionalization of the founder and the initial participants in the project is essential, since certain abilities are required in order to gain access to indispensable resources from international organizations and foundations, as well as from the few domestic sources of support available.*

Although the good will to want to do something for others is important, it is also essential to have the necessary background to be able to fulfill multiple requirements, in order to be able to formulate a project focused on volunteer action or acts of solidarity, especially, if it is planned to be a long-term project.

In terms of the *characteristics of the volunteers*, we found that the individual life experiences of the subjects, as well as their reasons for actively participating in these kinds of actions, *make it possible for us to locate at least three different types of volunteers.*

1. *Those who come from families where this kind of learning is an everyday way of expressing commitment to others.* In this case, it may be the mother, father, or

both, or perhaps grandparents or an aunt or uncle who is engaged in these activities on an everyday basis and so it is seen as something natural, when one is socialized in this context, to continue this family tradition into adult life.

2. *Those who combine a complex mix of religious values, education, and some event in their life that is the stimulating factor leading them to enter into the path of volunteer actions.* Here a certain vocation or "calling" appears to transform their personal or family problem into something including others in similar situations.

3. *Those whose social concerns are assumed as a personal responsibility to contribute to transforming situations of profound social inequality.* These are people whose ideas were formed in specific contexts or moments of our history and, as a result, they have a different perspective on what they will do in life.

Although these are the types that emerge from the analysis, we consider that *the most important finding is the one concerning the role that the family of origin plays as a transmitter of a series of values and principles that will be put into practice throughout the subject's life.*

In this regard, the mother's role stands out in terms of teachings a mix of religious and ethical values that are taken up by their daughters and translated into a commitment, motivation, or form of personal redemption when favoring the growth of others.

For men, at least in the set of cases analyzed, this does not happen, since they perceive the volunteer actions they perform as having a social character related to the community. We think it would be necessary to delve more deeply into these kinds of findings in order to gain deeper understanding of these processes, since women were the majority of those interviewed, outnumbering men three to one.

We also found that *the majority of people involved in volunteer actions or acts of solidarity, independent of their position within the organizational structure, were in the productive stage of their lives and also were engaged in some economic activity to make a living,* although there is also a section of retired women or housewives who dedicate part of their time to activities for third parties. This demystifies the idea that volunteer actions are mainly performed by women from more comfortable middle or upper sectors or people with idle time that is filled in this way.

Another interesting point is the finding regarding the *mobility of those who participate in the organizations.* According to the information gathered, the participants in the organizations usually stay in the same organization for long periods of time, i.e., *mobility is almost zero.* Moreover, it was observed that a multiplier effect exists, that is to say, that several of them participated in two organizations.

Given the characteristics of the subjects and their individual histories, the time devoted to these kinds of long-term commitments is variable. The information indicates that there are at least *two different ways of devoting time and making one's knowledge available to others.*

(a) Those who devote 7 to 10 h a day, i.e., almost a complete working day or a little more, to volunteer actions over some period of time that may last as long as three years. These kinds of people have practically decided to dedicate their lives to guarantee the fulfillment of the organization's objectives, even at the cost of not being able to enter the labor market and having to depend on others (family members) in order to survive.

(b) People who have devoted between an hour and a half and 10 h a week over periods of time of more than a decade of engaging in this activity. In this case, it is also a personal decision to devote specific times to these kinds of actions, where the aim is to fulfill the responsibilities acquired. This may be one or two times a week or on the weekends, depending on their available time. What is evident in the cases analyzed is that once the decision is made, the responsibility is fulfilled.

Regarding the type of activities the volunteers participate in, it was found that these are related to the kind of responsibility they have in the organizational structure. The founder undertakes activities to motivate the participants, consolidate the support networks, and raise funds for an activity in which the director participates at times. The directors, few of whom are volunteers, maintain the daily operations and do annual planning in collaboration with the trust or foundation, when one is involved. They also coordinate the actions of those below them. The coordinators, only a few of whom are volunteers, are the ones who execute the activities and at the same time pay attention to distributing tasks. The volunteers are the ones dealing directly with the organization's users. In this group, there are people with previously assigned responsibilities and also personnel who basically help with whatever is needed.

It should be pointed out that another finding is the difference between organizations made up only of volunteers and those that include both paid and volunteer personnel.

1. In the case of *organizations made up only of volunteers, where decisions are usually made by consensus, the members of the organization interchange responsibilities, since the aim is for everyone to get experience and get to know about the organization.* In these cases, the motivation to continue, although personal, found a path to follow thanks to the interaction with a group in similar conditions. In general, everyone involved is considered to be equal in terms of abilities.

2. *In the organizations that began due to promotion by a group or person and then became an entity with important participation on the part of paid personnel, the volunteers were usually located at the bottom of the organizational structure or outside of it. That is to say, the structure consists of paid personnel.* In these cases it was observed that the volunteers are employed for diverse tasks and offer their help due to personal interest. This implies that the volunteers are not recognized as subjects with possibilities of carrying out concrete responsibilities over long periods of time.

Here it is important to point out that several of the organizations do not consider the volunteers to be trained personnel. Moreover, it is not thought that their professionalization is required in order for them to make contributions and take advantage of these available human resources. In regard to this, it might be pointed out that it is still necessary for the organizations themselves, and especially their administrative and coordinating cadre, to have a clear idea of what it means for a person to devote their time to helping others without pay. In the few cases in which the volunteers were incorporated into the structure, it seemed that there was a special motivation to be responsible for undertaking specific matters. This is something to be learnt from volunteer organizations.

Another finding worth mentioning is the attitude the interviewees had toward the volunteer work they perform. These are people who can be included among "typical and intense volunteers" with a certain degree of clarity about what they contribute to the organization, which is a result of their own decision and of a commitment they have assumed. *For most of the people included in this group, these activities give them pleasure, satisfaction, a raison d'être, and they say that their main motivation for acting is giving themselves to help and support others.* Others consider that they know what needs to be done for society and what should be done to improve the social environment surrounding them.

To summarize, it might be mentioned that volunteer actions are defined by the subjects as the act of giving, helping, or assisting others, believing in what one is doing and, especially, thinking about what needs to be done. In this regard, saying that this is done "to help others" is in fact a deeply-rooted conviction among participants in volunteer actions and acts of solidarity that has to do with the entire context they have experienced. In regard to "what needs to be done", there is a clear perspective that is expressed by an important number of those interviewed. To the degree they participate in these actions, they realize that their commitment and activities alone are not enough in a country with such urgent social needs to be solved. It may be said that volunteer solidarity actions are a scarce commodity. What is available is not enough, it is necessary to increase the amount. It is, without a doubt, necessary to deepen this analysis. There are still large gaps in our knowledge in this area in the case of Mexico. For the moment, we think that, although many questions have been answered, a broad range of new questions have been generated that open new paths for investigation.

Challenges and Recommendations for Promoting Volunteer Activity and Participation in Acts of Solidarity

Challenges

Individual Volunteer/Solidarity Actions in Mexico

The analysis of the phenomenon of volunteer actions and acts of solidarity requires greater exploration and in-depth investigation to clarify the reasons why many of these activities are carried out in an isolated way. The fact that 21% of the total universe of 66% of citizens acting in solidarity, i.e., *about one fourth of the current solidarity and volunteer activities in Mexico, are carried out in an isolated way* obliges us to look for reasons and new hypotheses that provide us with new scenarios to explain these numbers.

The first hypothesis – corroborated by other Mexican studies already mentioned – is that Mexicans do not usually work in groups or associations. This may be due to the lack of confidence in others in order to work in groups or to not being accustomed to doing so. The second hypothesis would have to do with the fiscal and legal difficulties in forming formal groups or associations. This is reflected in the results of the study themselves. They show that most of those who act as volunteers or express solidarity do so informally. The third hypothesis would have to do with Mexican religious customs, predominantly reflecting the Catholic tradition, in which acts of solidarity or assistance to others are not considered to be public, but rather private actions.[3] At this time, these hypotheses remain as possible explanations of the data uncovered by our investigation and require greater reflection and study to be confirmed. The challenge in this first point is to find the primary causes of this reality so that society as a whole may take the corresponding measures.

Perception and Awareness of Volunteer Actions and Acts of Solidarity

Several myths about volunteer activity in Mexico are shattered by this investigation. On one hand, the survey shows us that all socioeconomic and educational levels participate equally in solidarity activities and, on the other hand, the case studies indicate that most people who participate in these activities through groups are in the productive stage of their lives and engage in some type of economic activity to make a living.

Many individuals do not consider themselves as volunteers although they fulfill our definition's profile. The generosity of Mexican people is evident in this study, but it is not shown in an organized way. It is possible that this may reflect a mistaken perception of volunteers in the popular imagination, where volunteer actions and acts of solidarity are thought only to be found within groups that provide services to third parties, generally the society's most vulnerable groups. It is also probable that what is necessary – as a further challenge – is to inform the public in general about the wide range of activities and possibilities where they can currently contribute, as well as indicating the benefits received by volunteers due to their actions.

Visibility and Promotion of Volunteer Actions and Group Organization

We think that the more public and evident the current contribution of volunteer action is and the more its potential and scope for future contributions are

---

[3] It is the Catholic tradition to serve one's fellow men but based on the premise that *your right hand doesn't know what your left hand is doing*. Many people are not interested in others knowing about what they do, how much time they devote, or how much they contribute. They do not consider these to be volunteer actions but rather religious or moral duties.

emphasized, the greater participation of people in these activities. There is a challenge to promote group membership and organization, if the aim is to encourage greater citizen participation in solidarity and volunteer activities and help to forge more volunteerism. In our survey, 76% of the total Mexican population say that they do not belong to a group and 24% say they do. This does not mean membership, just participation, and the group they belong to is not necessarily an NPO. In terms of volunteer actions and acts of solidarity, out of the 66% of the Mexican adult population responded positively to the question on volunteer activity and acts of solidarity in our survey. Of these, only 44% volunteer through a formal gourp or legal institution.

The need for a participative and associative culture of volunteerism and solidarity was one of the main themes motivating this investigation. One of the difficulties encountered by people when organizing groups for solidarity activities may be the lack of identifying volunteer action as a social value or the mistrust about participating that persists for the average Mexican person.[4] Another explanation of the lack of group participation is possibly rooted in the legal and fiscal difficulties that exist in Mexico and check this kind of spontaneous participation. The following recommendations come from the data and contributions of this study and may be useful for different sectors of the society.

Recommendations

For the Government

The government can play a fundamental role in providing local and national infrastructure for volunteer action. Support for legal and fiscal promotion has involved slow and unfinished processes with tendencies toward regulation and control. Perhaps one of the biggest challenges we face at this moment is the new civil society/government relationship, which is moving away from the corporativism and clientelism of the past. There is a need to provide real and tangible support, if there is real interest in greater social participation to encourage democracy and building greater social responsibility among the citizens in Mexico. Volunteer groups have traditionally provided Mexican society with services for human and social needs not covered or inadequately covered by the state. In this way, they have called attention to specific problems that are often ignored by the authorities. There are several key factors that the government needs to consider if it decides to give more support to NPOs and, specifically, to volunteer actions and acts of solidarity. We point out a few suggestions in this section:

Development of *public policies to promote these activities*, including:

---

[4]It is true that Mexicans generally mistrust others and trust those closest to them. When answering the question in our survey, *Would you say that most people can or can't be trusted?*, 79% said they can not be trusted and 19% said they could.

1. *Strategic development* of these actions with a defined and identifiable governmental connection to attend to these activities with possibilities for including all stakeholders in order to reach decisions by consensus with shared responsibility between the government and the citizens.
2. *Recognition and independence of volunteer actions,* in addition to resisting the temptation to use volunteer and solidarity activities for the government's own ends by means of clearly delimiting governmental and civil society activities. This would make it possible to have the freedom to form coalitions with NPOs when it is appropriate to do so – such as in cases of crisis or natural disaster – since the function of the activities of the third sector is to join in governmental social efforts and responsibilities, not replace them.
3. *Promote a culture of participation and solidarity from childhood.* The most important finding coming out of the case studies is the impact of family environment on participating in solidarity and volunteer activities. Both in community centers and in public schools, the government has the opportunity to create volunteer action programs during the first formative years so as to make solidarity activities for others a habit and part of the culture.
4. *Promote propitious environments and create visible supports.*
   (a) National and local support with budget resources for infrastructure for volunteer initiatives by means of research about the sector.
   (b) Promotion by public servants of these kinds of activities.
   (c) Promotion of volunteer actions for young people. The development of specific educational programs and encouraging volunteer activities among young people, as well as systems that accredit this type of work. This is a vehicle for acquiring life experience and technical abilities as well as creating awareness about common problems.
   (d) Promote an image of working together with private enterprise. Grant recognition and different incentives to highlight the contributions of volunteerism and solidarity to the country's development. Encourage the creation of joint initiatives with companies that promote volunteer participation. Tax incentives could also be offered to companies for supporting volunteer actions on the part of their employees.
5. *International level.* Governments can influence and demand that multilateral and international organization develop volunteer action strategies by acting together with them or asking organizations like the UN or the World Bank to develop plans and programs to promote volunteer action.

Legal and fiscal support as well as appropriate public policy on the part of the government contributes to generating confidence and participation in these activities. Legal protection for volunteers, tax incentives for donations and contributions are some key points that serve to encourage giving at all social levels. Moreover, increased citizen participation should be sought in all aspects of public administration: from planning and the creation of policy to providing services that contribute to transparency, accountability, and evaluations to keep society informed.

For the Nonprofit Sector

Companies

Some companies in Mexico promote volunteer action groups and specific volunteer programs. It may be said that this is not yet a common business practice. However, there are companies that have corporate social responsibility programs[5] that channel donations to causes of importance, which do not necessarily involve their employees in volunteer actions. Some companies organize activities or allow their employees' work time for these labors. At times, they may donate a small amount if their employees participate as volunteers in community action groups. There is no data available about the effectiveness of these activities linked to corporations. What was captured through our study was the availability of people for solidarity or volunteer work in places close to their homes or workplaces. 71% of the population says that it would be either very likely or somewhat likely that they would do something for others as a volunteer if access to these activities was closer by. This leaves a lot to think about in terms of possibilities for developing programs where people are willing to participate as volunteers as another option for corporate social responsibility.

Volunteer Groups

NPOs in Mexico face great difficulty since competition for operational and survival funds are a problem and a constant challenge, as has already been demonstrated. Also, the lack of knowledge about the sector, and the lack of articulation among the organizations themselves may be an obstacle to their growth. From the point of view of volunteer actions and acts of solidarity, we can identify two great challenges for the third sector in Mexico.

The first is to invite a larger number of people to participate in their organizations so as to promote community solutions by means of joint volunteer actions and acts of solidarity. In the Cemefi's ENSAV survey, most of the people who participated in organizations were invited: 21% found them on their own, 20% were invited by a member of the group, and 16% were invited by a relative or acquaintance. If the sector really wants to grow, it should break with the exclusivity of the existing organizations and include more people who want to consciously contribute to the common good and causes through volunteer actions and acts of solidarity.

With this investigation, we hope to make it clear that individuals can contribute not only money but also other resources such as the time, talent, energy, and their experience, which are elements without quantitative measurement. However, as the case studies

---

[5] CSR is the acronym for these corporate practices.

in this investigation show, when there is a solid commitment on the part of individuals to improve the conditions around them, the achievements are exponential.

The second challenge for the sector lies in institutionalizing and professionalizing volunteer activities. Clarity on the roles of volunteers in the organizations is a focal point of attention. Our study clearly reveals that those volunteers who hold important posts in an organization consider themselves to be an indispensable part of it and act in accordance with that belief. Volunteer activity can be a source of learning and gaining new abilities for individuals who perform it. However, structures are required to increase the value and take advantage of their labor, and not just to retain them, but search out actions to increase participation in their organizations.

Solidarity Participation

It might be mentioned here that the ENSAV survey tells us that family members of half those interviewed (45%) have also done something for others. The interviews in the qualitative part of the study corroborate this and emphasize the importance of the family in the case of Mexico in terms of a repetition of generous solidarity gestures. People who observe these kinds of activities in the family tend to repeat these actions and attitudes. One of the recommendations coming out of this study is to look for ways to incorporate these activities into the family environment.

The information for this Mexican study corresponds to information from other countries where family upbringing and volunteer actions in the family lead to people having a favorable disposition toward engaging in these kinds of activities. It is important to mention the relevant role of institutions like the church and school in these kinds of activities. In Mexico, the groups that individuals belong to most often come from religious contexts. This is the first activity mentioned by those interviewed, and it is the one where there is most solidarity and volunteer activity in the country. This subject requires more investigation and is a pending matter for future studies.

Implications and Final Reflections

This investigation indicates that volunteer work and activity have profound implications for Mexican society. It produces a series of benefits for the individuals who engage in it in five respects:

Development of social capital, good government, and democracy. Social capital is one of the products of volunteer associations, since this generates norms of reciprocity and trust. Solidarity and volunteer activities have to do with the formation of horizontal networks of participation, especially when there are face to face relationships in volunteer service to others. Insofar as there is a well-known lack of trust in strangers in the case of Mexico, it is possible to demonstrate with this study that, among the people interviewed, volunteer work and activity help to create friendships (bringing strangers together) and promote ways of learning new things, contributing in this way to resolving situations of inequality and of forming social networks. Of those interviewed, 53% say they have made friends through volunteer work and 56% admit having learned something.

Those interviewed in this study are committed to their activities and believe that "something has to be done" to solve some community problems afflicting the country, and they act as responsible citizens of society through their volunteer participation.

Citizens' personal development. Solidarity and volunteer participation is not just about giving to others; it is also important to recognize that tangible and intangible benefits are obtained, such as friendship ties, knowledge about other people and situations, the experience of generosity and reciprocity, learning new abilities, work experience, as well as the personal satisfaction and pleasure that – the volunteers interviewed in the cases studies tell us – are also the result of this work.

Economic benefits provided. The parameters developed for our investigation have only focused on collecting information about solidarity and volunteer activities. It has been mentioned that Mexicans contribute the equivalent of 27 days of work a year. If this is multiplied by the corresponding minimum wages and compared to the total GNP for community, social, and personal services, which is a category similar to solidarity activities, the contribution would be equal to 4.7% of the GNP for 2004. This is a considerable economic contribution.

Integration of youth and excluded sectors. Mexicans over 18 years old were surveyed in the 2005 ENSAV. Although the largest number of people who do something for others are in the 30–49 age group (43%), 25% are youth (18–29), and 33% are over 50 years old. These numbers indicate the same tendency as was found in the 15 case studies of organizations, where we see that the largest number of people engaged in these activities are of productive age and at an economically active time in their lives.

Solidarity and volunteer activity creates conditions for equity and inclusion. These experiences – in which young people, retired people, and people with varied abilities or who are disabled participate – remove the image of these people as only being recipients of help and demonstrate that they too can participate in solving common problems. In order for volunteer actions to contribute more effectively to social integration, it is important to open volunteer and solidarity roles and opportunities in social organizations for young people and citizens in excluded groups.

Promotion of future employment. Volunteer action can play an important role in increasing employment opportunities for those who need them. For those looking for paid employment, these kinds of actions may, in addition to increasing self-esteem, open access to work relationship networks and provide new specific abilities for the labor market. These activities often lead to the creation of services related to social needs. A world-wide example is the creation of both public and private health-sector employment based on innovative responses by volunteers to HIV/AIDS.

In conclusion, we could say that there are great demonstrations of generosity among Mexicans through their volunteer actions and acts of solidarity. However, these need encouragement, organization, and promotion in the home, at school, and in the larger social environment so as to develop responsible and aware citizens to build a more independent, organized, and effective civil society. The promotion of social responsibility and the path to participation in all fields of action – on the part of both government and civil society – as well as the creation of a socially responsible citizenry, depends on a greater understanding of activities like those described here.

We have demonstrated that those who consider themselves to be volunteers and to those who act in solidarity with others obtain a series of often intangible benefits that are sufficient to maintain their commitment to this activity, at times on a full-time basis, and in other cases on an individual basis. We have discovered that, generally speaking, there is a great lack of awareness in Mexico about the possibilities that exist for participation in acts of solidarity and volunteer action. There is also a need to reveal the potential of these activities for present-day society and for future generations by means of promoting opportunities for participation so that those who wish to focus their energy on volunteer activity may do so.

We are aware that these results represent the first step to a more profound knowledge of the world of solidarity and volunteer activity in Mexico. The definitions chosen for this investigation were broad, in accordance with international parameters, with the intention of obtaining information that would make possible comparisons with other countries and also reflect the reality of Mexico.

A series of questions to be answered by future research have been uncovered by this exploratory and descriptive study. Many questions remain unanswered about this activity in Mexico. In general terms, we could say that we still need to find out more about the ethics, the representative character, and the social impact of these activities. Another pending matter is getting to know more about the professionalization of volunteers in these organizations, as well as the processes involving those engaging in volunteer solidarity work for others who do not belong to social organizations.

New questions for research and related issues about these activities arise at the same time as the following issues need to be resolved. What is the most effective way to take advantage of volunteer work and time? What are the relationships like between volunteers and employees within the same organization? Why do many Mexicans choose to engage in volunteer work in an isolated way? What are the mechanisms that people expressing solidarity use to consolidate a civil society organization in Mexico? It is our hope and expectation that this study may stimulate interest among experts on the subject and establish a point of departure for generating greater knowledge in this regard.

The development of citizenship and participation must correspond to our customs and social norms. We know that, in the end, we act according to what matters to us, in consequence with our scale of values. In a much broader sense, the recently deceased anthropologist Clifford Geertz tells us that for actions to be part of a culture, they need to become integrated with everyday life, since the "ways of society are the substance of culture."[6] In order for volunteer actions and acts of solidarity to become everyday values and guide our behavior to really become that "substance," Geertz mentions, it will be essential to create more opportunities for giving and helping others that are within the reach of everyone.

---

[6] Geertz, C. (1973). *La interpretación de las culturas*. Barcelona: Gedisa, p. 38.

Biography

Jacqueline Butcher (Editor)

President of the Board of Directors of the Centro Mexicano para la Filantropía (Cemefi, Mexican Center for Philanthropy) for the period 2006–2010 and president of the International Society for Third Sector Research (ISTR) for 2007–2008. Dr. Butcher has published numerous articles and chapters in books on the subject of volunteer action and citizen participation. She is on the Editorial Board of *Voluntas* and *Prometeo* and currently a member of the Technical Expert Group on the Measurement of Volunteer Work at the Center for Civil Society Studies at Johns Hopkins University and the International Labor Organization (ILO). She belongs to the Citizen Consultation Council of the National DIF System, an advisory Board presided by the First Lady of Mexico, Margarita Zavala.

Miguel Basáñez

President of the Global Quality Research Corp., a public opinion survey company established in Princeton. Doctorate in Political Science from the London School of Economics. He was president of the World Association for Public Opinion Research (WAPOR, 1998–2000) and is founding president of the magazine *Este País*. He is a member of the Board of Directors of the World Values Survey. He has been a professor since 1970 and is the author or coauthor of nine books and more than 100 articles on surveys, politics, and values.

Ernesto Benavides

He is the director of Social Training of the Tecnológico de Monterrey System. Masters in Science and Administration, and doctoral candidate in Social Anthropology from the Universidad de Salamanca, Spain. His work covers methodological design, implementation, and evaluation of university volunteer programs, community social service, citizen education, and university social responsibility. He is a pioneer in Mexico in implementing the "Service-Learning" teaching technique in the context of university educational models.

María Guadalupe Serna

She is a full time professor and researcher at Instituto de Investigaciones Dr. José María Luis Mora, CONACYT System CPI, and member of the National System of Researchers in Mexico. She holds a doctorate in Social Science, with a specialization in Social Anthropology. In her research, she has focused on analyzing economic organizations and has several publications. Since 1980 she has been a professor at several higher education institutions.

Gustavo Verduzco

Bachelor's degree in Sociology from the Political and Social Science Department of the Universidad Autónoma de México. Doctorate in Sociology from the University of Texas, Austin (1980).

He has been a professor and researcher for El Colegio de México since 1983. He was director of the Center for Sociological Studies of that institution (2000–2006). He is a member of the National System of Researchers in Mexico, level III. His work includes the book *Organizations no lucrativas: visión de su trayectoria en México*, published jointly by El Colegio de México and the Centro Mexicano para la Filantropía, 2003.

Appendix I
Methodological Note and Questionnaire for the ENSAV

Miguel Basáñez, Jacqueline Butcher, and Gustavo Verduzco

Universe: Residents of Mexico, 18 and over located throughout the country.

Basis of sample: Electoral sections of the Federal Electoral Institute, updated to the elections of 2003.

Sampling procedure: It was a multistage sample to complete complex interviews. Elements with unequal probabilities (proportional by size-PBS) were selected in the first stage. These were the Primary Sampling Units (PSU-electoral section). The method applied was simple random selection within the first conglomerate (defined as a function of the number of PSUs desired divided by the number of registered voters in the electoral sections as a whole) to get *it started*, and then this method was systematically applied to each one of the conglomerates until there were 150 PSUs or beginning points.

The second stage consisted of selecting the Secondary Sampling Units (SSU-blocks in the beginning points) in each PSU. These SSUs were determined by applying the method of systematic selection as a function of the residential characteristics of each area.

The third stage of sampling is concerned with the selection of the Tertiary Sampling Units (TSU-residences) in the SSUs where the interview would be performed. This selection was systematic and defined by the number of homes/houses on each block.

The last stage of sampling was the selection of the people to be interviewed. We used the last birthday as a method of control with a variable for gender, in accordance with the estimates obtained from the parameters for the population of interest.

An additional sample of 25 PSUs or beginning points was also obtained by means of the same steps already described, for the electoral sections of the state of Chihuahua.

The final purpose of the sampling process both at a national level and in the case of Chihuahua, was to do 10 interviews in each of the PSUs or beginning points selected.

Size of the Sample and Margin of Error: For the national survey, with 1500 cases, the theoretical margin of error for the sample as a whole was ±2.5% at a confidence level of 95%. The estimations for the additional sample in Chihuahua have a theoretical error margin of ±5.7%.

The No Response Rate (NRR), noted in the beginning point record sheets, did not exceed the estimated 10%, which implies no significant changes in the error margin estimate.

Field Work and Dates: The interviews were performed between August 27 and September 12, 2005.

The interviews involved the participation of 45 interviewers, 10 field supervisors (supervision for revisiting homes, and telephone supervision), 3 coders, 5 people to type in the data, 1 person responsible for processing data, and 2 general coordinators.

Supervision: There was supervision for 30% of the sample. Of this, 20% of the supervision was performed when the questionnaires were applied, 5% during the return home visit, and 5% by telephone.

Data Processing: The codification, capture, data base processing, and preparation of reports were completed from September 12 to 24, 2005. All the data reported were processed using SPSS (Statistical Package for Social Sciences) software.

Questionnaire Used for the ENSAV
_____

VERSION 8.2 - AUGUST 24

GQR-CEMEFIL APPLICATION: 050826-0904

FOLIO: |___|___|___|___|___|

LOCALITY: BEGINNING POINT CODE: |___|___|___|___|___|

STATE: _____

TYPE: (1) Urban (2) Semi-rural (3) Rural

DATE OF INTERVIEW: |_0_|___||___|___|___|

TIME INTERVIEW WAS BEGAN: |___|___| : |___|___|

INTERVIEWER'S CODE AND NAME: |___|___|___|

_____
SIZE OF LOCALITY: **1** 2.5m-/ **2** 2.5-5/ **3** 5-10/ **4** 10-25/ **5** 25-50/ **6** 50-100/ **7** 100-250/ **8** 250-500/ **9** 500-1M/ **10** 1M-5M/ **11** 5M+

Good morning/afternoon/evening. I am _____ from the Public Opinion Studies Center. We are doing a survey about the ways in which people give and receive help and services. We are interviewing 1,500 people all over the country. This house was randomly selected, but I need to interview a <u>member of the family</u> (NOT DOMESTIC HELP) over 18 years of age. Who is the person who had or is going to have a birthday closest to today's date who is here now? Are you that person? (NO): Could you call them?
(BEGIN AGAIN) (YES): I don't need your name, just sincere responses.

F1. Were you born after September 1987? 1. **NO** /2. **YES:** (ASK FOR ANOTHER MEMBER OF THE HOUSEHOLD OVER 18 AND BEGIN AGAIN).

F2. Do you or someone in your home work for **(1)** an advertising agency (THANK AND END); **(2)** opinion or marking surveys (THANK AND END); **(3)** communication media (THANK AND END); **(4)** none (CONTINUE).

I'm going to ask you about help in terms of time or services that you give or have given to other people who are not part of your family, without receiving payment for that activity and which you have done in a voluntary way. Is that clear or should I repeat it? It can be help of any kind, such as: teaching how to read; organizing a neighborhood meeting; a school or church party; a sports team; a collection for the Red Cross or a clinic; helping a sick person who is not your relative; lending a neighbor a hand; helping with a pilgrimage or a political group; a project for the community; [IN RURAL AREAS ADD] or helping to bring in a harvest. Anything that is to benefit others, without payment for you and done in a voluntary way. Is that clear or should I repeat it?

1. Have you ever done something for others without being paid? / **(1) NO:** NO ONE, IN NO WAY? ARE YOU SURE? TRY TO REMEMBER... (IF THEY DO NOT REMEMBER, READ 3–4 CATEGORIES FROM THE TABLE – NONE OF THESE? READ ANOTHER 3–4 CATEGORIES – NONE OF THESE? GO TO Q15 / **(2) YES** (CONTINUE): 1) Which do you remember? (DO NOT READ. NOTE AT THE TOP OF EACH COLUMN AND CODE THE 1ST IN COL. 1. Any others? [ASK UNTIL YOU GET ALL THOSE REMEMBERED AND NOTE THE 2ND IN COL. 2, ETC. AT THE END, ASK ABOUT THE ONES NOT MENTIONED.]

		1st	2nd	3rd	4th	5th	6th	7th	8th
A	**Church** or religious group (construction, cleaning, prayer, etc.)								
B	**School** (students, parents, teachers, etc.)								
C	**Sports** or recreation								
D	**Young people or children** (boy scouts, guides, youth clubs, etc.)								
E	**Poor**								
F	**Sick people** (Red Cross, hospitals, etc.)								
G	**Orphans, elderly, indigenous people, disabled**								
H	**Neighbors**, communities, ejidos								
I	**Human rights**								
J	**Ecology**, environment, or animals								
K	**Art**, music, or culture								
L	**Professional associations or unions**								
M	**Government** (projects and activities)								
N	**Women**								
O	**Trade union**								
P	**Political groups** or parties								
Q	**Citizen causes**								
R	Other:								

2. How long ago or in what year did you **begin** [if you remember]… (READ FIRST
    ONE MENTIONED FOR Q #1)? And the second one…? And the third one…?
    (ASK ABOUT ALL THOSE MENTIONED IN THE PRECEDING QUESTION
    AND NOTE THIS IN TABLE 2. DON'T READ OR APPLY THE CODES AT
    THE TOP OF THE TABLES. IF THEY MENTION THE YEAR, NOTE IT IN
    THE LEFT MARGIN):
3. How long did you continue doing it or what year did you **stop** doing it?: First the
    one about… (READ THE FIRST ONE MENTIONED FROM TABLE Q #1)?
    And the second one…? And the third one…? (ASK ABOUT ALL THOSE
    MENTIONED IN THE PRECEDING QUESTION AND NOTE THIS IN
    TABLE 3. DON'T READ OR APPLY THE CODES AT THE TOP OF THE
    TABLES. IF THEY MENTION THE YEAR, NOTE IT IN THE LEFT
    MARGIN):

1 Less than 3 months / **2** from 3 to 6 months / **3** from 6 to 12 months / **4** from
1 to 3 years / **5** from 3 to 5 years / **6** from 5 to 10 years /**7** from 10 to 15 years/
8 from 15 to 20 years / **9** from 20 to 30 years / **10** More than 30 years / **11**
Continues doing it / **12** NC / NA

Q #2 BEGAN	1	2	3	4	5	6	7	8	9	10	11	12
1st												
2nd												
3rd												
4th												
5th												
6th												
7th												
8th												

Q #3 F FINISHED	1	2	3	4	5	6	7	8	9	10	11	12
1st												
2nd												
3rd												
4th												
5th												
6th												
7th												
8th												

4. How **frequently** did you do each one?: The one about… (READ THE FIRST
    ONE MENTIONED FROM TABLE Q #1)? And the second one…? And the
    third one…? (ASK ABOUT ALL THOSE MENTIONED IN THE PREVIOUS
    QUESTION AND NOTE IN TABLE 4) (DO NOT READ): **1** Every day / **2** 2 or
    3 times a week / **3** Once a week / **4** Every two weeks / **5** Every month / **6** Every
    2–3 months / **7** 3–4 times a year / **8** 1–2 times a year / **9** Only sporadically / **10**
    NC/NA
5. On the average, about how much time do you dedicate a week to the first one?:
    The one about… (READ THE FIRST ONE MENTIONED FROM TABLE Q
    #1)? And the second one…? And the third one…? (ASK ABOUT ALL THOSE
    MENTIONED IN THE PREVIOUS QUESTION AND NOTE IN TABLE 5)

(DO NOT READ): **1** Sporadically / **2** Less than 1 h / **3** 1–3 h / **4** 3–6 h / **5** 6–9 h / **6** 9–12 h / **7** more than 12 h a week / **8** NC/NA

Q #4 FREQUENCY	1	2	3	4	5	6	7	8	9	10
1st										
2nd										
3rd										
4th										
5th										
6th										
7th										
8th										

Q #5 HOURS	1	2	3	4	5	6	7	8
1st								
2nd								
3rd								
4th								
5th								
6th								
7th								
8th								

6. **About the last activity you have done (did):** You said it was [is] ... (USE TABLE Q #1 TO RECONFIRM). We're going to talk in greater detail. What, concretely, did/do you do? (NOTE, DO NOT READ, AND CODE): ___

Advice, advising	1
Personal attention or care/Accompany	2
Manpower (physical work)	3
Teaching or training	4
Information campaigns	5
Raising funds	6

Planning, research, strategies	7
Administrative support (office work)	8
Public relations	9
Organizing events, parties, etc.	10
Other _____	11
NC/NA	12

7. How do or did you provide that volunteer service: **1** Through an institution or organized group (SUCH AS A CHURCH, CLINIC, SENIOR CARE HOME, SCHOOL, HOSPITAL, ASSOCIATION, OR SOMETHING SIMILAR)?; or **2** Something more informal? (LIKE A GROUP OF FRIENDS); or **3** With neighbors, fellow employees, or acquaintances?; or **4** By yourself (FOR ONE OR MORE PEOPLE)? (DO NOT READ) **5** Other. How? _____ _____ **6** NC/NA

8. How did you begin? Did someone invite you? (DO NOT READ): **1** A relative or acquaintance; **2** a member of that group; **3** a member of another group; **4** an ad on TV, radio, or in the newspaper; **5** an ad on the Internet; **6** through school; **7** looked for it on their own; **8** Other (DESCRIBE) _____ _____; **9** NC/NA (DO NOT READ)

9. Do you continue to participate in the same activity? **YES** (CIRCLE #10) / **NO** Why did you stop doing it? (SPECIFY AND CODE)_____ _____

1	Lack of time
2	Moved
3	No longer interested
4	Work / studies
5	Helps in other ways
6	Health problems
7	Prefers to donate money
8	Other:
9	NC / NA
10	Still does it now

10. How old were you when you began your volunteer activities? (SPECIFY) _____ / 99 NC/NA

11. How old were you when you started your most recent activity? (SPECIFY) _____ / 99 NC/NA

12. In general, have you made new friends through your volunteer activity? 1 **YES**; 2 **NO**; 3 NC-NA

13. (MULTIPLE) Do you think you learned something new through volunteer activities? **1** NO, nothing in particular; (YES) What? (DO NOT READ): **2** greater knowledge of others; **3** knowledge of the country; **4** knowledge of those who suffer; **5** other _____; **6** NC/NA

14. There are many reasons to do something to benefit others. What are yours? (DO NOT READ, SPECIFY, AND CODE ONLY ONE)_____

To help their children in school	1
Because of religious beliefs	2
It's a way to feel useful	3
To do something worthwhile	4
Necessary to repay the community	5
Those who have should give to those who do not have	6
Help the needy	7
Meet people/make friends	8
Desire to help others	9
The government is incompetent	10
Their friends are already participating there	11
To be recognized, appreciated by others	12
The government does not offer support and something must be done	13
Other:	14

15. **(ONLY FOR THOSE WHO DO NOT HELP)** (MULTIPLE) What would you say is the main reason you have not contributed any type of help? (DO NOT READ) Any other reason? ... Another?

1	Lack of time
2	Lack of motivation, desire/lack of trust
3	Doesn't want to commit to those kinds of things
4	Work/studies
5	Helps in other ways
6	Has other priorities/pressing needs
7	Doesn't think helping does much good
8	Doesn't make enough money
9	Doesn't know how to get involved
10	Health problems
11	Prefers to donate money
12	Other:
13	NC/NA
14	**DOES VOLUNTEER WORK**

16. (MULTIPLE) In your immediate family (spouse, children, parents, brothers, or sisters), does someone do or has someone done volunteer service? (DO NOT READ): **1 (NO)** (GO TO Q #19); **(YES)** Who? **2** spouse; **3** children; **4** parents; **5** brothers or sisters; **6** everyone; **7** NC/NA

17. A total of how many do or have done it? (SPECIFY) _____ / 99 NC/NA

18. Have you invited other people, relatives, or friends to devote part of their time to helping others? **(YES)** Have you gotten them to participate? **(YES)** Who? (DO NOT READ): **1** relatives; **2** relatives and friends; **3** relatives, friends, and others; **4** strangers; **5** has invited without success; **6** has not invited; **7** NA

19. (MULTIPLE) What activities have you invited them to? **1 None; 2 YES** (CODE IN TABLE BELOW, NUMBERING THE ORDER MENTIONED):

A	**Church** or religious group (construction, cleaning, worship, etc.)	
B	**School** (students, parents, teachers, etc.)	
C	**Sports** or recreation	
D	**Young people or children** (boy scouts, guides, youth clubs, etc.)	
E	**Poor**	
F	**Sick people** (Red Cross, hospitals, etc.)	
G	**Orphans, elderly, indigenous people, disabled**	
H	**Neighbors**, communities, ejidos	
I	**Human rights**	
J	**Ecology**, environment, or animals	
K	**Art**, music, or culture	
L	**Professional associations or unions**	
M	**Government** (projects and activities)	
N	**Women**	
O	**Trade union**	
P	**Political groups** or parties	
Q	**Citizen causes**	
R	Other:	

20. **(MULTIPLE)** Now we are going to talk about help with money, clothes, food, furniture, or something similar. <u>We are not going to talk about your time.</u> Is this clear or should I repeat it? Are you in the habit of giving money or things to people who <u>are not your relatives</u>?: **1 (NO)** (GO TO Q #24); **(YES)**: What do you mainly give? **2** money / **3** clothes / **4** food / **5** furniture / **6** other: (SPECIFY) _____; **7** No answer

21. **(MULTIPLE)** How do you usually give: through a group of friends; directly; a religious or other organization; in some other way? (DO NOT READ): **1** The church; **2** religious group; **3** non-religious organization; **4** group of friends; **5** directly; **6** other; which one? _____; **7** NC/NA

22. Did you say you have given money? **1 (NO)** (GO TO Q #24) / **(YES)** On the average, how much do you give a month? (EVEN IF THEY DO NOT GIVE MONTHLY, CALCULATE ON A MONTHLY BASIS): **2** $ _____ **3** NC/NA

23. How do you give it? (DO NOT READ): **1** coins / **2** bills / **3** check / **4** credit card / **5** internet / **6** monthly payment / **7** membership fee / **8** other (SPECIFY) ____

Now I'm going to ask you to tell me if you have **received any support** from **anyone**: a private organization, the government, the church, someone who is not a relative.

For example, clothes, food, housing, medicine, medical devices, scholarships, free classes or training courses, pilgrimage without payment, or anything else.

24. (MULTIPLE) Have you received any help?: **1** (**NO**) (GO TO Q #27); (**YES**) Who? (DON'T READ): **2** training; **3** classes; **4** scholarship; **5** medicine; **6** medical devices; **7** free pilgrimage; **8** food; **9** housing; **10** clothes; **11** furniture; **12** other service; **13** donation in kind; what? (SPECIFY) ___.

25. (MULTIPLE) Who did you receive it from? (DO NOT READ): **1** church; **2** government;

   3 private organization, which one?_____;

   4 political organizations, which one? _____ ;

   5 if any other kind of organization, which one? _____;

   6 person (not a relative) _____;

   7 other, what? _____;

26. (MULTIPLE) Do you remember when you received it? (DO NOT READ): **1** less than 3 months; **2** 3–6 months; **3** 6–12 months; **4** 1–3 years; **5** 3–5 years; **6** 5–10 years; **7** more than 10 years; **8** Doesn't remember; **9** NC.

27 (MULTIPLE) Do you belong to any group? (**NO**) (INSIST: SPORTS, ASSOCIATION, POLITICAL, PROFESSIONAL, RELIGIOUS, TRADE UNION, COMMUNITY, SAVINGS BANKS, ANYTHING) **1** (**NO**), none (GO TO Q #29) **2** (**YES**) Which one, what's it called? (FILL IN NAME):

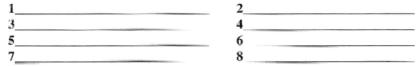

28. Regarding the first group, (READ NAME IN Q #27), is it an institution or organized group (LIKE A CHURCH, CLINIC, REST HOME, SCHOOL, HOSPITAL, ASSOCIATION, ETC.) or, something more informal like a group of friends or neighbors, fellow employees, acquaintances, or what is it? (DO NOT READ AND INCLUDE CODE IN THE LOWER TABLE IN THE APPROPRIATE PLACE) And the 2nd? ,,, and the 3rd? (ASK ABOUT ALL THOSE MENTIONED): **1** institution or organized group / **2** group of friends / **3** group of neighbors/fellow employees/acquaintances / **4** other / **5** NC/NA

		1	2	3	4	5	6	7	8
A	**Church** or religious group (construction, cleaning, worship, etc.)								
B	**School** (students, parents, teachers, etc.)								
C	**Sports** or recreation								
D	**Young people or children** (boy scouts, guides, youth clubs, etc.)								
E	**Poor**								
F	**Sick people** (Red Cross, hospitals, etc.)								
G	**Orphans, elderly, indigenous people, disabled**								
H	**Neighbors**, communities, ejidos								
I	**Human rights**								
J	**Ecology**, environment, or animals								
K	**Art**, music, or culture								
L	**Professional associations or unions**								
M	**Government** (projects and activities)								
N	**Women**								
O	**Trade union**								
P	**Political groups** or parties								
Q	**Citizen causes**								
R	Other:								

29. Now I'm going to read you the names of some institutions. Tell me for each one, how much do you trust them? a lot, some, a little, not at all? (READ AND CIRCLE THE ANSWER FOR EACH QUESTION)

	A lot	Some	A little	Not at all	Not certain	Does not know
a. Church	1	2	3	4	5	6
b. Television	1	2	3	4	5	6
c. Large companies	1	2	3	4	5	6
d. Government	1	2	3	4	5	6
e. Army	1	2	3	4	5	6
f. Schools	1	2	3	4	5	6
g. Hospitals	1	2	3	4	5	6
h. Political parties	1	2	3	4	5	6
i. Unions	1	2	3	4	5	6
j. Groups of neighbors	1	2	3	4	5	6
k. Red Cross	1	2	3	4	5	6
l. Telethon	1	2	3	4	5	6
m. Azteca Foundation	1	2	3	4	5	6
n. CNDH	1	2	3	4	5	6

30. In general terms, would you say that most people can or cannot be trusted when dealing with people? **1.** They can be trusted / **2** They cannot be trusted / **0** NC/NA

31. To finish up, I'm going to read you a list of some activities and you tell me if you do them **(1)** regularly, **(2)** once in a while, **(3)** you once did them, **(4)** you might do them, or **(5)** you would never do them / (DO NOT READ) **(6)** NS/NA (READ PHRASES AND RECORD)

	1	2	3	4	5	6
1. Attend church or parish activities	A	A	A	A	A	A
2. Attend neighborhood, community, or school activities	C	C	C	C	C	C
3. Keep informed about what's happening in the country	D	D	D	D	D	D
4. Vote in elections	E	E	E	E	E	E
5. Being a member of some group	F	F	F	F	F	F
6. Attend meetings of your group	G	G	G	G	G	G
7. Participate in neighborhood, community, or school decisions	I	I	I	I	I	I
8. Sign a petition	J	J	J	J	J	J
9. Participate in an unauthorized strike	L	L	L	L	L	L

32. If you think about **all** your free time during the week and on the weekend, about how many hours of free time do you have every week? _____ (NOTE AND CODE): **1** less than 3 hours / **2** 3–6 h / **3** 6–9 h / **4** more than 10 h a week / **5** NC/NA

33. If there was some way that you could give a few minutes of your time during the week to some because you like near your home or work, how likely or unlikely is it that you would do so? (DON'T READ BUT INSIST: VERY OR SOMEWHAT) **1** Very likely / **2** Somewhat likely / **3** Neither likely or unlikely / **4** Somewhat unlikely (GO TO Q #35) / **5** Very unlikely (GO TO Q #35) **6** NC/NA

34. If you could do it, how much time do you think you could devote per week? (NOTE AND CODE) _____ **1** less than 3 h / **2** 3–6 h / **3** 6–9 h / **4** more than 10 h a week / **5** NC/NA

35. During the last 12 months, was your family able to save? Was it barely enough or did you spend some of your savings or have to borrow? **1** Could save / **2** Barely enough / **3** Spent savings / **4** Had to borrow / **5** NC/NA

36. What do you think your personal economic situation will be like in a year: better or worse? (DO NOT READ BUT INSIST: MUCH OR SOMEWHAT) **1** Much better / **2** somewhat better / **3** the same / **4** somewhat worse / **5** much worse / **6** NC

37. On a scale from 1 to 10, where 1 means "it depends completely on you," 10 means "it depends completely on the general situation," and you can pick any number in between, what does your personal economic situation improving depend on?

1   2   3   4   5   6   7   8   9   10

Depends on me   Depends on the general situation

38. How much do you find out about the news through...? (READ EACH OPTION): a lot, some, a little, not at all?

	1 A lot	2 Some	3 A little	4 Not at all	5 NC/NA
Television					
Radio					
Newspapers					
Talking to people					

39. How many hours of television per day do you watch on the average? _____

40. Do you believe in a religion? (**NO**) How would you describe your beliefs: nonbeliever, free thinker, agnostic, atheist, or what? (**YES**) Which one? (DO NOT READ): **01** Anglican; **02** Adventist; **03** Baptist; **04** Catholic; **05** Christian; **06** Evangelical; **07** Lutheran; **08** Light of the World; **09** Mennonite; **10** Methodist; **11** Mormon; **12** Orthodox; **13** Pentecostal; **14** Presbyterian; **15** Protestant; **16** Jehovah's Witness; **17** End Times; **18** free thinker; **19** agnostic; **20** atheist; **21** nonbeliever; **22** none; **23** NC/NA / **24** other (SPECIFY): _____

41. How often do you go to church or religious services? (DON'T READ): **1** More than once a week; **2** Once a week; **3** Once a month; **4** Only on special occasions; **5** Never or almost never; **6** NC/NA

Finally, just a little general information.

42. (RECORD WITHOUT ASKING) Interviewee's gender: **1** Man / **2** Woman

43. What year were you born? _____ (IF DOES NOT REMEMBER) About how old are you? (RECORD): _____

44. How many grades did you complete in school? (RECORD): _____

45. What is your marital status? (DO NOT READ): **1** Married / **2** Living together / **3** Divorced / **4** Separated / **5** Widow(er) / **6** Single (never married) / **9** No answer

46. Do you have children? **1** YES; **2** NO; **3** NC-NA

47. a. How many? (RECORD) ___ **b.** How many are under 18? (RECORD) _____

48. How many people live in your home / residence, including you? _____

49. Do you have a job now? (IF ANSWER IS "YES") How many hours do you work a week? (IF HAS MORE THAN ONE JOB: ONLY FOR THE MAIN JOB)

Yes	DO NOT
1) Full time / 30 hours a week or more	6) Retired/pensioned
2) Part time / less than 30 hours a week	7) Housewife without other work
3) Self-employed in store or workshop	8) Student
4) Self-employed on street	9) Unemployed
5) Self-employed in country	10) Other _____

50. Do you work for the public sector, private sector, or are you self-employed?
1 Public / **2** Private / **3** Self-employed / **4** Doesn't work / **5** NC/NA (DO NOT READ)

51. What is your **main** occupation or activity? (DO NOT READ. IF HAS MORE THAN ONE JOB, ONLY THE MAIN ONE)

1 Employer/manager in workplace with more than 10 employees

2 Employer/manager in workplace with less than 10 employees

3 Professional (lawyer, accountant, etc.)

4 Supervisor of non-manual work in shop or office.

5 Non-manual worker in shop or office, under supervision

6 Teacher/educator

7 Supervisor / foreman of manual workers

8 Skilled manual worker (plumber, electrician, etc.)

9 Semi-skilled manual worker (apprentice, helper, etc.)

10 Unskilled manual worker (laborer, etc.)

11 Farmer/*Ejidatario*

12 Peasant/Rural day laborer

13 Member of police or armed forces

14 Attends to household

15 Never has had a job

16 Other (SPECIFY): _____

52. How many light bulbs do you have in your house? _____

53. In your house, do you have…? (**1** = Yes / **2** = No / **0** = NC/NA) **a.** Telephone _____ / **b.** Microwave _____ / **c.** Computer _____ / **d.** Internet _____

54. Approximately, what is your households total combined monthly gross income $_____ (RECORD)

55. Generally speaking, do you consider yourself to be a supporter of the PRI, PAN, PRD, or as an independent? (INSIST: A LOT OR SOMEWHAT) **1** Support the PRI somewhat / **2** Support the PRI a lot / **3** Support the PAN somewhat / **4** Support the PAN a lot / **5** Support the PRD somewhat / **6** Support the PRD a lot / **7** Somewhat independent / **8** Very independent / **9** No party / **10** Other _____ / **11**) NC/NA

That's all. Thank you very much for your time. Time when finished _____

In case my supervisor needs to check my work, could you give me your first name so as to be able to ask for you? (RECORD) _____ Do you have a phone number where you can be reached? _____

The complete survey may be accessed at the Cemefi Webpage: http://www.cemefi.org

Appendix II
Survey Graphics

Miguel Basáñez

1) Have you ever done something for others without being paid?

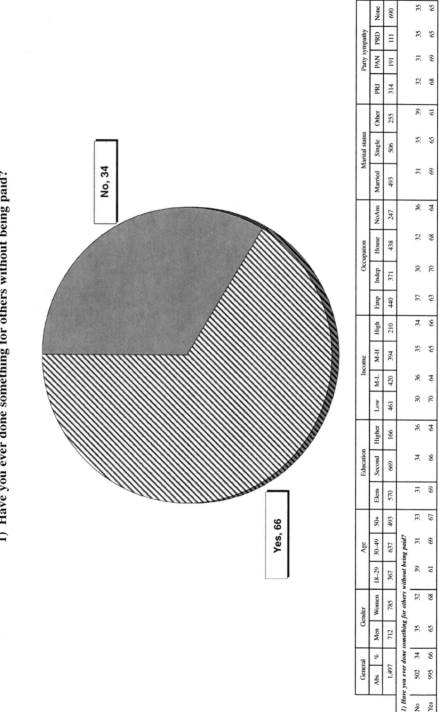

No, 34

Yes, 66

	General		Gender		Age			Education			Income				Occupation				Marital status			Party sympathy			
	Abs	%	Men	Women	18–29	30–49	50+	Elem	Second	Higher	Low	M-L	M-H	High	Emp	Indep	House	NoAns	Married	Single	Other	PRI	PAN	PRD	None
	1,497		712	785	367	637	493	570	669	166	461	420	394	210	440	371	438	247	493	506	255	314	191	111	690
1) Have you ever done something for others without being paid?																									
No	502	34	35	32	39	31	33	31	34	36	30	36	35	34	37	30	32	36	31	35	39	32	31	35	35
Yes	995	66	65	68	61	69	67	69	66	64	70	64	65	66	63	70	68	64	69	65	61	68	69	65	65

1) Which do you remember?: multiple

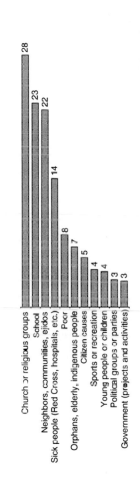

Church or religious groups	28
School	23
Neighbors, communities, ejidos	22
Sick people (Red Cross, hospitals, etc.)	14
Poor	8
Orphans, elderly, indigenous people	7
Citizen causes	5
Sports or recreation	4
Young people or children	4
Political groups or parties	3
Government (projects and activities)	3

	General		Gender		Age			Education			Income				Occupation				Marital status			Party sympathy			
	Abs	%	Men	Women	18–29	30–49	50+	Elem	Second	Higher	Low	M-L	M-H	High	Emp	Indep	House	NoAns	Married	Single	Other	PRI	PAN	PRD	None
	1,497		712	785	357	637	493	570	659	166	461	420	394	210	440	371	438	247	463	506	255	314	191	111	690
1) Which do you remember?: multiple																									
Church or religious groups	417	28	23	32	23	26	34	34	24	19	35	26	26	20	23	23	33	26	30	26	23	30	27	21	28
School	338	23	20	25	20	25	21	2	20	25	27	22	19	21	19	23	25	23	24	22	21	23	21	27	25
Neighbors, communities, ejidos	327	22	25	19	20	20	26	2	20	24	26	21	21	19	21	28	18	22	23	22	18	22	20	20	25
Sick people (Red Cross, hospitals, etc.)	213	14	10	18	13	14	16	1	15	11	16	12	15	12	11	16	16	14	16	14	10	16	12	11	13
Poor	120	8	6	10	6	9	9		8	10	8	6	9	10	8	7	9	7	9	6	6	8	11	5	6
Orphans, elderly, indigenous people	100	7	5	9	4	7	6		8	7	7	6	6	8	5	6	9	6	3	8	5	7	8	3	5
Citizen causes	82	5	7	4	4	5	4		6	5	6	4	6	7	5	6	4	5	5	5	5	6	6	6	5
Sports or recreation	62	4	7	2	5	4	4		4	11	3	3	5	8	5	6	1	5	4	7	2	4	3	4	5
Young people or children	59	4	5	3	2	5	3		3	8	3	4	4	6	6	5	4	4	3	5	3	3	3	6	4
Political groups or parties	45	3	4	2	2	3	3		3	5	3	3	2	3	4	2	2	4	3	2	3	6	3	7	1
Government projects and activities	43	3	4	1	2	3	4		4	2	3	3	3	2	3	5	3	3	4	2	1	3	1	6	3
Other	81	5	7	4	8	5	4		6	14	2	5	9	7	6	8	3	4	5	8	4	4	4	5	7

2) How long ago did you begin and in what year [if you remember]? multiple

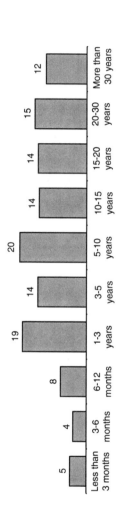

	Less than 3 months	3-6 months	6-12 months	1-3 years	3-5 years	5-10 years	10-15 years	15-20 years	20-30 years	More than 30 years
	5	4	8	19	14	20	14	14	15	12

2) How long ago did you begin and in what year [if you remember]? multiple

	General		Gender		Age			Education			Income				Occupation				Marital status			Party sympathy			
	Abs	%	Men	Women	18-29	30-49	50+	Elem	Second	Higher	Low	M-L	M-H	High	Emp	Indep	House	NoAns	Married	Single	Other	PRI	PAN	PRD	None
	1,497		712	785	367	637	493	570	669	166	461	420	394	210	440	371	438	247	493	506	255	314	191	111	690
Less than 3 months	74	5	3	6	6	5	4	5	5	4	5	5	6	6	6	5	5	5	5	6	3	5	2	5	5
3-6 months	60	4	2	5	6	5	2	4	4	3	3	3	4	4	5	4	5	3	4	5	4	5	4	1	4
6-12 months	114	8	7	8	15	6	4	7	8	9	8	5	10	6	8	9	8	6	7	13	4	4	5	6	10
1-3 years	280	19	17	20	29	19	11	17	20	23	23	15	19	16	16	18	21	21	18	26	14	17	19	23	17
3-5 years	214	14	15	14	18	16	9	12	16	20	13	11	17	20	15	14	13	14	13	20	11	12	14	17	14
5-10 years	293	20	19	20	26	21	13	18	22	20	19	20	20	20	17	23	21	17	20	23	15	17	19	27	21
10-15 years	209	14	14	14	8	18	13	12	14	18	16	15	12	10	13	18	13	12	17	11	9	13	12	11	16
15-20 years	214	14	16	12	1	20	17	15	12	23	15	14	12	19	19	17	10	10	18	8	11	18	15	17	14
20-30 years	228	15	15	15	0	15	27	20	11	6	20	12	14	16	13	22	13	13	19	6	14	22	19	10	13
More than 30 years	180	12	14	11	0	3	32	19	6	6	15	13	11	6	7	13	13	19	14	3	14	18	6	4	13
Continue doing it	8	1	1	1	0	1	1	0	1	1	0	0	0	1	1	0	1	1	1	0	0	0	1	2	0
Average (years)	8	13	14	12	4	11	21	16	10	11	14	13	12	11	12	14	12	14	14	7	15	16	12	10	13

3) How long did you continue doing it or what year did you stop doing it?: multiple

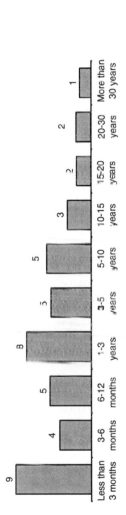

	Less than 3 months	3-6 months	6-12 months	1-3 years	3-5 years	5-10 years	10-15 years	15-20 years	20-30 years	More than 30 years
	9	4	5	8	5	5	3	2	2	1

	General		Gender		Age			Education			Income				Occupation				Marital status			Party sympathy			
	Abs	%	Men	Women	18–29	30–49	50+	Elem	Second	Higher	Low	M-L	M-H	High	Emp	Indep	House	NoAns	Married	Single	Other	PRI	PAN	PRD	None
	1,497		712	785	367	637	493	579	669	146	461	420	394	210	449	371	438	247	493	506	255	314	191	111	690
3) How long did you continue doing it or what year did you stop doing it?: multiple																									
Less than 3 months	139	9	11	8	15	9	6	9	9	8	9	9	11	9	8	13	6	10	9	13	7	7	7	13	12
3-6 months	58	4	3	4	4	4	4	4	4	2	4	3	5	4	2	4	5	7	4	4	3	3	5	3	4
6-12 months	76	5	4	6	7	5	3	4	4	8	6	4	5	6	5	4	6	6	5	6	5	8	7	5	4
1-3 years	119	8	9	7	11	7	8	6	9	13	5	6	10	11	8	7	9	6	8	11	6	6	13	5	8
3-5 years	74	5	4	6	5	5	5	4	5	7	7	5	4	6	5	5	4	6	4	7	5	4	10	5	4
5-10 years	82	5	6	5	3	5	8	7	5	8	3	3	2	3	5	6	5	6	6	3	6	7	6	5	6
10-15 years	44	3	3	3	1	2	6	3	3	4	2	1	2	3	3	3	3	4	3	2	2	3	3	5	3
15-20 years	27	2	2	3	0	1	4	3	1	0	2	1	2	4	3	1	1	2	2	1	2	2	1	5	1
20-30 years	28	2	2	1	0	1	5	2	2	1	2	2	2	0	2	1	2	5	2	0	1	1	1	0	2
More than 30 years	21	1	2	1	1	0	4	2	0	1	2	1	2	0	0	1	2	4	2	0	1	1	1	2	2
Continue doing it	1,212	81	77	85	64	90	82	87	87	87	92	75	73	72	78	97	79	65	90	73	60	87	64	73	81
Average (years)	6		6	6	3	4	10	8	4	4	6	6	6	5	2	5	6	9	7	3	6	6	4	6	6

4) How frequently did you do each one?: multiple

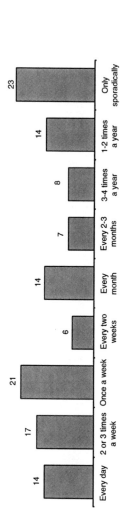

4) How frequently did you do each one?: multiple

	General		Gender		Age			Education			Income				Occupation				Marital status			Party sympathy			
	Abs	%	Men	Women	18–29	30–49	50+	Elem	Second	Higher	Low	M-L	M-H	High	Emp	Indep	House	NoAns	Married	Single	Other	PRI	PAN	PRD	None
	1,497		712	785	367	637	493	570	669	166	461	420	394	210	440	371	438	247	493	506	255	314	191	111	690
NO RESPONSE	502	34	35	32	39	31	33	31	34	36	30	36	35	34	37	30	32	36	35	35	39	32	31	35	35
Every day	214	14	13	15	10	15	16	13	16	13	14	14	15	14	12	16	11	22	15	14	12	14	14	17	14
2 or 3 times a week	248	17	14	19	16	16	17	15	16	22	16	15	16	15	15	18	18	16	17	16	15	18	23	17	13
Once a week	317	21	20	22	22	22	20	21	21	28	20	18	24	26	20	20	23	21	23	20	16	19	23	14	21
Every 2 weeks	95	6	6	6	6	7	7	8	5	7	8	5	7	4	5	8	7	5	7	7	5	6	6	5	6
Every month	217	14	13	16	13	14	16	14	13	18	16	12	17	13	13	19	14	11	16	9	14	13	16	20	15
Every 2–3 months	112	7	8	7	6	9	6	10	5	12	10	6	6	7	5	12	8	3	9	7	5	7	7	5	9
3–4 times a year	114	8	9	7	5	8	9	8	7	14	9	11	5	3	8	11	6	4	8	9	5	8	8	8	9
1–2 times a year	211	14	17	12	12	14	16	16	12	14	16	14	11	14	15	17	11	14	14	14	15	16	9	13	16
Only sporadically	344	23	23	23	19	23	26	26	24	15	29	19	24	18	22	22	23	27	26	24	13	29	14	22	24
Average (days a year)	*49*		*45*	*52*	*42*	*51*	*51*	*45*	*54*	*47*	*45*	*48*	*51*	*55*	*43*	*49*	*45*	*66*	*49*	*50*	*48*	*48*	*53*	*57*	*46*

5) On the average, about how much time do you dedicate a week: multiple

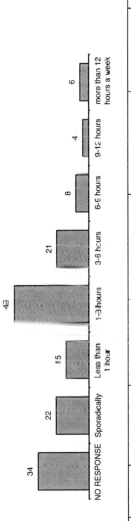

Bars: NO RESPONSE 34 · Sporadically 22 · Less than 1 hour 15 · 1-3 hours 49 · 3-6 hours 21 · 6-9 hours 8 · 9-12 hours 4 · more than 12 hours a week 6

5) On the average, about how much time do you dedicate a week: multiple

		General		Gender		Age			Education			Income				Occupation				Marital status			Party sympathy			
		Abs	%	Men	Women	18-29	30-49	50+	Elem	Second	Higher	Low	M-L	M-H	High	Emp	Indep	House	NoAns	Married	Single	Other	PRI	PAN	PRD	None
		1,497		712	785	367	637	493	570	666	Es	461	420	394	210	440	371	438	247	493	506	255	314	191	111	690
NO RESPONSE		502	34	35	32	39	31	33	31	34	36	32	36	35	34	37	30	32	36	31	35	39	32	31	35	35
Sporadically		324	22	20	23	19	21	25	26	15	15	20	16	24	20	21	15	26	27	25	20	14	24	16	17	20
Less than 1 h		225	15	12	18	12	16	16	15	15	19	17	15	18	14	15	15	16	12	17	12	12	15	14	14	14
1-3 h		734	49	42	56	41	54	48	59	49	60	56	50	45	44	41	62	55	36	52	45	45	52	53	45	51
3-6 h		316	21	27	16	21	19	25	23	29	28	21	21	20	22	19	26	14	26	22	25	15	24	19	19	21
6-9 h		127	8	11	6	7	9	9	9	8	7	5	5	8	10	8	12	7	7	10	7	6	7	5	12	10
9-12 h		57	4	5	3	3	3	5	4	7	7	4	4	3	3	4	3	1	6	4	3	3	3	3	5	4
more than 12 h a week		87	6	8	4	6	6	5	5	7		5	5	7	8	6	5	3	8	6	8	4	6	4	10	6
Average (hours)			3.3	3.9	2.8	3.5	3.5	3.3	3.1		3.4	3.2	3.4	3.3	3.6	3.6	3.5	2.5	3.7	3.2	3.7	3.2	3.3	3.0	4.0	3.5

6) Concerning the most recent activity... What did or do you do concretely? Multiple

Bar chart — percentages:

- Manpower (physical work): 30
- Personal attention or care / Accompany: 12
- Raising funds: 9
- Teaching or training: 9
- Organizing events, parties, etc.: 7
- Advice, advising: 5
- Information campaigns: 2
- Administrative support (office work): 1
- Planning, research, strategies: 1
- Other: 1
- Public relations: 1

6) Concerning the most recent activity... What did or do you do concretely? Multiple

	General		Gender		Age			Education			Income				Occupation				Marital status			Party sympathy			
	Abs	%	Men	Women	18–29	30–49	50+	Elem	Second	Higher	Low	M-L	M-H	High	Emp	Indep	House	NoAns	Married	Single	Other	PRI	PAN	PRD	None
	1,497		712	785	367	637	493	570	669	166	461	420	394	210	440	371	438	247	493	506	255	314	191	111	690
Manpower (physical work)	450	30	33	28	27	32	30	36	27	16	39	31	25	19	28	35	31	25	31	28	30	32	23	25	34
Personal attention or care/Accompany	177	12	7	16	11	12	12	12	13	7	11	13	13	10	9	11	16	11	13	13	9	12	13	8	13
Raising funds	139	9	8	11	8	9	10	9	9	11	9	7	10	11	10	7	11	8	9	8	11	7	11	10	7
Teaching or training	131	9	9	8	12	8	7	6	10	18	7	6	11	12	8	9	7	13	9	12	6	6	9	10	10
Organizing events, parties, etc.	101	7	6	8	5	9	5	7	7	7	6	7	7	6	6	6	9	5	8	5	6	8	12	5	5
Advice, advising	75	5	6	4	5	5	5	4	5	11	3	5	5	10	6	6	2	6	5	7	4	5	5	5	4
Information campaigns	27	2	2	2	2	2	5	2	2	3	1	2	2	3	2	2	0	2	2	4	2	2	3	4	1
Administrative support (office work)	20	1	2	1	1	2	1	1	1	2	1	2	2	1	1	2	2	2	1	2	1	2	2	1	1
Planning, research, strategies	18	1	2	1	1	1	2	1	1	1	1	1	2	2	0	1	0	2	1	2	1	1	1	4	1
Other	9	1	0	1	1	1	0	0	0	2	0	0	1	0	0	0	1	2	1	1	0	0	1	2	0
Public relations	8	1	0	1	1	0	0	1	1	0	0	1	0	0	1	0	1	0	1	1	0	1	0	1	0

7) How do or did you provide that volunteer service?

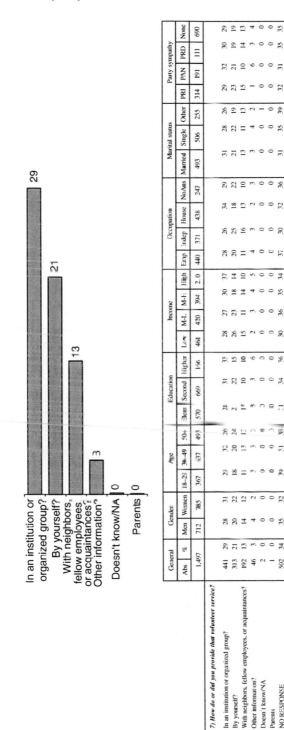

In an institution or organized group?	29
By yourself?	21
With neighbors, fellow employees, or acquaintances?	13
Other information?	3
Doesn't know/NA	0
Parents	0

	General		Gender		Age			Education			Income				Occupation				Marital status			Party sympathy			
	Abs	%	Men	Women	18-29	30-49	50+	Elem	Second	Higher	Low	M-L	M-H	High	Emp	Indep	House	NoAns	Married	Single	Other	PRI	PAN	PRD	None
	1,497		712	785	367	637	493	570	669	196	461	420	394	2.0	440	371	438	247	493	506	255	314	191	111	690
7) How do or did you provide that volunteer service?																									
In an institution or organized group?	441	29	28	31	29	32	26	28	31	33	28	27	30	37	28	26	34	29	31	28	26	29	32	30	29
By yourself?	313	21	20	22	18	20	24	2	22	15	26	23	18	14	20	25	18	22	21	22	19	23	21	19	19
With neighbors, fellow employees, or acquaintances?	192	13	14	12	11	13	12	1	10	10	15	11	14	10	11	16	13	10	13	11	13	15	10	14	13
Other information?	46	3	4	2	3	3	3	3	3	6	2	3	4	5	4	3	2	3	3	4	2	1	6	3	4
Doesn't know/NA	2	0	0	0	0	0	0	0	0	0	0	0	0	0	0	0	0	0	0	0	0	0	0	0	0
Parents	1	0	0	0	0	0	0	0	0	0	0	0	0	0	0	0	0	0	0	0	0	0	0	0	0
NO RESPONSE	502	34	35	32	39	31	35	31	34	36	30	36	35	34	37	30	32	36	31	35	39	32	31	35	35

8) How did you begin? Did someone invite you?

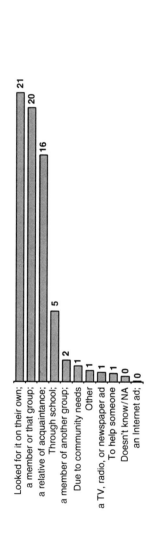

Looked for it on their own;	21
a member or that group;	20
a relative of acquaintance;	16
Through school;	5
a member of another group;	2
Due to community needs	1
Other	1
a TV, radio, or newspaper ad	1
To help someone	1
Doesn't know/NA	0
an Internet ad;	0

8) How did you begin? Did someone invite you?

	General		Gender		Age			Education			Income				Occupation				Marital status			Party sympathy			
	Abs	%	Men	Women	18–29	30–49	50+	Elem	Second	Higher	Low	M-L	M-H	High	Emp	Indep	House	NoAns	Married	Single	Other	PRI	PAN	PRD	None
	1,497		712	785	367	637	493	570	669	166	461	420	394	210	440	371	438	247	493	506	255	314	191	111	690
Looked for it on their own;	308	21	20	21	16	21	23	22	20	19	24	20	20	16	21	20	20	21	21	20	20	19	19	20	20
a member of that group;	292	20	20	19	18	22	17	20	20	17	18	19	21	20	19	22	21	14	21	17	18	20	23	21	20
a relative or acquaintance;	242	16	15	17	17	15	18	17	15	17	17	16	14	18	13	19	16	19	16	18	14	20	18	12	14
Through school;	75	5	4	6	5	7	3	4	6	4	5	5	5	4	5	4	6	5	5	6	5	4	4	7	5
a member of another group;	23	2	2	1	2	1	2	1	1	3	2	1	2	1	2	1	1	2	2	1	1	1	2	4	2
Due to community needs	17	1	2	0	1	1	2	1	1	1	2	0	1	2	1	2	0	–	1	1	2	3	2	2	1
Other	12	1	1	1	–	1	–	1	1	1	1	–	1	1	1	–	1	2	1	–	1	–	–	1	–
a TV, radio, or newspaper ad	10	1	0	1	1	1	0	0	1	1	1	1	0	–	1	0	1	0	1	0	1	1	2	0	1
To help someone	9	1	1	0	0	0	0	1	1	–	0	1	0	1	0	0	–	1	0	0	0	1	–	0	–
Doesn't know/NA	6	0	0	0	1	0	0	1	0	0	0	0	0	0	0	0	0	0	0	0	0	0	0	0	0
an Internet ad;	1	0	0	0	0	0	0	0	0	0	0	0	0	0	0	0	0	0	0	0	0	0	0	0	0
NO RESPONSE	502	34	35	32	39	31	33	31	34	36	30	36	35	34	37	30	32	36	31	35	39	32	31	35	35

9) Do you continue to participate in the same activity? Why did you stop doing so?

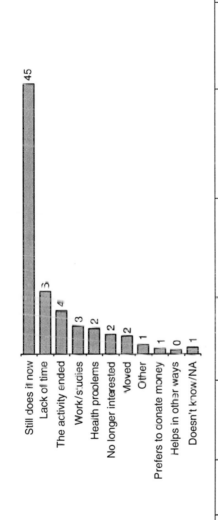

	Still does it now	45
Lack of time	6
The activity ended	4
Work/studies	3
Health problems	2
No longer interested	2
Moved	2
Other	1
Prefers to donate money	1
Helps in other ways	0
Doesn't know/NA	1

9) Do you continue to participate in the same activity? Why did you stop doing so?

	General		Gender		Age			Education			Income				Occupation				Marital status			Party sympathy			
	Abs	%	Men	Women	18-29	30-49	50+	Elem	Second	Higher	Low	M-L	M-H	High	Emp	Indep	House	NoAns	Married	Single	Other	PRI	PAN	PRD	None
	1,497		712	785	367	637	493	570	669	160	461	420	394	210	440	371	<38	247	493	506	255	314	191	111	690
Still does it now	676	45	43	47	39	40	44	49	44	44	51	44	43	40	43	50	49	35	49	42	36	48	42	40	44
Lack of time	90	6	5	7	9	5	5	4	7	7	6	5	5	9	4	6	6	6	7	6	5	5	6	8	6
The activity ended	62	4	5	3	3	5	4	5	4	2	5	3	4	4	5	5	5	4	4	3	5	3	5	5	6
Work / studies	40	3	3	2	4	3	1	2	3	5	2	3	2	5	5	2	2	3	2	5	3	1	4	2	3
Health problems	36	2	3	2	0	1	6	3		4	3	2	2	2	0	3	1	7	2	2	3	4	4	1	1
No longer interested	28	2	1	1	1	1	3	2	2	4	1	2	2	2	1	1	1	4	2	1	3	2	3	3	3
Moved	26	2	1	3	2	2	0	1	1	2	2	2	2	0	2	1	3	1	1	1	4	2	3	3	2
Other:	13	1	1	1	1	1	1	1		0	0	0	1	1	1	1	1	1	1	2	0	1	1	0	2
Prefers to donate money	8	1	1	1	0	1	1	0		1	0	0	0	0	0	1	1	0	0	1	0	0	1	1	0
Helps in other ways	6	0	0	1	0	0	1	0		1	0	1	1	1	0	1	0	0	0	0	0	0	1	1	1
Doesn't know/NA	10	1	1	1	1	0	1	0		1	0	1	0	1	1	1	0	1	0	1	1	1	1	1	1
NO RESPONSE	502	34	35	32	39	31	33	31	34	36	33	36	35	34	37	30	32	36	31	35	39	32	31	35	35

10) How old were you when you began your volunteer activities?

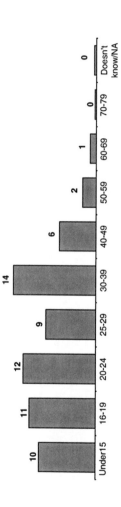

	General		Gender		Age			Education			Income				Occupation				Marital status			Party sympathy			
	Abs	%	Men	Women	18–29	30–49	50+	Elem	Second	Higher	Low	M-L	M-H	High	Emp	Indep	House	NoAns	Married	Single	Other	PRI	PAN	PRD	None
	1,497	27	712	785	367	637	493	570	669	166	461	420	394	210	440	371	438	247	493	506	255	314	191	111	690
10) How old were you when you began your volunteer activities?																									
NO RESPONSE	502	34	35	32	39	31	33	31	34	36	30	36	35	34	37	30	32	36	31	35	39	32	31	35	35
Under 15	145	10	10	9	17	7	8	9	11	9	9	7	12	11	9	9	10	12	8	16	8	9	6	5	13
16–19	170	11	14	9	23	8	6	9	14	13	14	10	9	12	12	12	9	14	9	25	5	10	10	10	13
20–24	186	12	13	12	17	14	7	11	13	17	12	12	14	11	15	13	10	11	13	12	12	12	15	14	12
25–29	128	9	7	10	4	11	9	11	8	8	8	10	7	9	13	7	12	6	10	4	7	10	9	4	9
30–39	212	14	11	17	0	22	14	15	14	11	14	14	16	12	13	17	16	8	16	5	17	18	16	14	12
40–49	94	6	6	6	0	6	11	9	4	4	7	7	5	6	5	7	7	7	7	2	7	6	7	10	5
50–59	35	2	2	3	0	0	7	3	1	2	4	2	2	1	1	3	3	2	3	0	3	2	3	5	2
60–69	16	1	1	1	0	0	3	2	0	1	2	1	1	2	0	1	1	3	1	0	0	0	0	3	1
70–79	4	0	0	0	0	0	1	0	0	0	0	0	0	0	0	0	0	0	0	0	1	0	1	1	0
Doesn't know/NA	5	0	1	0	0	0	0	0	0	1	1	0	0	0	0	1	0	0	0	0	0	0	1	0	0
Average (hours)		*27*	*27*	*28*	*18*	*27*	*34*	*29*	*25*	*25*	*28*	*28*	*26*	*27*	*25*	*28*	*28*	*27*	*29*	*20*	*29*	*27*	*30*	*32*	*25*

11) How old were you when you started your most recent activity?

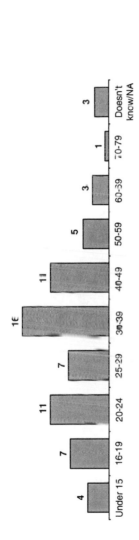

	General		Gender		Age			Education			Income				Occupation				Marital status			Party sympathy			
	Abs	%	Men	Women	18-29	30-49	40+	Elem	Second	Higher	Low	M-L	M-H	High	Emp	Indep	House	NoAns	Married	Single	Other	PRI	PAN	PRD	None
	1,497		712	785	367	637	493	570	669		461	420	394	210	440	371	438	247	493	506	255	314	191	111	690
11) How old were you when you started your most recent activity?																									
NO RESPONSE	502	34	35	32	39	31	33	31	34	36	30	36	35	34	37	30	32	36	31	35	39	32	31	35	35
Under 15	59	4	4	3	8	2	3	2	4	1	3	4	5	5	3	3	4	6	2	6	4	4	2	2	5
16-19	106	7	8	6	19	3	3	4	10	12	8	5	7	10	8	6	5	11	4	22	3	5	5	5	9
20-24	161	11	12	10	22	9	5	8	14	9	12	10	13	6	12	12	7	12	9	16	12	10	8	11	12
25-29	111	7	6	8	9	9	4	7	8	9	6	9	6	9	8	6	9	6	8	6	5	9	7	6	8
30-39	236	16	13	18	0	28	13	16	16	2	17	15	15	15	15	20	18	8	18	8	16	18	20	13	13
40-49	159	11	10	11	0	18	13	14	8	4	9	11	12	11	11	13	11	7	13	2	10	11	13	11	9
50-59	70	5	5	5	0	3	14	7	2	4	6	5	3	3	3	5	6	4	6	1	3	5	4	6	4
60-69	45	3	3	3	0	0	9	5	1	0	5	2	2	2	1	2	3	6	4	0	4	3	4	1	2
70-79	10	1	1	1	0	0	2	1	0	0	1	1	0	0	1	0	0	2	1	0	1	0	1	1	0
Doesn't know/NA	38	3	3	3	2	1	4	3	2	4	2	3	2	3	1	4	3	2	2	0	3	2	6	2	2
Average (hours)	38	33	33	34	20	33	44	38	25	42	35	33	32	32	32	34	35	33	36	23	34	34	36	38	31

12) In general, have you made new friends through your volunteer activity?

Yes, 53

No, 10

Doesn't know/NA, 3

12) In general, have you made new friends through your volunteer activity?

	General		Gender		Age			Education			Income				Occupation				Marital status			Party sympathy			
	Abs	%	Men	Women	18–29	30–49	50+	Elem	Second	Higher	Low	M-L	M-H	High	Emp	Indep	House	NoAns	Married	Single	Other	PRI	PAN	PRD	None
	1,497		712	785	367	637	493	570	669	166	461	420	394	210	440	371	438	247	493	506	255	314	191	111	690
Yes	794	53	52	54	49	55	54	54	52	54	58	48	54	50	51	57	53	51	55	52	50	55	55	59	50
DO NOT	149	10	9	11	9	10	10	11	9	8	9	12	8	11	8	11	11	10	10	9	9	9	10	6	11
Doesn't know/NA	52	3	4	3	3	4	3	3	4	2	3	4	4	4	4	3	3	2	4	4	2	4	4	0	3
NO RESPONSE	502	34	35	32	39	31	33	31	34	36	30	36	35	34	37	30	32	36	31	35	39	32	31	35	35

13) Do you think you learned something new through volunteer activities for others? Multiple

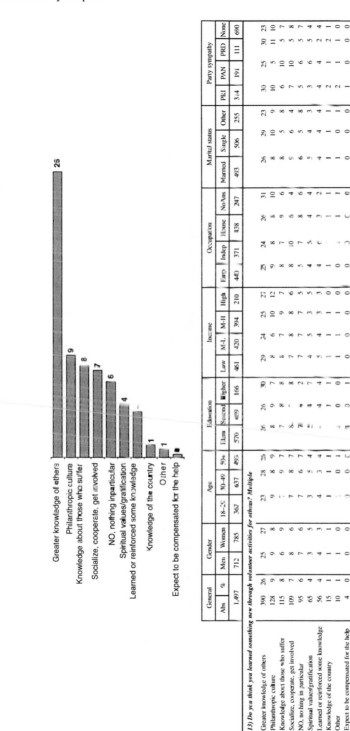

13) Do you think you learned something new through volunteer activities for others? Multiple

	General		Gender		Age			Education			Income				Occupation				Marital status			Party sympathy			
	Abs	%	Men	Women	18–25	30–49	50+	Elem	Second	Higher	Low	M-L	M-H	High	Emp	Indep	House	NoAns	Married	Single	Other	PRI	PAN	PRD	None
	1,497		712	785	367	637	493	570	659	166	461	420	394	210	440	371	438	247	493	506	255	314	191	111	690
Greater knowledge of others	390	26	25	27	23	28	25	26	26	30	29	24	25	27	25	24	26	31	26	29	23	30	25	30	23
Philanthropic culture	128	9	9	8	9	8	9	9	9	7	8	6	10	12	9	8	8	10	8	10	9	10	5	11	10
Knowledge about those who suffer	115	8	6	9	6	9	7	7	7	8	8	8	9	7	8	7	9	6	8	5	8	6	10	5	7
Socialize, cooperate, get involved	109	7	8	6	7	8	7	8	7	8	7	8	8	6	8	10	6	4	5	6	4	7	10	5	8
NO, nothing in particular	95	6	7	6	7	6	6	6	6	2	7	7	7	5	5	7	8	6	6	5	8	5	6	5	7
Spiritual values/gratification	65	4	3	5	3	5	4	4	4	7	4	5	3	3	4	5	4	4	5	4	3	3	6	5	4
Learned or reinforced some knowledge	56	4	4	3	4	3	3	4	4	4	5	4	3	3	4	4	3	2	4	4	4	4	4	4	4
Knowledge of the country	15	1	1	1	1	1	1	1	1	1	1	1	1	0	0	1	1	1	1	1	1	2	2	2	1
Other	10	1	1	0	1	0	1	1	1	0	1	0	1	0	0	1	1	1	1	0	1	2	1	0	0
Expect to be compensated for the help	4	0	0	0	0	0	0	0	0	1	0	0	0	0	0	0	0	0	0	0	0	1	0	0	0

14) There are many reasons to do something to benefit others. What are yours?

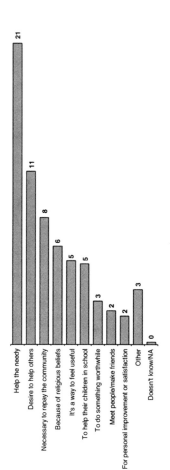

14) There are many reasons to do something to benefit others. What are yours?

	General		Gender		Age			Education			Income				Occupation				Marital status			Party sympathy			
	Abs	%	Men	Women	18–29	30–49	50+	Elem	Second	Higher	Low	M-L	M-H	High	Emp	Indep	House	NoAns	Married	Single	Other	PRI	PAN	PRD	None
	1,497		712	785	367	637	493	570	669	166	461	420	394	210	440	371	438	247	493	506	255	314	191	111	690
Help the needy	309	21	19	22	20	22	20	22	20	20	20	20	20	24	17	22	24	19	22	22	16	19	24	19	20
Desire to help others	164	11	12	10	8	13	11	11	10	17	11	10	12	12	13	12	9	11	11	12	9	11	11	12	12
Necessary to repay the community	120	8	11	6	7	8	9	9	8	4	10	8	7	5	9	9	6	9	8	6	10	12	7	9	7
Because of religious beliefs	93	6	5	7	6	6	7	9	5	4	9	6	6	3	5	6	8	6	7	6	5	6	9	5	5
It's a way to feel useful	79	5	5	5	4	5	6	4	6	8	5	4	6	6	5	7	5	4	5	6	5	4	6	4	6
To help their children in school	76	5	3	7	4	8	3	6	5	1	6	6	4	3	5	3	8	4	5	2	7	5	5	5	5
To do something worthwhile	41	3	3	3	2	2	4	2	3	2	2	2	3	2	2	3	3	4	3	2	2	3	2	1	3
Meet people/make friends	32	2	2	1	3	2	2	2	3	3	3	2	2	2	2	2	1	3	2	4	1	3	2	4	2
For personal improvement or satisfaction	27	2	2	2	3	2	1	1	3	3	1	2	2	5	2	2	3	2	2	3	2	2	1	2	2
Other	52	3	3	4	4	3	4	3	4	4	4	3	4	2	4	3	4	2	4	3	3	4	2	5	3
Doesn't know/NA	2	0	0	0	0	0	0	0	0	0	0	0	0	0	0	0	0	0	0	0	0	0	0	0	0
NO RESPONSE	502	34	35	32	39	31	33	31	34	36	30	36	35	34	37	30	32	36	31	35	39	32	31	35	35

15) What is the main reason you have not contributed any kind of help?: multiple

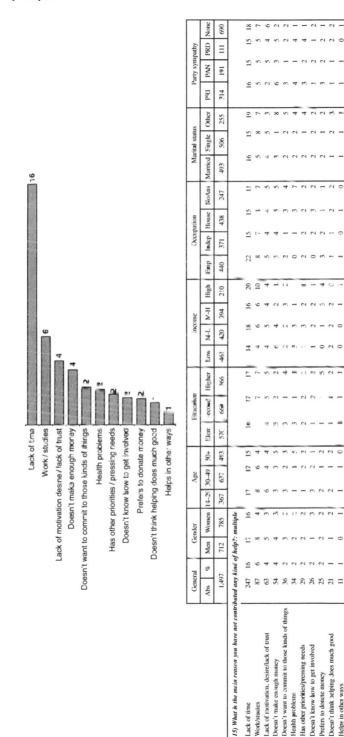

15) What is the main reason you have not contributed any kind of help?: multiple

	General		Gender		Age			Education			Income				Occupation				Marital status			Party sympathy			
	Abs	%	Men	Women	14-29	30-49	50+	Elem	Second	Higher	Low	M-L	M-H	High	Emp	Indep	House	NoAns	Married	Single	Other	PRI	PAN	PRD	None
	1,497		712	785	367	637	493	570	669	966	461	420	394	210	440	371	438	247	493	506	255	714	191	111	690
Lack of time	247	16	17	15	17	17	15	16	17	17	14	18	16	20	22	15	15	11	16	16	19	16	15	15	18
Work/studies	87	6	8	4	8	6	4	7	7	7	4	6	6	10	8	7	1	7	5	8	7	5	5	5	7
Lack of motivation, desire/lack of trust	63	4	5	3	6	4	4	5	5	5	6	5	4	4	5	4	4	5	4	4	3	2	5	4	6
Doesn't make enough money	54	4	4	4	3	3	5	5	2	2	6	4	2	1	3	4	4	5	3	1	3	6	3	5	2
Doesn't want to commit to those kinds of things	36	2	3	3	3	2	1	3	3	4	3	3	3	2	2	1	3	4	2	2	5	3	3	2	2
Health problems	34	2	2	2	1	1	5	3	1	1	3	3	1	1	0	2	3	7	2	1	4	4	1	4	1
Has other priorities/pressing needs	29	2	2	2	1	2	2	2	2	2	1	2	2	2	2	2	1	2	2	2	2	1	2	1	2
Doesn't know how to get involved	26	2	2	3	3	2	1	1	1	2	1	1	2	1	0	2	3	1	2	2	2	3	2	2	2
Prefers to donate money	25	2	1	2	2	2	2	1	2	5	2	1	3	4	3	1	2	2	2	1	2	1	2	1	2
Doesn't think helping does much good	21	1	1	2	1	1	1	1	1	2	2	1	2	0	1	0	1	2	1	2	3	1	1	0	2
Helps in other ways	11	1	0	1	1	1	0	1	1	0	0	1	1	1	1	1	1	0	1	0	1	1	1	0	1
Other:	9	1	0	1	1	0	1	1	1	0	1	1	1	0	0	0	1	0	0	0	2	1	0	0	1

16) In your immediate family, does anyone do or has anyone done volunteer service? Multiple

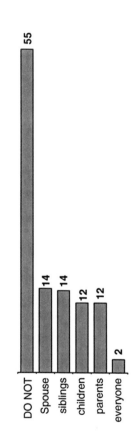

DO NOT	55
Spouse	14
siblings	14
children	12
parents	12
everyone	2

16) In your immediate family, does anyone do or has anyone done volunteer service? Multiple

	General		Gender		Age			Education			Income				Occupation				Marital status			Party sympathy			
	Abs	%	Men	Women	18–29	30–49	50+	Elem	Second	Higher	Low	M-L	M-H	High	Emp	Indep	House	NoAns	Married	Single	Other	PRI	PAN	PRD	None
	1,497	55	712	785	367	637	493	570	669	166	461	420	394	210	440	371	438	247	493	506	255	314	191	111	690
DO NOT	822	55	53	57	56	55	54	55	53	55	55	57	54	50	52	51	58	60	54	52	61	54	56	59	53
Spouse	213	14	16	13	8	16	16	17	12	15	15	12	14	16	15	16	14	9	20	1	1	18	13	14	14
Siblings	208	14	16	12	17	16	9	12	16	18	13	13	14	16	18	15	10	13	12	24	10	12	14	16	15
Children	177	12	12	12	1	9	23	15	8	10	12	12	11	12	8	15	13	10	15	2	13	16	11	12	10
Parents	177	12	13	10	22	12	4	8	16	14	11	9	15	13	14	12	9	12	8	26	9	9	11	8	14
Everyone	34	2	2	3	2	2	3	2	3	1	2	3	2	3	2	3	2	2	2	2	3	2	3	1	3

17) A total of how many do or have done it?

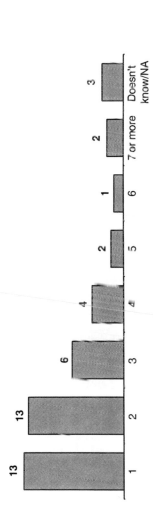

17) A total of how many do or have done it?

	General		Gender		Age			Education			Income				Occupation				Marital status			Party sympathy			
	Abs	%	Men	Women	18–29	30–49	50+	Elem	Second	Higher	Low	M-L	M-H	High	Emp	Indep	House	NoAns	Married	Single	Other	PRI	PAN	PRD	None
	1,497		712	785	367	637	493	570	669	156	465	420	394	210	440	371	438	247	493	506	255	314	191	111	690
NO RESPONSE	822	55	53	57	56	55	54	55	53	55	55	57	54	50	52	51	58	60	54	52	61	54	56	59	53
1	199	13	13	14	14	14	11	14	14	12	14	13	14	13	14	13	14	11	14	14	11	10	12	14	16
2	190	13	13	12	14	12	12	11	14	11	12	11	14	15	13	13	12	14	13	15	9	15	14	11	11
3	103	7	9	5	4	6	1	7	6	7	7	6	7	6	7	10	5	6	8	4	7	9	9	3	7
4	63	4	6	3	4	5	4	4	5	3	3	5	4	5	5	4	2	4	4	4	5	6	3	5	5
5	25	2	2	2	1	1	2	1	1	1	1	1	2	2	1	3	1	2	1	2	1	2	1	1	2
6	19	1	1	1	2	3	3	2	2	1	2	2	2	3	3	2	3	0	2	2	2	1	0	2	2
7 or more	33	2	2	2	4	2	4	2	2	3	3	2	2	3	3	3	3	1	2	5	3	2	3	2	2
Doesn't know/NA	43	3	2	3		2	2		3									2						5	3
Average		1.1	1.2	1.0	1.0	1.2	1.2	1.1	1.1	1.1	1.1	1.0	1.1	1.3	1.2	1.2	1.0	0.9	1.1	1.2	1.0	1.2	1.1	1.0	1.1

18) Have you invited other people to devote part of their time to helping others?

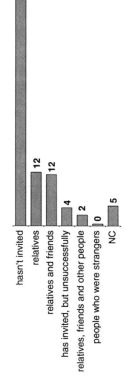

hasn't invited — 65
relatives — 12
relatives and friends — 12
has invited, but unsuccessfully — 4
relatives, friends and other people — 2
people who were strangers — 0
NC — 5

	General		Gender		Age			Education			Income				Occupation				Marital status			Party sympathy			
	Abs	%	Men	Women	18–29	30–49	50+	Elem	Second	Higher	Low	M-L	M-H	High	Emp	Indep	House	NoAns	Married	Single	Other	PRI	PAN	PRD	None
	1,497		712	785	367	637	493	570	669	166	461	420	394	210	440	371	438	247	493	506	255	314	191	111	690
18) Have you invited other people to devote part of their time to helping others?																									
Hasn't invited	970	65	64	66	66	64	65	64	64	66	64	64	67	63	64	61	66	69	62	64	73	63	62	63	68
Relatives	181	12	13	11	9	14	12	12	13	13	13	11	13	11	14	13	13	8	14	9	8	14	14	9	10
Relatives and friends	173	12	13	10	14	11	11	10	12	12	10	12	10	16	13	13	8	12	12	15	7	11	12	15	11
Has invited, but unsuccessfully	61	4	3	5	3	4	5	5	4	3	4	5	4	3	3	5	5	3	4	3	5	4	6	3	3
Relatives, friends, and other people	37	2	2	3	1	3	3	4	2	2	2	2	1	2	2	4	3	2	3	2	1	3	2	4	3
People who were strangers	7	0	0	0	0	1	0	1	0	0	0	1	1	0	0	1	1	0	1	0	0	0	2	2	0
NC	68	5	5	4	6	4	4	6	4	3	4	5	5	4	4	4	5	6	4	6	5	4	4	5	4

19) What activities have you invited them to? (multiple)

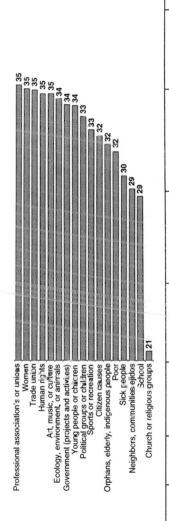

	Professional associations or unions	35
	Women	35
	Trade union	35
	Human rights	35
	Art, music, or culture	35
	Ecology, environment, or animals	34
	Government (projects and activities)	34
	Young people or children	34
	Political groups or children	33
	Sports or recreation	33
	Citizen causes	33
	Orphans, elderly, indigenous people	32
	Poor	32
	Sick people	30
	Neighbors, communities ejidos	29
	School	29
	Church or religious groups	21

19) What activities have you invited them to? (multiple)

	General		Gender		Age			Education			Income				Occupation				Marital status			Party sympathy			
	Abs	%	Men	Women	18–29	30–49	50+	Elem	Second	Higher	Low	M-L	M-H	High	Emp	Indep	House	NoAns	Married	Single	Other	PRI	PAN	PRD	None
	1,497		712	785	367	677	493	570	669	185	461	429	344	210	440	371	438	247	493	506	255	314	191	111	690
Professional associations or unions	527	35	36	34	34	36	35	36	35	34	36	36	33	37	35	36	36	31	38	38	36	37	38	37	32
Women	524	35	36	34	33	36	35	36	36	34	36	36	33	37	36	39	34	31	37	37	36	36	38	37	32
Trade union	523	35	36	34	34	36	36	35	36	33	36	36	32	36	35	39	34	30	37	37	36	36	38	37	32
Human rights	520	35	36	34	33	35	35	35	36	34	36	35	32	35	35	39	34	30	37	37	36	36	38	36	31
Art, music, or culture	520	35	35	34	33	35	35	36	35	33	36	36	32	35	35	38	34	31	37	37	36	37	38	37	31
Ecology, environment, or animals	516	34	35	34	32	34	35	35	35	33	36	35	32	36	35	37	34	30	36	34	34	36	38	35	30
Government (projects and activities)	511	34	35	34	33	33	35	35	35	33	35	35	31	36	35	37	34	31	36	36	35	35	37	35	31
Young people or children	510	34	35	33	33	34	35	35	35	32	35	35	32	33	35	38	33	30	35	35	35	33	36	37	31
Political groups of parties	501	33	33	34	31	34	34	34	34	30	34	34	32	33	34	37	33	28	35	35	35	33	36	36	30
Sports or recreation	490	33	32	34	30	34	34	34	34	25	34	34	30	33	32	36	34	28	34	34	33	33	36	33	30
Citizen causes	485	32	32	32	31	33	33	33	33	31	32	34	31	31	32	36	32	28	34	34	34	33	36	33	30
Orphans, elderly, indigenous people	478	32	34	30	31	32	33	34	32	31	32	33	30	30	33	34	31	30	33	34	34	32	34	34	30
Poor	472	32	34	29	31	32	32	33	32	31	32	32	29	30	33	34	31	30	33	33	31	34	34	34	29
Sick people	452	30	32	28	29	32	32	31	30	30	29	31	29	32	31	32	29	28	32	31	31	31	34	32	28
Neighbors, communities, ejidos	441	29	28	30	29	31	31	29	31	32	29	30	29	31	31	30	30	26	31	30	30	28	34	28	27
School	435	29	31	27	29	32	16	29	30	27	29	29	28	31	30	34	26	25	31	32	22	30	34	26	26
Church or religious groups	307	21	23	18	23	22	22	19	23	27	18	21	18	27	23	25	16	18	21	26	15	20	23	27	19
Other:	515	34	35	34	33	35	34	34	36	33	35	35	32	36	35	37	34	30	36	36	27	36	37	36	31

20) Are you in the habit of giving money or things to people who aren't your relatives?: multiple

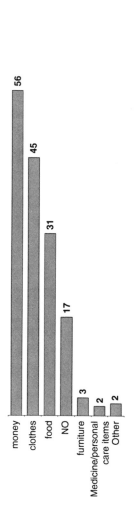

money   56
clothes   45
food   31
NO   17
furniture   3
Medicine/personal care items   2
Other   2

20) Are you in the habit of giving money or things to people who aren't your relatives?: multiple

	General		Gender		Age			Education			Income				Occupation				Marital status			Party sympathy			
	Abs	%	Men	Women	18–29	30–49	50+	Elem	Second	Higher	Low	M-L	M-H	High	Emp	Indep	House	NoAns	Married	Single	Other	PRI	PAN	PRD	None
	1,497	56	712	785	367	637	493	570	669	166	461	420	394	210	440	371	438	247	493	506	255	314	191	111	690
Money	841	56	59	54	56	54	59	55	55	69	46	58	60	67	58	54	52	62	55	58	55	58	59	56	56
Clothes	668	45	37	52	46	45	43	39	51	49	38	46	48	49	46	42	49	40	47	44	38	37	42	43	49
Food	471	31	27	36	26	31	37	35	30	23	34	33	30	25	29	36	34	24	34	26	28	33	29	23	31
NO	254	17	19	15	17	17	16	17	17	12	23	15	15	10	18	17	16	19	16	15	23	20	20	17	13
Furniture	46	3	4	2	3	3	3	2	2	4	2	2	5	4	4	3	3	2	4	2	1	1	2	4	4
Medicine / personal care items	25	2	2	2	1	2	2	2	2	2	2	1	2	1	3	1	2	0	2	1	2	1	0	4	2
Other:	32	2	3	2	3	2	2	1	3	5	2	2	3	3	2	3	1	3	2	1	2	2	2	5	2

21) How do you usually give? : multiple

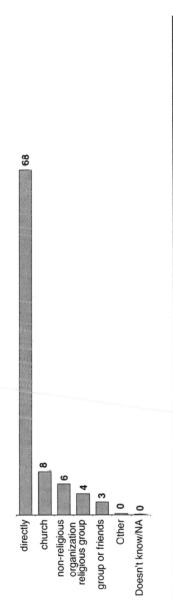

directly	68
church	8
non-religious organization	6
religious group	4
group or friends	3
Other	0
Doesn't know/NA	0

21) How do you usually give? : multiple

	General		Gender		Age			Education			Income				Occupation				Marital status			Party sympathy			
	Abs	%	Men	Women	18–29	30–49	50+	Elem	Second	Higher	Low	M-L	M-H	High	Emp	Indep	House	No Ans	Married	Single	Other	PRI	PAN	PRD	None
	1,497		712	785	367	637	403	570	669	156	451	420	364	210	440	371	438	247	493	506	255	314	191	111	690
Directly	1,014	68	67	69	68	68	67	68	68	68	63	71	72	67	67	66	68	71	68	68	67	66	65	68	70
Church	127	8	7	10	8	7	10	9	8	8	8	8	10	8	7	8	11	6	10	10	7	10	8	10	8
Non-religious organization	91	6	6	6	6	6	5	5	6	13	6	6	6	13	8	7	4	5	6	9	5	6	5	5	7
Religious group	63	4	3	5	4	3	5	5	3	2	5	4	4	4	3	4	6	3	4	4	4	4	3	5	4
Group of friends	38	3	2	3	4	3	2	2	1	4	3	2	2	4	1	3	3	2	3	3	3	2	4	4	3
Other	4	0	1	0	0	0	0	0	0	0	0	0	0	0	0	1	0	0	0	0	2	1	0	0	0
Doesn't know/NA	2	0	0	0	0	0	0	0	0	1	0	0	0	1	0	0	0	0	0	0	0	0	0	0	0

22) Did you say you have given money?

Doesn't know/NA, 4

No, 25

Yes, 54

	General		Gender		Age			Education			Income				Occupation				Marital status			Party sympathy			
	Abs	%	Men	Women	18–29	30–49	50+	Elem	Second	Higher	Low	M-L	M-H	High	Emp	Indep	House	NoAns	Married	Single	Other	PRI	PAN	PRD	None
	1,497		712	785	367	637	493	570	669	166	461	420	394	210	440	371	438	247	493	506	255	314	191	111	690
22) Did you say you have given money?																									
No	376	25	21	29	25	27	23	26	25	20	29	24	24	20	22	28	30	19	27	24	22	20	21	27	29
Yes	812	54	56	52	55	52	56	54	53	66	45	55	58	67	56	52	51	60	54	57	52	57	55	53	53
Doesn't know/NA	55	4	3	4	3	3	4	3	5	2	3	6	3	3	5	3	4	3	3	3	4	3	3	3	5
NO RESPONSE	254	17	19	15	17	17	16	17	17	12	23	15	15	10	18	17	16	19	16	15	23	20	20	17	13

22b) On the average, how much do you give a month?

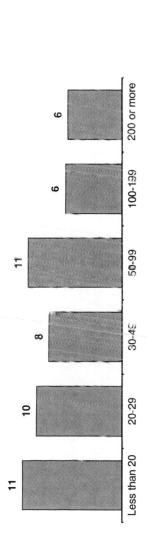

	Less than 20	20-29	30-49	50-99	100-139	200 or more
	11	10	8	11	6	6

22b) On the average, how much do you give a month?

	General		Gender		Age			Education			Income				Occupation				Marital status			Party sympathy			
	Abs	%	Men	Women	18–29	30–49	50+	Elem	Second	Higher	Low	M-L	M-H	High	Emp	Inde»	Hous»	NoAns	Married	Single	Other	PRI	PAN	PRD	None
	1,497		712	785	367	637	493	570	569	166	461	423	394	210	440	377	438	247	493	505	255	314	191	111	690
NO RESPONSE	630	42	40	44	42	44	40	43	42	42	52	40	39	39	43	44	45	37	43	39	44	39	41	44	42
Less than 20	170	11	11	11	11	9	15	16	8	8	15	11	9	9	9	12	13	12	12	12	9	10	10	8	13
20–29	146	10	10	10	10	10	10	13	8	4	9	12	9	9	9	9	11	11	10	10	10	10	8	12	11
30–49	125	8	8	8	10	9	6	9	8	8	7	7	13	8	9	8	8	9	8	10	8	10	4	9	9
50–99	161	11	11	11	13	9	11	8	12	14	8	7	14	10	10	12	9	12	10	11	13	11	14	5	9
100–199	97	6	8	6	6	7	5	4	8	11	3	5	7	14	8	5	5	8	7	6	5	7	9	9	5
200 or more	93	6	8	5	5	7	6	3	7	1	2	6	5	15	11	4	3	7	6	6	7	7	4	8	4
Doesn't know/NA	75	5	4	5	4	5	6	4	6	6	4	6	5	5	6	5	5	4	5	5	5	4	4	5	6
Average		46	52	41	44	48	45	51	51	80	23	45	52	85	62	38	34	53	45	46	49	52	60	52	37

23) How do you give it?

	48
Coins	
bills	5
Doesn't know/NA	4
monthly payment	1
check	0
credit card	0
Different promotion	0
Other	0

	General		Gender		Age			Education			Income				Occupation				Marital status			Party sympathy			
	Abs	%	Men	Women	18–29	30–49	50+	Elem	Second	Higher	Low	M-L	M-H	High	Emp	Indep	House	NoAns	Married	Single	Other	PRI	PAN	PRD	None
	1,497		712	785	367	637	493	570	669	166	461	420	394	210	440	371	438	247	493	506	255	314	191	111	690
23) How do you give it?																									
NO RESPONSE	630	42	40	44	42	44	40	43	42	32	52	40	39	30	40	44	45	37	43	39	44	39	41	44	42
Coins	715	48	50	46	49	46	50	49	46	51	41	48	52	55	47	48	46	52	47	51	47	51	47	49	47
Bills	73	5	5	5	5	5	5	4	5	7	3	6	4	8	6	3	5	6	5	5	4	4	6	5	5
Doesn't know/NA	55	4	3	4	3	3	4	3	5	2	3	6	3	3	5	3	4	3	3	3	4	3	3	3	5
Monthly payment	8	1	1	1	1	0	0	0	0	2	0	0	0	1	1	1	0	0	1	1	0	1	1	0	0
Check	6	0	1	0	0	0	0	0	0	4	0	0	0	2	0	0	0	0	0	0	0	1	1	0	0
Credit card	4	0	0	1	0	0	0	0	0	1	0	0	1	0	0	1	0	1	0	0	0	0	0	0	0
Different promotions	4	0	0	0	0	0	0	0	0	1	0	0	0	0	0	0	0	0	0	0	0	0	1	0	0
Other	2	0	0	0	0	0	0	0	0	0	0	0	0	0	0	0	0	0	0	0	0	0	1	0	0

24) Have you received any help?: multiple

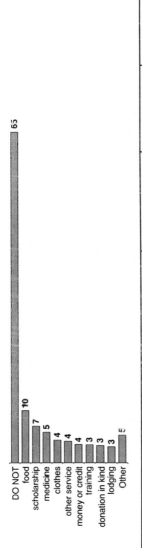

24) Have you received any help?: multiple			
DO NOT	65		
food	10		
scholarship	7		
medicine	5		
clothes	4		
other service	4		
money or credit	4		
training	3		
donation in kind	3		
lodging	3		
Other	5		

	General		Gender		Age			Education			Income				Occupation				Marital status			Party sympathy			
	Abs	%	Men	Women	18–29	30–49	50+	Elem	Second	Higher	Low	M-L	M-H	High	Emp	Indep	House	No/Ans	Married	Single	Other	PRI	PAN	PRD	None
	1,497		712	785	367	637	493	570	669	16	461	420	394	210	440	371	438	247	493	506	255	314	191	111	690
DO NOT	967	65	65	64	64	70	58	61	68	70	51	64	66	68	71	71	66	56	67	62	61	60	69	59	64
Food	152	10	8	12	6	8	16	14	7	2	16	10	7	4	5	10	14	13	9	8	14	14	9	16	8
Scholarship	107	7	6	8	10	7	5	6	6	1	5	8	9	7	7	8	8	9	7	10	6	7	7	6	8
Medicine	89	6	5	7	7	5	7	5	6	1	6	7	6	3	4	5	6	4	6	5	8	10	2	5	6
Clothes	66	4	3	6	4	3	5	5	3	1	6	5	3	4	3	5	6	4	3	5	7	6	4	4	6
Other service	63	4	4	4	3	3	6	5	3	4	5	5	4	4	3	6	3	5	4	4	6	2	4	4	4
Money or credit	54	4	4	3	4	3	4	3	3	7	1	4	4	2	6	4	2	4	3	5	4	5	3	9	5
Training	53	4	5	3	4	3	4	4	4	7	2	3	3	4	6	4	2	4	3	5	3	5	4	4	4
Donation in kind	50	3	2	4	1	3	4	3	4	3	4	4	3	6	2	2	4	2	4	2	3	2	4	3	3
Lodging	47	3	4	2	4	3	5	3	2	4	4	3	3	8	3	5	4	3	2	3	5	5	3	4	3
Other	81	5	7	4	3	5	8	7	4	4	4	5	6	8	6	5	4	7	6	5	6	8	5	6	5

25) Who did you receive it from?: multiple

	government	17
	person (not related)	11
	church	4
	political organization	2
	private organization	2
	other kind of organization	1
	Other	1

	General		Gender		Age			Education			Income				Occupation				Marital status			Party sympathy			
	Abs	%	Men	Women	18–29	30–49	50+	Elem	Second	Higher	Low	M-L	M-H	High	Emp	Indep	House	NoAns	Married	Single	Other	PRI	PAN	PRD	None
	1,497		712	785	367	637	493	570	669	166	461	420	394	210	440	371	438	247	493	506	255	314	191	111	690
25) Who did you receive it from?: multiple																									
Government	248	17	15	18	15	15	19	20	13	13	19	18	15	12	12	17	19	20	16	16	17	21	14	15	17
Person (not related)	164	11	11	11	12	8	14	12	10	10	14	9	9	12	10	14	9	12	9	14	14	11	8	16	11
Church	64	4	4	5	3	4	6	5	4	2	4	5	5	3	3	4	5	6	3	5	6	6	4	2	4
Political organization	30	2	3	2	1	2	3	2	2	1	2	3	2	3	2	2	2	3	2	1	3	4	3	5	1
Private organization	23	2	2	1	2	2	1	2	2	4	0	1	1	2	2	2	1	2	2	2	0	1	1	1	2
Other kind of organization	19	1	1	1	1	1	2	1	1	1	1	1	1	1	1	1	1	1	1	1	1	2	0	3	1
Other	15	1	1	1	1	1	1	1	1	1	1	1	1	2	1	1	1	1	1	1	0	1	2	0	1

26) Do you remember when you received it?: multiple

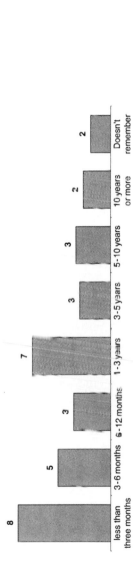

	less than three months	3-6 months	6-12 months	1-3 years	3-5 years	5-10 years	10 years or more	Doesn't remember
value	8	5	3	7	3	3	2	2

26) Do you remember when you received it?: multiple

	General		Gender		Age			Education			Income				Occupation				Marital status			Party sympathy			
	Abs	%	Men	Women	18–29	30–49	50+	Elem	Second	Higher	Low	M-L	M-H	High	Emp	Indep	House	NoAns	Married	Single	Other	PRI	PAN	PRD	None
	1,497		712	785	367	637	463	570	569	156	61	420	394	210	440	371	438	247	493	506	255	314	191	111	690
Less than three months	125	8	6	10	10	7	9	9	7	5	11	8	8	5	5	5	9	13	7	12	8	6	9	5	9
3-6 months	71	5	6	4	2	5	5	5	4	2	6	4	5	4	4	7	4	5	4	5	6	5	4	9	6
6-12 months	50	3	3	4	3	5	4	5	3	4	5	4	2	0	3	2	5	2	3	2	5	4	3	4	3
1–3 years	106	7	6	8	9	6	8	7	6	4	7	7	7	7	6	6	8	10	6	9	7	9	7	6	7
3–5 years	42	3	3	3	4	3	3	3	3	4	3	2	3	4	3	4	3	2	2	2	4	3	3	5	3
5–10 years	47	3	4	3	2	4	5	2	2	4	3	4	2	4	4	4	3	4	4	2	3	5	4	3	3
10 years or more	37	2	3	2	1	2	2	2	2	2	1	1	2	3	1	3	1	2	3	2	2	3	1	5	2
Doesn't remember	27	2	2	2	2	2	2	2	2	2	2	2	3	3	2	3	1	2	3	2	3	2	2	2	2
Average (years)	2.9		3.4	2.5	2.4	2.2	3.9	2.7	2.9	4.8	2.5	2.9	2.9	4.1	3.5	3.4	2.3	2.6	3.3	2.4	2.5	3.0	3.8	3.8	2.6

27) Do you belong to some group?

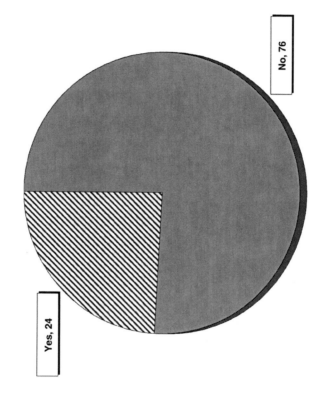

Yes, 24

No, 76

	General		Gender		Age			Education			Income				Occupation				Marital status				Party sympathy			
	Abs	%	Men	Women	18–29	30–49	50+	Elem	Second	Higher	Low	M-L	M-H	High	Emp	Indep	House	NoAns	Married	Single	Other	PRI	PAN	PRD	None
	1,497		712	785	367	637	493	570	669	166	461	420	394	210	440	371	438	247	493	506	255	314	191	111	690
27) Do you belong to some group?																									
No	1,135	76	73	78	77	75	75	78	75	67	79	81	73	66	75	73	78	78	73	76	84	75	72	69	78
Yes	362	24	27	22	23	25	25	22	25	33	21	19	27	34	25	27	22	22	27	24	16	25	28	31	22

27) Group belonged to: multiple

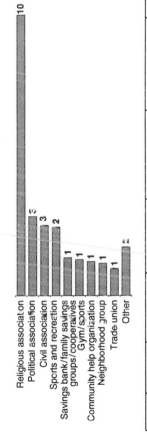

Religious association	10
Political association	3
Civil association	3
Sports and recreation	2
Savings bank/family savings groups/cooperatives	1
Gym/sports	1
Community help organization	1
Neighborhood group	1
Trade union	1
Other	

27) Group belonged to: multiple	General		Gender		Age			Education			Income				Occupation				Marital status			Party sympathy			
	Abs	%	Men	Women	18–29	30–49	50+	Elem	Second	Higher	Low	M-L	M-H	High	Emp	indep	House	NoAns	Married	Single	Other	PRI	PAN	PRD	None
	1,497		712	785	367	637	493	570	669	66	461	429	334	210	440	371	438	247	493	506	255	314	191	111	690
Religious association	156	10	8	13	8	10	13	12	9	8	11	10	10	11	8	10	15	8	12	9	7	10	16	9	10
Political association	44	3	4	2	2	3	3	3	3	5	3	2	3	4	4	4	1	3	2	2	2	6	3	9	0
Civil association	39	3	4	2	2	3	3	3	3	4	1	2	3	6	3	4	1	2	3	3	3	2	2	4	3
Sports and recreation	38	3	4	1	4	3	1	1	3	5	2	2	4	4	4	2	1	3	2	2	1	3	2	2	3
Savings bank/family savings group/cooperatives	21	1	1	1	1	2	1	2	2	1	1	1	2	2	2	2	2	0	1	1	2	1	1	2	2
Gym/Sports	20	1	2	1	1	1	1	1	2	2	2	0	2	3	1	2	0	2	1	3	1	0	2	3	2
Community help organization	19	1	1	1	2	1	1	1	2	2	2	1	2	1	2	2	1	1	1	3	1	0	0	1	1
Neighborhood group	18	1	2	0	1	2	1	1	1	3	2	1	2	2	2	2	0	0	1	1	0	1	2	1	1
Trade union	15	1	2	2	0	1	1	1	1	3	2	3	2	2	1	2	1	1	2	1	1	3	0	3	2
Other	27	2	2	2	2	2	2	2	2	1	2	1	2	3	3	3	2	2	2	2	1	3	2	1	1

28a) And the first group, is it a...? multiple

Church or religious group (construction, cleaning, prayer, etc.): 11
Sports or recreation: 4
Political groups or parties: 3
Neighbors, communities, ejidos: 2
School (students, parents, teachers, etc.): 1
Trade union: 1
Citizen causes: 1
Sick people (Red Cross, hospitals, etc.): 1
Other: 4

28a) And the first group, is it a...? multiple	General		Gender		Age			Education			Income				Occupation				Marital status			Party sympathy			
	Abs	%	Men	Women	18–29	30–49	50+	Elem	Second	Higher	Low	M-L	M-H	High	Emp	Indep	House	NoAns	Married	Single	Other	PRI	PAN	PRD	None
	1,497		712	785	367	637	493	570	669	166	461	420	394	210	440	371	438	247	493	506	255	314	191	111	690
Church or religious group (construction, cleaning, prayer, etc.)	169	11	9	13	9	10	14	14	10	8	13	10	11	11	9	12	15	10	13	13	8	11	15	9	11
Sports or recreation	60	4	6	2	8	4	2	1	5	10	3	2	5	9	6	4	1	6	3	9	2	4	4	4	4
Political groups or parties	38	3	4	1	2	3	2	2	3	4	3	2	2	4	3	4	1	2	3	2	2	6	3	5	0
Neighbors, communities, ejidos	28	2	3	1	1	3	3	1	3	1	1	2	2	2	2	4	1	1	2	2	1	1	3	2	2
School (students, parents, teachers, etc.)	16	1	1	1	1	1	1	1	1	2	1	1	2	1	2	2	2	1	1	1	1	1	1	3	1
Trade union	11	1	1	0	0	1	1	0	1	3	0	0	1	2	2	1	0	0	1	0	0	2	0	1	1
Citizen causes	10	1	1	1	1	1	0	0	0	2	0	1	1	2	1	1	1	0	1	1	0	0	0	0	1
Sick people (Red Cross, hospitals, etc.)	9	1	0	1	1	1	0	0	1	1	0	1	1	1	1	1	0	0	0	0	1	0	0	0	0
Other	60	4	5	3	4	4	4	3	4	6	2	3	6	7	5	5	4	2	5	4	2	4	5	7	3

28b) And the first group, is it a...? multiple

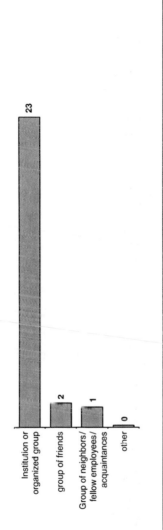

Institution or organized group	23
group of friends	2
Group of neighbors/fellow employees/acquaintances	1
other	0

28b) And the first group, is it a...? multiple

	General		Gender		Age			Education			Income				Occupation				Marital status			Party sympathy			
	Abs	%	Men	Women	18–29	30–49	50+	Elem	Second	Higher	Low	M-L	M-H	High	Emp	Indep	House	NoAns	Married	Single	Other	PRI	PAN	PRD	None
	1,497		712	785	367	637	493	570	692	166	461	420	394	210	440	371	438	247	493	506	255	314	191	111	690
Institution or organized group	338	23	24	21	24	23	24	21	23	31	20	19	24	33	23	25	21	20	26	22	14	24	26	29	20
Group of friends	23	2	2	1	2	2	2	1	2	2	2	1	2	1	2	2	0	1	1	3	1	2	2	1	1
Group of neighbors/fellow employees/ acquaintances	19	1	2	1	2	1	1	1	2	2	0	1	3	1	1	2	1	0	1	1	2	1	2	1	1
Other	2	0	0	0	0	0	0	0	0	1	0	0	1	0	0	0	0	0	0	0	0	0	1	0	0

29) Tell me for each one, who much do you trust them? % a lot/some (−) little/not at all

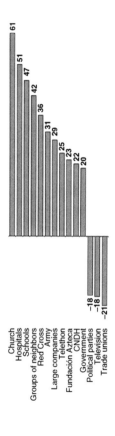

29) Tell me for each one, who much do you trust them? % a lot/some (−) little/not at all

	General		Gender		Age			Education			Income				Occupation				Marital status			Party sympathy			
	Abs	%	Men	Women	18–29	30–49	50+	Elem	Second	Higher	Low	M-L	M-H	High	Emp	Indep	House	NoAns	Married	Single	Other	PRI	PAN	PRD	None
	1,497		712	785	367	637	493	570	669	166	461	420	394	210	440	371	438	247	493	506	255	314	191	111	690
Church		61	53	68	59	57	67	72	55	43	66	59	60	53	51	60	74	55	67	47	56	76	73	42	50
Hospitals		51	54	49	53	53	47	51	51	47	50	55	52	48	53	54	51	45	54	48	46	60	58	41	47
Schools		47	46	47	54	47	41	46	47	42	49	40	48	53	48	46	46	46	43	48	56	48	46	50	45
Groups of neighbors		42	45	40	44	45	37	39	46	40	44	35	44	50	50	34	37	38	40	50	41	53	42	49	33
Red Cross		36	38	34	43	35	32	35	36	40	36	34	37	40	38	34	35	37	34	41	39	42	31	43	31
Army		31	38	25	40	34	21	25	34	43	29	21	38	45	35	30	25	38	27	38	38	38	36	23	28
Large companies		29	33	25	41	34	13	16	35	57	16	23	38	53	39	26	21	29	25	34	35	34	38	23	24
Telethon		25	25	24	34	28	14	29	24	26	22	22	30	26	30	20	25	29	24	29	23	30	35	14	21
Fundación Azteca		23	25	22	36	26	9	22	26	26	16	21	31	25	30	20	22	21	21	33	17	27	32	15	19
CNDH		23	23	22	25	27	6	15	27	30	16	16	28	32	30	19	16	19	19	30	21	22	21	17	23
Government		22	28	16	25	22	17	18	17	38	15	19	24	29	20	18	18	28	15	30	29	36	42	17	8
Political parties		−18	−12	−22	−9	−22	−19	−13	−23	−8	−20	−18	−16	−12	−17	−22	−18	−12	−22	−16	−6	5	10	−7	−37
Television		−18	−16	−19	−14	−15	−25	−20	−15	−17	−22	−18	−15	−13	−20	−14	−18	−18	−18	−21	−13	−4	−4	−24	−30
Trade unions		−21	−19	−22	−1	−24	−30	−26	−17	−11	−23	−20	−19	−18	−25	−23	−20	−9	−27	−4	−18	−11	−12	−23	−28

30) Would you say that most people can or can't be trusted?

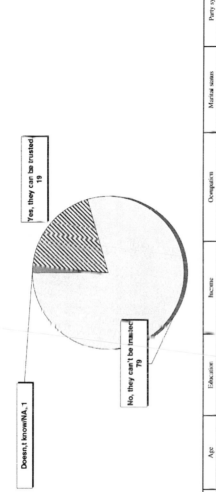

Doesn,t know/NA, 1

Yes, they can be trusted 19

No, they can't be trusted 79

	General		Gender		Age			Education			Income				Occupation				Marital status			Party sympathy			
	Abs	%	Men	Women	18–29	30–49	50+	Elem	Second	Higher	Low	M-L	M-H	High	Emp	Indep	House	NoAns	Married	Single	Other	PRI	PAN	PRD	None
	1,497		712	785	367	637	493	570	669	185	461	420	394	210	440	371	438	247	493	506	255	314	191	111	690
30) Would you say that most people can or can't be trusted?																									
Doesn't know/NA	21	1	1	2	2	2	1	1	2	2	1	2	2	0	3	0	1	2	1	2	1	1	4	1	1
Yes, they can be trusted	288	19	22	15	16	18	23	18	13	29	19	18	22	18	21	21	15	23	19	20	19	19	29	22	16
No, they can't be trusted	1,188	79	77	82	82	80	76	81	80	69	80	80	76	81	76	79	83	78	80	78	80	81	67	77	83

31) Some activities, and tell me if... (% regularly)

	Vote in elections	58
Keep informed about what's happening in the country		47
Some activities and tell me if... Attending church or parish activities		35
Attending neighborhood, community, or school activities		22
Participating in neighborhood, community, or school decisions		22
Being a member of some group		18
Attending meetings of your group		18
Signing a petition		15
Participating in an unauthorized strike		1

	General		Gender		Age			Education			Income				Occupation				Marital status			Party sympathy			
	Abs	%	Men	Women	18–29	30–49	50+	Elem	Second	Higher	Low	M-L	M-H	High	Emp	Indep	House	NoAns	Married	Single	Other	PRI	PAN	PRD	None
	1,497		712	785	367	637	493	570	669	166	461	420	394	210	440	371	438	247	493	506	255	314	191	111	690
31) Some activities, and tell me if... (% regularly)																									
Vote in elections	870	58	58	58	46	62	62	59	55	66	55	59	58	63	61	59	58	51	62	52	52	68	67	60	56
Keep informed about what's happening in the country	707	47	52	43	46	51	44	41	50	69	39	46	50	62	53	44	43	48	50	47	41	45	53	52	51
Some activities and tell me if... Attending church or parish activities	525	35	31	39	27	34	43	41	32	25	38	36	35	29	28	40	41	31	39	29	27	34	41	25	35
Attending neighborhood, community, or school activities	330	22	22	22	20	23	22	26	20	19	24	21	23	19	17	28	25	16	26	20	13	25	17	23	23
Participating in neighborhood, community, or school decisions	328	22	24	20	19	24	22	23	22	21	23	22	22	21	22	28	21	13	27	17	12	26	16	22	23
Being a member of some group	267	18	21	15	16	17	21	15	19	27	15	15	20	23	21	21	15	13	21	17	10	18	19	23	16
Attending meetings of your group	263	18	20	16	16	17	19	16	19	26	15	16	20	21	20	20	15	13	21	17	8	19	20	20	16
Signing a petition	230	15	17	14	13	16	16	16	13	23	14	15	17	18	17	18	13	12	19	12	10	21	13	20	14
Participating in an unauthorized strike	18	1	2	1	1	1	1	1	1	1	1	1	1	2	2	2	0	0	1	2	1	2	1	3	1

32) On the average, about how many hours of free time do you have a week?

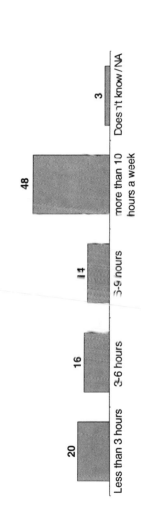

	Less than 3 hours	3-6 hours	3-9 hours	more than 10 hours a week	Does'n't know/NA
	20	16	14	48	3

32) On the average, about how many hours of free time do you have a week?

	General		Gender		Age			Education			Income				Occupation				Marital status			Party sympathy			
	Abs	%	Men	Women	18–29	30–45	53+	Elem	Second	Higher	Low	M–L	M–H	High	Emp	Indep	House	NoAns	Married	Single	Other	PRI	PAN	PRD	None
	1,497		712	785	367	637	493	570	669	168	461	430	394	210	440	371	438	247	493	506	255	314	191	111	690
Less than 3 hours	293	20	15	15	14	19	24	24	16	28	23	19	19	16	20	21	23	9	22	11	19	15	20	17	22
3–6 h	234	16	16	15	19	16	12	15	16	4	16	16	16	13	18	16	14	13	15	16	16	17	14	12	16
6–9 h	205	14	14	13	12	17	11	12	15	11	15	15	12	13	16	13	13	11	14	15	10	14	16	10	13
more than 10 h a week	719	48	52	44	52	45	49	46	52	55	43	47	50	56	43	46	46	64	45	55	51	52	46	57	46
Doesn't know/NA	46	3	3	3	2	3	4	3	3	2	3	3	3	2	2	4	4	2	3	2	5	2	3	5	3
Average (hours)	8.1		8.6	7.7	8.5	8.0	8.1	7.8	8.2	8.6	7.7	8.1	8.2	8.8	7.8	7.9	7.9	9.5	7.9	8.9	8.3	8.5	8.0	8.8	7.9

33) If close to your home... how likely or unlikely is it that you would do it?

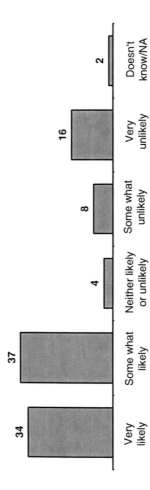

33) If close to your home... how likely or unlikely is it that you would do it?

	General		Gender		Age			Education			Income				Occupation				Marital status			Party sympathy			
	Abs	%	Men	Women	18–29	30–49	50+	Elem	Second	Higher	Low	M-L	M-H	High	Emp	Indep	House	NoAns	Married	Single	Other	PRI	PAN	PRD	None
	1,497		712	785	367	637	493	570	669	166	461	420	394	210	440	371	438	247	493	506	255	314	191	111	690
Very likely	507	34	34	34	36	34	32	30	37	43	28	36	37	34	33	37	33	33	34	38	30	35	36	32	31
Somewhat likely	553	37	35	38	39	41	29	42	36	29	42	33	35	38	36	36	41	34	38	37	33	36	37	38	38
Neither likely or unlikely	53	4	4	3	5	3	3	4	4	4	2	3	5	4	4	4	2	3	4	4	3	4	4	3	3
Somewhat unlikely	114	8	7	8	8	6	9	6	8	9	8	7	7	9	8	9	6	8	7	7	9	6	7	8	9
Very unlikely	245	16	18	15	10	14	25	15	14	16	17	18	15	13	18	15	13	20	15	12	23	18	16	18	17
Doesn't know/NA	25	2	2	2	1	2	2	2	1	1	2	1	1	1	2	1	2	2	2	1	3	1	2	2	2
Likely (-) unlikely		*47*	*44*	*49*	*56*	*56*	*28*	*50*	*50*	*46*	*45*	*44*	*50*	*50*	*43*	*48*	*54*	*39*	*49*	*57*	*31*	*47*	*50*	*43*	*43*

34) If you could do it, how much time do you think you could devote a week?

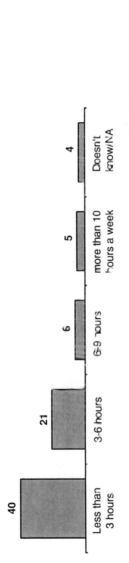

40	21	6	5	4
Less than 3 hours	3-6 hours	6-9 hours	more than 10 hours a week	Doesn't know/NA

34) If you could do it, how much time do you think you could devote a week?

	General		Gender		Age			Education			Income				Occupation				Marital status			Party sympathy			
	Abs	%	Men	Women	18-29	30-49	50+	Elem	Second	higher	Low	M-L	M-H	High	Emp	Indep	House	NoAns	Married	Single	Other	PRI	PAN	PRD	None
	1,497		712	785	367	637	493	570	569	166	46	420	392	210	440	371	438	247	493	566	255	314	191	111	690
NO RESPONSE	359	24	25	23	19	20	33	22	22	34	25	25	22	22	26	24	24	23	23	19	32	24	23	26	26
Less than 3 h	602	40	36	44	41	44	35	45	38	39	42	40	40	39	39	40	44	30	45	37	30	37	47	34	41
3-6 h	309	21	22	19	24	22	16	21	25	19	19	18	24	23	22	18	20	23	19	26	21	25	18	23	18
6-9 h	94	6	7	5	6	7	6	5		6	4	8	5	5	6	9	5	6	7	6	5	7	4	6	6
More than 10 h a week	74	5	5	5	7	4	4	4		6	4	5	5	6	4	5	5	9	3	9	5	6	4	6	5
Doesn't know/NA	59	4	5	3	2	4	5	4			4	4	5	4	4	5	3	4	4	3	6	2	4	3	4
Average (hours)	3.9		4.1	3.7	4.1	3.7	3.9	3.5	4.1	4.0	3.7	4.0	3.9	4.1	3.7	3.9	3.5	4.6	3.6	4.4	4.2	4.1	3.5	4.3	3.8

Appendix III
Technological Support for Gathering Qualitative Information

Ernesto Benavides

The purpose of this appendix is to describe the process started by the Instituto Tecnológico y de Estudios Superiores de Monterrey to gather the information corresponding to the qualitative phase of the investigation. The type of information technology used and the way the tool selected permitted constant interaction between the coordinator of the qualitative area, the technical coordinator, and the team that gathered the information is described.

Background

For the Tecnológico de Monterrey, knowledge and interaction with the different communities in the areas where their campuses are located is a constant point of attention. In this regard, the participation of the institution in this investigation on citizen action and solidarity service, which led to this book, was part of the concerns shared by all the members of our community.

The institution supported this investigation with professional personnel from the Social Training Program. During the qualitative phase, 12 professionals from different campuses participated, gathering information that included participant observation and indepth interviews with diverse people involved in various nonprofit organizations. The participation of our professionals with community development experience also opened up possibilities for developing social investigation abilities on the team. The coordinator of the qualitative area added anthropological tools to their experience in order to carry out the participant investigation and indepth interviews.

For the case studies, 12 organizations were picked from among a broad range of organizations that are located in different regions of Mexico and that have the common characteristic of having maintained a formal relationship with the Tecnológico de Monterrey for seven years through the "Institutional Strengthening" program. It promotes the development of quality social service by the students, which makes them "training partners" of the ITESM. These organizations have contributed to the institution by way of designing better ways of undertaking projects that receive service providers and volunteers. The close prior work relationship with the organizations studied made it possible to guarantee their formal and professional participation in the investigation. A technological platform licensed for use by the Instituto Tecnológico de Monterrey was also utilized by the work team and the coordinator of the qualitative area. This platform was coordinated with the person responsible for the technical area at the institution.

A close working relationship based on mutual respect was established while developing the investigation among the field investigators, the leader of the organization, and the people interviewed. This working relationship was affirmed in a verbal agreement in which the conditions and responsibilities of each one of the participants in gathering the information were established.

The Use of Information and Communication Technologies

The information and communication technological resources that were used in the investigation are analyzed in this section, structured around a collaboration work tool. Special emphasis is placed on the ability of the technological platform used to allow for interaction and communication among the members of the team that gathered the field information, the technical coordinator, and the coordinator of the qualitative area, as well as making it possible for the information to be available to all team members.

The idea of including the technological platform arose for the purpose of innovation in the ways of documenting, improving, and transferring information gathered in social investigations such as this one. Beyond simply storing information, the platform represented an innovation and contributed in an effective way in doing the field work.

The Technological Platform

The technological and communications platform employed consists of three elements:

1. Facilitating exchange of information, sending and receiving messages, files, data, or documents among the field investigators, the technical coordinator, and the area coordinator, without depending on direct contact or the limited interaction during certain meeting times.
2. Making possible information exchange through computers connected to a network, with the possibility of sharing content that each user may modify and the use of chat rooms. The result was fluid, daily interaction among the participants. In fact, this element was used a great deal during the initial phase of the investigation. It also makes possible synchronous collaboration among the actors involved in the field work.
3. Contributing to organizing the group activities during development of the investigation. This characteristic was very important, since it was possible to agree upon dates and a schedule for carrying out the activities, send instructions and reminders to the participants, organize and follow up on actions, control the

flow of activities undertaken, and to manage the tasks and documents in a well-structured process framework. Each actor was to have platform access privileges assigned by the technical coordinator. In practice, both the technical coordinator and the area coordinator could log on to review the information gathered, which smoothed the progress of the responsibilities of the team members. The area coordinator was able to guide the participants throughout the work of collecting data, answering questions, correcting interviews, and posing new questions.

The use of the technological platform made it possible to put into practice new ways of interacting with the team members on the part of the coordinator of the qualitative area, as well as making it possible to guide and review the information coming in and share experiences among all participants. This contributed to generating new knowledge about how to carry out interviews and take advantage of the experiences of others, thus facilitating the process of gathering information.

Characteristics of the Technological Platform

A platform was chosen that was easy to use, even for someone without previous experience in intensive use of information and communication technology collaborative work tools. This was favorable for accompanying and guiding the field investigators and providing different communication and information exchange options. The platform was permanently adapted to the design of the investigation and not the opposite. It also fostered both formal and informal simple interaction processes in small groups during the development of the data collection phase.

Communication between each field investigator and the area coordinator was documented at all times, so it is possible to use the chronologically ordered and saved files to tell how each interview developed from beginning to end. In fact, given the nature of the equipment, decisions were made during the process that made the communication and documentation process more efficient. The sequence of stages of work completed was registered and accessible for review at all times. This element is essential for replicating the experience in other investigations.

Each participant had the oportunity to identify where they were at each moment in regards to their coordination, advisory, or field work, which facilitated self-evaluation of the learning process that each member developed during the information gathering phase. The result was a series of synergies that favored quality field interviews, their transcription, and final satisfactory conclusion.

The platform made it possible for the technical coordinator and the area coordinator to find out about the degree of evolution of the overall process and what each field investigator was experiencing, so as to be able to provide them with the required support and advice in a timely way.

Another basic element is the fact that the platform is stable. This has to do with the technological infrastructure supporting the tool, the hardware, software, and human support resources. All of these are essential elements that made it possible to guarantee good results. This is due to prior experience of more than 10 years on the part of the Tecnológico de Monterrey, the institution that provided the technological platform.

The Use of *Blackboard* in this Investigation

The Tecnológico de Monterrey has developed ample experience in the use of this technology in order to facilitate educational processes and training of its professorial staff. This experience and the use rights to this tool made it possible to train the field investigators and the area coordinator, facilitating team integration and communication in order to collect field information.

Blackboard (Bb). In order to have access to the platform, a software license, an e-mail account and an access password are necessary. These elements were provided by the Tecnológico de Monterrey for the entire team involved in the process.

Those team members collecting the case study information, had student-category access, while the general coordinator, platform technical coordinator, and the area coordinator had instructor access.

The initial procedure consisted of the field investigators from the different campuses sending the information collected to the technological facilitator, who was responsible for uploading the information in folders. At first, none of the participants had access to the information sent by others. This proved to not be very learning efficient, so the strategy was modified so as to establish the most appropriate way for transferring information to all participants, which allowed the area coordinator to interact and share concerns with all those involved. A discussion board was opened for this purpose for all the team members.

In the initial phase, although the field investigators and the qualitative area coordinator had been trained to use this tool for specific purposes, the lack of practice and familiarity with it made feedback for each field investigator difficult. It was decided to use e-mail for feedback, which would be uploaded to the platform. As a result, parts of the process were not recorded. It was necessary to carry out some practice sessions to improve the process, which made it possible for the technological coordinator to establish the technological platform as the means of communication for the entire process. Control over use of the platform was obtained with this corrective measure, and the data that were being transferred, as well as the exchanges among the participants, began to be put in order.

Benefits from Using the Technological Platform

The following benefits were realized at the end of the process of gathering the information as a corollary to the technical coordination actions:

(a) A record of the data from each field investigator during the process was available to be checked so as to improve any aspect of the field investigation.

(b) Structured and accessible information, making the data related to the investigation, is available for the future, although it was not included in the final report because of space considerations. Similarly, it is possible to replicate the process, since files describing the process followed are available.

(c) All the aspects of the work, policies, instructions, working conditions, agreements, and support and reference materials were recorded and are easily accessible.

(d) Online feedback from the qualitative area coordinator. The information accumulated through the feedback to each investigator, in addition to being recorded, allows for future analytical and systematization exercises.

(e) Chats to reinforce some subject of general interest to the group or a part of the group. These exercises were very helpful and economical and provided simultaneous geographical coverage for the areas where each investigator was located. The results and process of discussion were accessible to all participants.

(f) Discussion forums. When it was necessary to open up a subject for discussion in which all actors needed to participate, this was done without the need to meet at the same time and place. The information for generating discussion in these forums was registered and each participant contributed at the time it was possible for them to do so. Once a discussion came to an end, the information derived from it was accessible for all participants to review.

(g) Recording information and the process of developing it. The information was safely recorded and saved and was also accessible.

(h) Teamwork. Effective communication was maintained among the participants, thus breaking through time and space barriers that are typical of a field investigation of this nature and degree of complexity.

    (i) Documentation of the entire field investigation process, which was an indispensable element for assuring the process of transferring this experience to new investigators.

In addition to complying with the methodological rigor demanded by the investigation, learning was also promoted by means of interchanges of opinions and points of view between field investigators. The importance of this interaction is not the quantity of interchanges and interventions but rather the degree of influence such interaction has on the participants' learning process. In summary, things were learned by all participants from joint reflection, the exchange of ideas, and analysis of a common subject, and an enriched outcome was obtained from this process.

By means of the synchronous communication developed during the phase of gathering information in the field, each participant improved their technique, expressed concerns, and received feedback, both directly from the area coordinator and from what their colleagues submitted in written form, so each participant was able to contribute their thoughts and experience throughout the process.

The Tecnológico de Monterrey contributed the technological platform and their experience with it without additional cost for this investigation. This was a key element allowing for the communication of information and thoughts among the participants. This experience has made it possible to establish connections between seasoned investigators and new generations in the Social Training area of the Instituto Tecnológico y de Estudios Superiores de Monterrey.

Information and communication technologies are promoting generational changes in different social environments, and the area of investigation is not the exception. The differences of the generations are significant. While the new generations incorporate the use of technology in most of their activities, older people are generally more cautious about its use.

Finally, it is worthwhile to emphasize the value added in this experience, its innovative character, the savings in terms of efficiency and time use, the spatial coverage, the quality of the feedback for each activity without time and space restrictions, the uniformity in response times, the continual improvement of the interactive process among all the participants, and the ability to do the work under uniform conditions in the current social environment.

Appendix IV
Interview Guide

María Guadalupe Serna

Interviews were performed with four types of people within the organizations analyzed for this study: the director or informal leader of the organization, the founder (when possible), the staff members or coordinators, and the volunteers. The volunteers were those the organizations themselves considered as such. The topics established were to be discussed by all those interviewed, independent of their position in the organization's structure. In order to gather the information, the results of the first interview were analyzed and other possible questions were discussed and formulated for a second interview. Then the topics about which information was collected were listed along with an explanation of each one and the possible questions to be asked.

1. *Socio Demographic Area:* General information about the person interviewed

Collecting information for the four groups interviewed:

- This refers to the subject's place in the social structure: place of birth, age, education, occupation, type of work done to make a living. Recording family background, such as their parents' and siblings' activities, etc.
- The following questions were suggested for this purpose: Where and when were you born? How many brothers and sisters do you have? What place are you in with regard to the ages of your brothers and sisters? What was the last year of schooling you completed? (depending on the response, information is gathered about the institution where they studied, if it was public or private, and the different courses of study). What kind of degree do you have? *(when applicable)*.
- What does your father do? What does your mother do? *(if applicable)* What do your brothers and sisters do? What work do you do? Are you married? *(if applicable)* What does your spouse do? Do you have any children? How many children do you have? *(if applicable)* How old are your children? What year of school are they in? How many years have you been in your current job? How did you get there? Did you have other jobs before? What were they?

2. *History of Activities Supporting Others:* Volunteer actions

Collecting information for the four groups interviewed.

- This refers to information required to find out how the subject interviewed has been involved in these kinds of activities of helping others in the course of their lives. This topic makes it possible to go into the way the subject has become involved in different activities, whom they have interacted with, and the role that people have played in this.

- Questions like: Who invited you to work? Why did you decide to accept? What attracted you? Or what did they offer you that attracted your attention and why did it attract your attention? Determine here whether they receive a salary for the work they do.
- Go on to questions that lead the subject to think about why they carry out the activity and what this process has been like. Example: From your point of view, what are the reasons for your participating in this organization? What importance do you give it? Then orient the questions toward the relevance this has for him or her.
- Delve further into the relevance. For this purpose, the questions are like: What do you think about what you do here? What kind of satisfaction have you felt? Does this kind of activity or work you do here have its ups and downs? What do you do when there are problems? How have you felt when things don't work out right? How have you tried to fix this?

Only for staff and volunteers

- We're interested in finding out what satisfaction the work they do gives them and if they have done the same thing or if there have been changes. You can ask: Is the work you do in this organization different than the work you did before? In what sense? What do you do here? Have you always done the same thing, or has it changed? How has it changed? Could you tell me a little about how your work here has changed?

3. *Creation and Development:* The process of forming an organization

Gathering information on the founder if they are also the director or leader.

- For this topic, we are interested in gathering information on the way the subject becomes committed to achieving concrete objectives and consolidates them. In this case we're referring to the person who created the organization and also leads it. Questions like: How was it decided to form this organization? Where did the idea come from? Could you tell me a little about this? Who contributed to forming it? Can you tell us a little about what support was received? What difficulties did you face?
- We need to generate information about how they carry out the planning process in order to participate more systematically in an activity pursuing a compelling objective. How was this organization planned? Who collaborated in this? When was the project begun? Can you tell me a little about its development? Have there been changes from the beginning up until now? How are the organization's activities organized? Who participates with you in this kind of organization? How are decisions made? Have you had any problems or disagreements with any of your collaborators? How have you dealt with this?
- In this case, the topic is to try to find out where the organization's funds come from and if it has carried out actions oriented toward achieving self-sufficiency.

What do you do to look for funds to be able to operate? Tell me a little about who financed it in the beginning and where the operating funds come from now. Do your donors have specific demands when they donate funds? What kind of demands? Do you inform them about the activities undertaken with the funds? How do you do this?

Creation and Development: The process of forming an organization.

Gathering information on the founder if they are not the director or leader.

- Generate information on the way the subject becomes committed to achieving concrete objectives and consolidates them. In this case we're referring to the person who formed the organization. Can you tell me a little about how it was decided to form this organization? Where did the idea come from? Who collaborated in this? Who supported it at the beginning? What was the beginning like? What difficulties did you face?
- Go more deeply into questions that help us understand how they carry out the planning process in order to participate more systematically in an activity pursuing a compelling objective. How was this organization planned? How it was finally formed? Who participated with you in this kind of organization? How were decisions made? How did you deal with conflicts that arose? What do you think of the organization now?
- In this case, the topic is to try to find out where the organization's funds come from and if it has carried out actions oriented toward achieving self-sufficiency. What did you do to look for funds to be able to operate? Who financed it? Did your donors have specific demands when they donate funds? What kind of demands? Did you inform them about the activities undertaken with the funds?

Creation and Development: The process of forming an organization.

Gathering information on the director or leader.

- This covers information on the way the subject becomes committed to achieving concrete objectives and consolidates them. In this case we're referring to the people who created the organization and who are themselves sometimes at the head of the activities. How was it decided to form this organization? Who collaborated in this? What support was received?
- In this case we're referring to how the planning process was carried out in order to participate more systematically in an activity pursuing a compelling objective. Of course, this includes the absence of a project. How was this organization planned? Have there been changes from the beginning up until now? How are the organization's activities organized? Who participates with you in this kind of organization? How are decisions made? Have you had any problems or disagreements with any of your collaborators? How have you dealt with this?
- In this case, the concern is to try to find out where the organization's funds come from and if it has carried out actions oriented toward achieving self-sufficiency. Do you know where the operational funds come from? Who finances it? Do your donors have specific demands when they donate funds? What kind of demands?

Do you inform them about the activities undertaken with the funds? What do you do in this regard?

Other Topics for Gathering Information about the Founder.

Reasons Why the Organization Was Formed. Where it's going.

- The purpose here is to determine the concerns they had in mind when creating the organization, and in what direction these were focused. The questions are like: What goals have you set yourself for the organization? Were your expectations fulfilled? Why did you stop participating? (If this is the case).

Changing Organizations: Mobility from one organization to another.

- In this point the aim is to determine whether the subject being interviewed formed several organizations or if this is the only one and what were the reasons leading them to form it. In this case, the questions should be directed toward delving into the different kinds of organizations in which they have been involved. Have you participated in other organizations? Have you formed another organization? Can you tell me a little about that experience? Why didn't you continue? How is this related to the organization you founded? Were you interested in achieving something specific?

Meaning and Perceptions of Their Activity: How the subject perceives what they do.

- This refers to the way the subject verbalizes what they do, what they do it for, and why they do it. In this sense, we are explicitly referring to the activity the subject develops or used to develop in the organization. Why do they consider the work they now do to be important? How do they contribute to this activity? Go a little more deeply into their reasons. Why do they do it? If they continue to participate, you can ask: What kind of new contribution can you make to the group now? Why do you continue to be interested? What kinds of activities do you undertake now? Why do you like to do them? What kind of activities did you participate in last week? Among the activities you participated in, which one was the most interesting to you?
- In this topic, particularly the reasons why the subject carries out specific activities are gone into, how they verbalize them, and what aspects share a relationship with their life plan. What do you think of people who do not participate in this kind of activity? And what do you think about those who participate? What benefits has participating in these kinds of unpaid activities brought you as a person? Have you ever thought of not participating in them anymore? Why?

Time Dedicated: week of activity dedicated to volunteer action.
(Only if they are still involved. If not, omit this).

- At this point, the time they dedicate to this kind of work should be gone into, as well as how they decide when they will do it, in terms of organizing all their activities. The questions are like: How much time do you devote to these kinds of activities? How much time per week do you devote to it? Do these kinds of activities sometimes interfere with your other responsibilities?

Other Topics for Gathering Information about the Director or Leader.

Reasons Why the Organization Was Formed. Where it's going.
- The purpose here is to determine the concerns they had in mind when creating the organization, and in what direction these were focused. The questions are like: What goals has the organization set itself? How does it pursue them? What do you think the organization is good for?

Decisions in the Organization: How are decisions made about what to do and how to do it?

- In this topic, we want to find out how decisions are made in the organization. Do you consult with some group when making decisions about what the organization is going to do? Have you encountered any problems? How have you dealt with this? Is it difficult for you to find people who want to work as volunteers? Why? Where do your volunteers come from? How do they approach the organization? What future plans do you have for the organization?

Changing Organizations: Mobility from one organization to another.

- Here the point is to try to get to know whether the subject interviewed has been in other organizations and to go into the reasons for changing organizations. In this case, the questions should be directed toward delving into the different kinds of organizations in which they have been involved: Have you been in another organization or organizations? What kind of activities were you engaged in, in each one of those organizations? Why did you decide to switch to another organization? What did the new organization offer you? How long have you been participating with the organization where you are now? Who invited you to participate? Why did you think participating in that organization was worthwhile?

Meaning and Perceptions of Their Activity: How the subject perceives what they do.

- This refers to the way the subject verbalizes what they do and why they do it. In this sense, we're explicitly referring to the activity the subject currently develops in the organization. Do you like what you do? Why? Do you think that it is useful? Why? What does this new activity give you or do for you? What kind of new contribution can you make to the group where you participate now? What kind of activities did you participate in yesterday? How did you feel when you did it? What kind of activities did you participate in last week? Among the activities you participated in, which one was the most interesting to you?
- In this topic, particularly the reasons why the subject carries out specific activities are gone into, how they verbalize them, and what aspects have a relationship with their life plan. What do you think of people who participate in this kind of activity? What benefits has participating in these kinds of unpaid activities brought you as a person? Have you ever thought of not participating in them anymore? Why? And what do you think about those who do not participate?

Time Dedicated: the number of hours dedicated to this activity.

- At this point, the time they dedicate to this kind of work should be gone into, as well as how they decide when they will do it, in terms of organizing all their activities. The questions are like: How much time do you devote to these kinds of activities? How much time per week do you devote to it? Do these kinds of activities sometimes interfere with your other responsibilities?

Other Topics for Gathering Information about Staff or Coordinators:

Changing Organizations: Mobility from one organization to another.

- Here the point is to try to get to know whether the subject has belonged to several organizations and to go into the reasons for doing so. In this case, the questions should be directed toward the different kinds of organizations in which they have been involved: Have you participated in other organizations? What kind? What kind of activities were you engaged in, in each one of those organizations? Why did you decide to switch to another organization? What did the new organization offer you? How long have you been participating in this organization? Who invited you to participate? Can you tell me a little about how this happened? Why did you think participating in that organization was worthwhile?

Meaning and Perceptions of Their Activity: How the subject perceives what they do.

- This refers to the way the subject verbalizes what they do, and why they do it. In this sense, we're explicitly referring to the activity the subject currently develops in the organization. Why do they consider the work they now do to be important? How do they contribute to this activity? What kind of new contribution can you make to the group where you participate now? What kind of activities did you participate in yesterday? How did you feel when you did it? What kind of activities did you participate in last week? Among the activities you participated in, which one was the most interesting to you?
- In this topic, particularly the reasons why the subject carries out specific activities are gone into, how they verbalize them, and which aspects have a relationship with their life plan. What do you think of people who do not participate in this kind of activity? What benefits has participating in these kinds of unpaid activities brought you as a person? Have you ever thought of not participating in them anymore? Why?

Time Dedicated and Activity: Volunteer work

- At this point, the time they dedicate to this kind of work should be gone into, as well as how they decide when they will do it, in terms of organizing all their activities. The questions are like: What do you do here? How many people are you in charge of? How is it organized? How much time do you devote to these kinds of activities? How much time per week do you devote to it? Do these kinds of activities sometimes interfere with your other responsibilities?

Creation and Development: The process of forming an organization.

- This covers information on the way the subject becomes committed to achieving compelling objectives and consolidates them. Do you know how this organization was formed? Who collaborated in this? Do you know something about this organization's history? Can you tell me a little about it?
- In this case we're referring to how the planning process was carried out in order to participate more systematically in an activity pursuing a compelling objective. Of course, this includes the absence of a project. Do you know how this organization was formed? Have there been changes from the beginning up until now? Do you know how the activities are organized? Who participates with you in this kind of organization? How are decisions made? Have you had any problems or disagreements with any of your collaborators? How have you dealt with this?
- In this case, the topic is to try to find out where the organization's funds come from and if it has carried out actions oriented toward achieving self-sufficiency. Do you know where the operational funds come from? Who finances it? Do your donors have specific demands when they donate funds? What kind of demands? Do you inform them about the activities undertaken with the funds? Do you know how this is done?

Reasons Why the Organization Was Formed. Where it's going.

- The purpose here is to determine the concerns they had in mind when creating the organization, and in what direction these were focused. The questions are like: Can you tell me why this organization was formed? What goals were set? What do you think the organization is good for? Why did you become interested in this organization? What goals do you have for participating in this organization? Do you see some relationship between your interests and those of the organization?

Decisions in the Organization: Who decides what to do and how to do it?

- In this topic, we try to determine whether the subject interviewed has any possibility of deciding about the actions carried out by the organization and what these possibilities are. Questions related to this topic: How are decisions made in this organization? Who participates? What role do you have in this? Do you have any ideas you would like to put into practice?

Other Topics for Volunteer Personnel:

Changing Organizations: Mobility from one organization to another.

- Here the point is to try to get to know whether the subjects interviewed have belonged to several organizations and to go into the reasons for doing so. In this case, the questions should be directed toward delving into the different kinds of organizations in which they have been involved. What kind of activities were you engaged in each one of those organizations? Why did you decide to switch to another organization? What did the new organization offer you? How long have you been participating with the organization where you are now? Who invited you to participate? Why did you think participating in that organization was worthwhile? Do you participate in other organizations at the same time? In which ones? How much time do you devote to each one of them? Why do you participate in several organizations simultaneously?

Meaning and Perceptions of Their Activity: How the subject perceives what they do.

- This refers to the way the subject verbalizes what they do, and why they do it. In this sense, we're explicitly referring to the activity the subject currently develops in the organization. Why do they consider important the work they now do? How do they contribute to this activity? What kind of new contribution can you make to the group where you participate now? What kind of activities did you participate in yesterday? How did you feel when you did it? What kind of activities did you participate last week? Among the activities you participated in, which one was the most interesting to you?
- In this topic, particularly the reasons why the subject carries out specific activities are gone into, how they verbalize them, and which aspects have a relationship with their life plan. What do you think of people who do not participate in this kind of activity? What benefits has participating in these kinds of unpaid activities brought you as a person? Have you ever thought of not participating in them anymore? Why?

Time Dedicated and Activity: Volunteer action

- At this point, the time they dedicate to this kind of work should be gone into, as well as how they decide when they will do it, in terms of organizing all their activities. The questions are like: What do you do in the organization? Have you done different things? Are you responsible for different things? How much time do you devote to these kinds of activities? How much time per week do you devote to it? Do these kinds of activities sometimes interfere with your other responsibilities?

Creation and Development: The process of forming an organization.

- This covers information on the way the subject becomes committed to achieving concrete objectives and consolidates them. Do you know how this organization was formed? Can you tell me a little about it? Why did you get interested in participating? What does this organization offer you?
- In this case we're referring to how the planning process was carried out in order to participate more systematically in an activity pursuing a concrete objective. Of course, this includes the absence of a project. Do you know how this organization was formed? Have there been changes from the beginning up until now? How are the activities organized? Who participates with you in this kind of organization? How are decisions made? Have you had any problems or disagreements with any of your collaborators? How have you dealt with this?
- In this case, the topic is to try to establish whether the subject interviewed knows where the funds for the organization's operations come from. Do you know who

contributes money to the organization? What is done to look for funds to be able to operate? Do you know if the donors have specific demands when they donate funds? What kind of demands? Are they informed about the activities undertaken with the funds? How is this done?

Reasons Why the Organization Was Formed. Where it's going.

- The goal is to determine whether the goals of the person interviewed have some relationship to the organization's goals. The questions are like: Can you tell me what purpose this organization was formed for? What goals have been set? What do you think the organization is good for? What goals do you have for participating in this organization? If they are different, why do you participate? If they are the same, go further into this subject.

Decisions in the Organization: Who decides what to do and how to do it?

- In this topic, we try to determine whether the subject interviewed has any opportunity for deciding about the actions carried out by the organization and what these opportunities are. Questions related to this topic: How are decisions made in this organization? Who participates? What role do you have in this? Do you have any ideas you would like to put into practice?

Index

Breinigsville, PA USA
26 February 2010
233177BV00009B/84/P